the COMPARATIVE study

A Structured Approach

the COMPARATIVE study

A Structured Approach

Naomi Kloss MA HDE

educate.ie

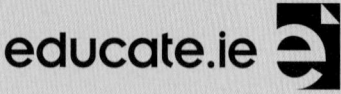

PUBLISHED BY:
Educate.ie
Walsh Educational Books Ltd
Castleisland, Co. Kerry, Ireland
www.educate.ie

EDITOR:
Eileen O'Carroll

PRODUCTION EDITOR:
Kieran O'Donoghue

DESIGN/ILLUSTRATIONS:
The Design Gang, Tralee

PRINTED AND BOUND BY:
Walsh Colour Print, Castleisland

Copyright © Naomi Kloss 2011

Without limiting the rights under copyright, this book is sold subject to the condition that it shall not, by way of trade or otherwise, be lent, resold, hired out, reproduced, stored in or introduced into a retrieval system, or transmitted, in any form or by any means (electronic, mechanical, photocopying, recording or otherwise), or otherwise circulated, without the publisher's prior consent, in any form other than that in which it is published and without a similar condition, including this condition, being imposed on the subsequent publisher.

The author and publisher have made every effort to trace all copyright holders, but if some have been inadvertently overlooked we would be happy to make the necessary arrangements at the first opportunity.

ISBN: 978-1-907772-56-6

Acknowledgements

I would like to thank the following for their help in compiling this textbook: Eileen O'Carroll, editor, for her excellent help and support and most especially for her apt and insightful structural suggestions. John O'Regan, for his very useful advice, constant help, and for providing inspiration for the title. Thanks too to Maryellen O'Keeffe, who offered an additional insight from an educational standpoint, and Peter Malone, editorial manager, who co-ordinated the different stages in the production of the book. Finally, the design team, whose design and illustrative material greatly enhance this textbook.

To all who have helped in any way, I am extremely grateful.

Naomi Kloss

  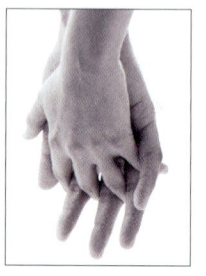 

EDITIONS USED

NOVELS

How Many Miles to Babylon?
– Jennifer Johnston (Penguin, 1974)

Tess of the D'Urbervilles
– Thomas Hardy (Harper Collins Children's Books, 2009)

Never Let Me Go
– Kazuo Ishiguro (Faber & Faber, 2005)

Emma
– Jane Austen (Penguin Books, 1994)

PLAYS

Sive
– John B. Keane (Progress House, 1985)

The Lonesome West
– Martin McDonagh (Methuen Press, 1977)

Dancing at Lughnasa
– Brian Friel (Faber & Faber, 1996)

A Doll's House
– Henrik Ibsen (Methuen Drama, 1989)

The Three Theban Plays
– Sophocles (Penguin Classics, 1984)

FILMS

Casablanca
– directed by Michael Curtiz (Warner Brothers, 1942)

The Constant Gardener
– directed by Fernando Meirelles (Focus Features, 2005)

Inside I'm Dancing
– directed by Damien O'Donnell (Universal Pictures, 2004)

32A
– directed by Marian Quinn (Janey Pictures, 2007)

As You Like It
– directed by Kenneth Branagh (HBO Films, 2006)

CONTENTS

Acknowledgements	5
Editions Used	7
How This Book Is Organised	12

1 Modes of Comparison — 19

2 Key Moments — 31

How Many Miles to Babylon?	*33*
Tess of the d'Urbervilles	*37*
Never Let Me Go	*44*
Emma	*48*
Sive	*52*
The Lonesome West	*56*
Dancing at Lughnasa	*63*
A Doll's House	*68*
Oedipus the King	*72*
Casablanca	*75*
The Constant Gardener	*77*
Inside I'm Dancing	*83*
32A	*85*
As You Like It	*90*

3 Theme or Issue: Isolation — 95

How Many Miles to Babylon?	*97*
Sive	*99*
A Doll's House	*102*
Casablanca	*105*
Inside I'm Dancing	*110*

| **4** | ***Theme or Issue:* Exploitation** | **115** |

Never Let Me Go	*116*
Sive	*120*
The Constant Gardener	*125*

| **5** | ***Theme or Issue:* Family Relationships** | **131** |

How Many Miles to Babylon?	*132*
The Lonesome West	*138*
Dancing at Lughnasa	*141*
32A	*144*

| **6** | **Answering the Theme or Issue Question** | **149** |

| **7** | **General Vision and Viewpoint** | **159** |

How Many Miles to Babylon?	*161*
The Lonesome West	*163*
Dancing at Lughnasa	*166*
A Doll's House	*170*
Never Let Me Go	*175*
The Constant Gardener	*179*
As You Like It	*182*
Inside I'm Dancing	*186*

| **8** | **Answering the General Vision and Viewpoint Question** | **191** |

| **9** | ***Literary Genre:* Novels** | **203** |

Tess of the d'Urbervilles	*205*
How Many Miles to Babylon?	*209*
Never Let Me Go	*214*

10 *Literary Genre:* Plays — 223

Oedipus the King — 225
A Doll's House — 228
Dancing at Lughnasa — 231
The Lonesome West — 237

11 *Literary Genre:* Film — 241

Inside I'm Dancing — 243
The Constant Gardener — 251

12 Answering the Literary Genre Question — 261

13 Cultural Context — 275

How Many Miles to Babylon? — 277
The Lonesome West — 280
Emma — 283
Tess of the d'Urbervilles — 287
Oedipus the King — 291
32A — 296
The Constant Gardener — 298
Casablanca — 301

14 Answering the Cultural Context Question — 305

How This Book Is Organised

This book examines the essential requirements of the comparative study (higher level) course for 2012 and 2013. *The Comparative Study: A Structured Approach* serves a two-fold purpose: it can either be used at the beginning of fifth year when students first encounter the set texts; or it can become a revision guide throughout sixth year.

This book will show you, the student, how to:
- Define the modes of comparison (Theme or Issue, General Vision and Viewpoint, Literary Genre and Cultural Context)
- Identify and comprehend the core aspects of each mode of comparison
- Plan, structure and shape a response to the challenges of the exam
- Bring together the reading of the texts with the requirement to compile your own comparative points, in a step-by-step process.

Key moments are illustrated throughout. A key moment is like an open door leading to further exploration of the text. All chapters provide classroom discussion exercises to enable you to formulate your own ideas while at the same time comparing the texts. Exemplars and full model essays are provided for some examination questions.

Chapter 1, Modes of Comparison, surveys the comparative study and forms a link between the Junior Certificate curriculum and the Leaving Certificate programme. It outlines the meaning of the terms 'theme or issue,' 'general vision and viewpoint,' 'literary genre' and 'cultural context.'

Chapter 2 details the important key moments in each text discussed throughout the book. The art of storytelling is centred on these pivotal moments which make or break a central character and propel the reader, audience or viewer more deeply into the story as it unfolds.

Chapter 3, Theme or Issue: Isolation, concentrates on Jennifer Johnston's *How Many Miles to Babylon?*, John B. Keane's *Sive*, Ibsen's *A Doll's House*, Michael Curtiz's *Casablanca* and Damien O'Donnell's *Inside I'm Dancing*. In *How Many Miles to Babylon?*, Alec is morally and emotionally alienated from his own class. To some extent, his isolation is self-imposed, but it is also created by others. Nora's and Sive's isolation is well conveyed in the closing stages of the plays discussed. In *Inside I'm Dancing*, Michael and Rory have to come to terms with societal prejudices that serve to isolate them from the community. In *Casablanca*, Rick's isolation is more self-imposed. He is aggrieved as the love of his life appears to reject him on that fateful day in Paris.

Chapter 4, Theme or Issue: Exploitation, explores how exploitation becomes an issue in *Sive*, Kazuo Ishiguro's novel *Never Let Me Go* and Fernando Meirelles' *The Constant Gardener*. The powerlessness of the main characters is clearly conveyed at every level possible. Sive is mercilessly exploited to serve others and she takes desperate measures in order to avoid her fate. Kathy, Tommy and Ruth's exploitation is graphically portrayed in *Never Let Me Go*. In *The Constant Gardener*, the exploitation of the poor and sick in Africa is highlighted and the collusion of the high commission with a ruthless pharmaceutical company is exposed.

Chapter 5, Theme or Issue: Family Relationships, details the central importance of this issue in *How Many Miles to Babylon?*, Martin McDonagh's *The Lonesome West*, Brian Friel's *Dancing at Lughnasa*, and Marian Quinn's *32A*. Alec's dysfunctional family is depicted, including his mother's role in emotionally blackmailing him to join the war. The warring brothers, Coleman and Valene, have to come to terms with their behaviour towards each other in *The Lonesome West*. In *Dancing at Lughnasa*, a family is broken apart due to unfavourable external conditions, while in the film *32A* Maeve and Ruth have to reconcile their growth to maturity with family difficulties.

Chapter 6, Answering the Theme or Issue Question, shows how to structure an answer to the theme or issue question in the examination. It targets the 2002 examination question and explores the theme of exploitation in *Never Let Me Go*, *Sive* and *The Constant Gardener*. It provides ten clear steps that can be used as a template in answering any theme or issue question.

Chapter 7, General Vision and Viewpoint, deals with this mode of comparison in *How Many Miles to Babylon?*, *The Lonesome West*, *Dancing at Lughnasa*, *A Doll's House*, *Never Let Me Go*, *The Constant Gardener*, Kenneth Branagh's *As You Like It* and Damien O'Donnell's *Inside I'm Dancing*. In *How Many Miles to Babylon?* a sombre note is struck, emphasised by Alec's pessimistic narration. In *The Lonesome West*, the alienation of modern life is graphically portrayed. Despite the pessimism, Valene and Coleman have a choice, highlighting the opportunity for individuals to have an active and positive impact on the wider world. In *Dancing at Lughnasa*, the immediate family circle offers a positive outlook on life. However, darker forces take over and the Mundy family falls apart due to factors outside their control. *A Doll's House* paints a mixed view of life. Nora breaks free of the suffocating influences of her husband, Helmer, and her late father and actively asserts the power of the individual to choose. However, her future survival is problematic and the text paints a negative view of marriage and relationships.

In *Never Let Me Go*, a relentlessly fatalistic note is struck, stressing the exploitative practices of the commanding figures in Kathy, Tommy and Ruth's lives. In *The Constant Gardener*, the glaring inequalities in African society emphasise the prevailing darkness surrounding the portrayal of life in this text, while Justin's search for the truth uncovers a deeper deception. In *As You Like It*, an optimistic note is struck when those who are banished find love, hope and wonder in the Forest of Arden. *Inside I'm Dancing* offers an optimistic view of life. Rory and Michael aim to live life to the full and realise the potential in every new situation. Both achieve independent living and battle successfully against society's prejudices towards the disabled.

Chapter 8, Answering the General Vision and Viewpoint Question, targets the 2010 examination paper though an examination of *How Many Miles to Babylon?*, *Sive* and *Inside I'm Dancing*. It also provides ten clear steps that can be used as a template for any general vision and viewpoint question.

Chapter 9, Literary Genre: Novels, explores the stylistic approach developed in Thomas Hardy's *Tess of the d'Urbervilles*, Jennifer Johnston's *How Many Miles to Babylon?* and Kazuo Ishiguro's *Never Let Me Go*. Some aspects of the novel are similar to the film and play: all involve characters, suspense and conflict. What makes the novel unique is its reliance on the printed word to convey the thoughts, the hopes, the emotions and the dreams of the central characters and their relationships and conflicts (internal or external). Like other art forms, the novel is a two-way process. The novelist creates a work of art while the reader actively responds to that creation.

Chapter 10, Literary Genre: Plays, looks at Sophocles' play *Oedipus the King*, *A Doll's House*, *Dancing at Lughnasa* and *The Lonesome West*. This chapter stresses the importance of a living performance, which depicts external conflicts as a means of propelling the drama and heightening the dramatic tension and suspense for the audience.

Chapter 11, Literary Genre: Film, examines some of the core aspects of this medium. It looks at Damien O'Donnell's *Inside I'm Dancing* and Fernando Meirelles' *The Constant Gardener*. The chapter addresses such issues as characterisation, the dramatisation of the moment by the actor, the acquired persona and certain technical issues.

Chapter 12, Answering the Literary Genre Question, targets the 2004 examination paper by comparing *How Many Miles to Babylon?*, *A Doll's House* and *Inside I'm Dancing*. It also outlines a ten-step approach to answering examination questions.

Chapter 13, Cultural Context, examines the social world of *How Many Miles to Babylon?*, *The Lonesome West*, *Tess of the d'Urbervilles*, Jane Austen's *Emma*, Sophocles' play *Oedipus the King*, as well as the films *32A*, *The Constant Gardener* and *Casablanca*. The discussion of *How Many Miles to Babylon?* explores not only the brutality of World War I, but the alienation of the central character, Alec, from his own privileged class. In *The Lonesome West*, we see a rural locality beset by family conflict and violence. The play highlights a deprived pocket of society which appears to have been left behind in the race for social and economic advancement. *Tess of the d'Urbervilles* highlights life in rural Dorchester in the late Victorian era where an isolated Tess struggles to cope with life's traumas, but is defeated. *Emma* is set in Highbury, in privileged society in the early nineteenth century. Jane Austen provides a social commentary on an elite society where a rigid formality stifles relationships. *Oedipus the King* highlights the family context and its immediate effect on the social and political life of Thebes. Oedipus's desire to discover his identity is the cause of his ruin. The gods' omnipotence and Greek piety are strongly emphasised.

Moving on to the films, *32A* looks at life in Ireland in the late 1970s from an exclusively female point of view and pays particular attention to the generation gap and wider social tensions. *The Constant Gardener* depicts a violent, despotic world where the deprived struggle for survival. Betrayal and corruption within the social elite is strongly conveyed. In *Casablanca*, the power of the Reich and the puppet Vichy régime darken the social world of the text. Refugees struggle to escape fascist tyranny in search of a new world.

Chapter 14, Answering the Cultural Context Question, looks at the 2009 examination question through a discussion of *Tess of the d'Urbervilles, Sive* and *Casablanca*. It highlights the necessity of providing as many comparative points between the texts as possible, as well as targeting the statement in the question. It provides ten clear steps that can be used as a template for any cultural context question.

At the end of several chapters in this book, a number of questions are offered. The questions are open-ended and allow for a range of opinions. All questions should be approached either as a forum for classroom discussion or as a written essay. In either case, students must back up their answers with clear reference to the texts themselves. Classroom activities are a necessary first step before embarking upon a comparative study essay. The ultimate aim is to encourage a thoughtful, independent approach to the English course, which is a prerequisite to achieving high marks in the final examination.

The editions of books used here are listed on p. 7. The versions of *Tess of the d'Urbervilles, Emma* and *Oedipus the King* may differ from the ones used in class. This will effect citations and page references.

Studying the comparative texts sets students on a journey of literary discovery. No text will ever be read in exactly the same light again. As you embark on the course you are encouraged to discover a new world of texts. Happy voyaging!

Modes of comparison

Modes of comparison

Comparisons are made constantly in everyday life. On the comparative course, you are required to compare three texts under certain modes of comparison. Before we discuss how to compare literary or visual texts, we should first try to establish how we make comparisons between everyday objects and ideas. Below is a list of topics which can be compared. Use the following link words or phrases in formulating your comparisons: 'likewise,' 'like,' 'in a similar way,' 'in a similar vein,' 'in the same way' and 'similarly' can be used to portray similarities; words or phrases such as 'in contrast to,' 'unlike' and 'whereas' can be used to depict differences.

Compare the following:

Flat / terraced house
Hedge / fence
Cheetah / elephant
Labrador / collie
Speed boat / fishing boat
Car / train
Aeroplane / helicopter
Soccer / table tennis
Gaelic football / swimming
Africa / Ireland

New York / Sahara Desert
Symphony / pop song
TV / radio
Book / journal
Art gallery / museum
Play / film
Diary / newspaper article
1940 / 2010
Nineteenth century / twentieth century

All books, plays and films bring the reader, audience and viewer on a voyage of discovery into worlds unknown. Each journey is special. As the reader pores through the pages of a novel, he or she follows the characters' own path of discovery. As the audience watches the production, the drama unfolds. As viewers settle down in front of the television, the actor's face conveys a range of different emotions. No novel, play or film is written or produced in exactly the same way. Each one has its own unique quality.

This chapter will:
- Define the key modes of comparison, illustrated by two Junior Certificate texts that are often studied.

Stories are at the heart of any text. Stories provide the tension, the spellbinding moments when all is or seems lost. No work is ever produced without the story in mind.

Many works of fiction contain moments of truth, of deceit or intrigue, love or heart-rending brutality. Take a moment to think back to the Junior Certificate course where many of these moments are represented in the texts studied. The very best of novels, plays or films include moments of suspense and tension. In Shakespeare's *Merchant of Venice*, for example, Shylock is stunned to discover how the bond he held so dear is being used in court against him. In *Romeo and Juliet*, the tragic events unfold to a heart-rending conclusion. A distraught Juliet awakes to find Romeo dead beside her. Moments later, she takes her own life. Unforgettable moments like these occur in many texts.

- Name a book you have read recently, or a film or play you have watched.
- What is it about this work of fiction that kept you gripped?
- What makes it a good piece of entertainment?

Each work of art creates characters. Characters are the real drivers of good drama. It helps if the central characters are likeable, or if one character conveys the thoughts of the audience. An audience or a viewer experiences a text differently from a reader. Films or plays are more accessible. The facial expressions of an actor can convey visually what would take a paragraph in a book to represent.

In Shakespeare's *Merchant of Venice*, Shylock strolls with confidence into a packed courtroom where a resigned Antonio is in the dock. At the end of this scene Shylock appears fearful and anxious and tries to bolt from the court. The emotional impact of this scene is told within minutes, but things unfold differently in a novel.

Works of fiction rely on the reader's imagination. Authors strive hard to create the right impression through their choice of words. It is through words that the reader is made aware of the innermost thoughts of the central characters. The words (or language) are designed to spirit the reader into the setting of a text. Language also provides emotional impact and strengthens the development of a particular theme.

Theme or Issue

Each text has a theme that runs through the plot and subplots. In *Romeo and Juliet* the theme is romantic love. In the *Merchant of Venice*, revenge, love and hate are some of the main themes. There are also key moments in each of these texts that draw these themes together. Your task is to identify the theme which appears in all three texts. In examining the texts, you should show how the writer, playwright or director uses the central characters to drive the plot, while also developing this theme.

Love and hate are at the core of most, if not all texts. Many characters may search for recognition or acceptance, while others may become isolated from their communities. Themes run from the beginning to the end of the novel, play or film. It is important to show how the theme is presented, but the overall design of the text also needs to be taken into account.

Many texts have a central theme. **Chapter 3** explores the theme of isolation. Isolation encompasses such ideas as segregation, separateness and removal from others. Some social circumstances might leave a character segregated from others. For other characters, like Michael and Rory in Damien O'Donnell's film *Inside I'm Dancing*, their isolation is due to physical disability. This chapter defines the meaning of the term 'isolation' and shows how it relates to some of the texts on the 2012 and 2013 courses and how the theme is developed by identifying pivotal moments within the texts.

Chapter 4 explores the theme of exploitation. This is a very controversial theme. In a harrowing and thought-provoking way, texts such as Kazuo Ishiguro's novel *Never Let Me Go*, John B. Keane's play *Sive* and Fernando Meirelles' film *The Constant Gardener* explore the theme of the subjection of others by a powerful social group in society. Many of the characters in these works respond passively to their plight. Chapter 4 defines the meaning of the term and how it is demonstrated in these texts, and identifies pivotal moments that explore this theme most powerfully.

Chapter 5 highlights the theme of family relationships as a central issue in many of the texts on the course. 'Family' is defined in diverse ways, especially in modern society, but in this chapter family is defined as a group of people who are related by birth or adoption. The diversity of families is reflected in texts such as Brian Friel's play *Dancing at Lughnasa*, Martin McDonagh's *The Lonesome West*, Jennifer Johnston's *How Many Miles to Babylon?* and the film *32A*, directed by Marian Quinn. In exploring this theme, different family structures can be compared and contrasted. Chapter 5 defines the meaning of 'family' and shows how it is described throughout these texts. It also identifies pivotal moments that highlight the complexity of family relationships.

Chapter 6 looks at how to compare the treatment of a theme by outlining a step-by-step approach to formulating your answer. It highlights the prescriptive importance of understanding the question and its demands on your answer. It emphasises that planning an answer is not an optional extra, but an essential requirement for a balanced and well-structured answer. The ten-step approach to the question on the theme or issue section is a guide to producing an effective and well-planned answer to the increased challenges of the comparative course.

General Vision and Viewpoint

Look outside right now. It might be a bright sunny day, or a cloudy one. The weather is often linked to mood. People appear much happier basking in the summer sunshine than they do when diving in and out between showers.

Watching the weather is not unlike charting the overall general vision and viewpoint of a novel, play or film. The writer, playwright and director have their own insights into life, which colour and shape the text. The level of optimism or pessimism of the author or director is conveyed in the text and influences how it is written and the overall approach taken.

The overall vision of Shakespeare's *Romeo and Juliet* is very pessimistic. Both Romeo and Juliet struggle against the odds. It is a tragedy. However, there is one small note of optimism. Their tragic deaths result in an end to the conflict between the two feuding families. Peace blossoms in Verona. The overall vision of the *Merchant of Venice* is very different. Antonio's life is spared and Shylock is ultimately defeated. This creates a more optimistic vision, for most of the central characters at least.

Never underestimate the importance of general vision and viewpoint as a mode of comparison. It is essential that you learn to define your terms. Studying general vision and viewpoint invites you, the student, to become a literary detective. Any detective has to search for clues to solve the most mysterious of crimes and you are on a similar quest. It is essential that you determine not just the level of optimism or pessimism, but how it is communicated in your chosen texts. The general vision and viewpoint chapters will assess:

- The opening scene: what does it say about life and its experiences?
- What do the characters in each of the texts have to say about life?
- Do these viewpoints change substantially as the plot progresses?
- Is there any hope expressed throughout the texts? If so, where? If not, why not?
- To what extent are the characters free to make their own choices? Such freedom to manoeuvre can emphasise in the clearest fashion the overall optimism of any text.
- What is the closing scene like?
- What aspects of life are concentrated on and why are they seen to be so important?

Many texts are explored in this mode of comparison, including Jennifer Johnston's *How Many Miles to Babylon?*, Martin McDonagh's *The Lonesome West*, Brian Friel's *Dancing at Lughnasa* and films such as Damien O'Donnell's *Inside I'm Dancing* and Kenneth Branagh's adaptation of Shakespeare's *As You Like It*.

A fatalistic approach accentuates the pessimism of a text, while the portrayal of a character's single-minded resolve to battle against insurmountable odds emphasises an optimistic and positive approach to life and its experiences. In *How Many Miles to Babylon?* Alec's bleak assessment of the harrowing brutality of the battlefield in Flanders accentuates the prevailing atmosphere of doom and gloom. Hopelessness prevails. Contrast this with the hopeful determination depicted in Kenneth Branagh's film *As You Like It*, or Nora's independence in *A Doll's House*. The chapters on general vision and viewpoint demonstrate how to get the most from this examination question.

Literary Genre

Literary genre is the overall style of the text. A novel is a work of imagination which attempts to draw the reader into the story through the exploration of the psychology of a central character. What makes the novel unique is its reliance on the printed word to convey the thoughts, hopes and dreams of the central characters, while a play focuses more on the external conflicts between characters. Instead of deep-seated analysis of the inner world of a leading character, a play, by contrast, relies on the visual depiction of a character's actions and gestures to portray their inner conflicts. Literary genre examines the ways in which the telling of a story differs through the variety of genres.

In relation to novels, the following aspects of literary genre are explored:
- Is the title significant? Does it contain social commentary?
- Who is the narrator of this text?
- How are the main characters developed?
- What is the central series of events in the story and how are they organised?
- What stimulates the reader to read on? What are the key moments that create the most tension and suspense?
- What is the plot and subplot and how do they ignite and sustain interest?
- What is described and how is it described?
- How is dialogue used?

In relation to plays, the following aspects of literary genre are explored:
- Is the title significant? Does it contain social commentary?
- Is there a narrator? Whose point of view is being emphasised?
- How are the characters developed?
- In what sequence is the story told?
- What is the plot and subplot?
- What key moments emphasise the external conflicts between the characters?

- What clues are given in the playwright's stage directions?
- Is imagery or symbolism used in the play?
- What special sound effects are used?
- How effective is the use of dialogue in propelling the drama?

In relation to films, the following aspects of literary genre are explored:
- What is the significance of the title? Does it contain social commentary?
- Is the camera the narrator?
- How are characters and motivation developed?
- How does the actor, the acquired persona, dramatise the moment?
- What is the story and the overall direction of the plot?
- Is there unity or disunity in the overall design?
- What is the power of the moving image? Instant accessibility?
- How are special effects (lighting and sound) used?
- What is the impact of the dialogue?

The literary genre chapters outline these differences in the telling of the tale and how their use has an impact on the reader's or audience's experience of the story. These chapters will assess texts as diverse as *How Many Miles to Babylon?*, *The Lonesome West*, *A Doll's House* and *Tess of the d'Urbervilles*. These chapters will also offer guidelines on how to approach the Leaving Certificate paper.

Cultural Context

Places are importance in popular imagination. Contrast, for example, the feelings conjured up by images of a local park in comparison to a bustling city street. The powerful effect of how the location of the book, play or film operates in a text can provide much of the drama in itself.

Cultural context is a broad term. To understand cultural context you need to look at the following:
- Setting
- Family
- Class
- Poverty
- The role of women

- Marriage
- Religion
- Violence
- The powerful
- The powerless.

As the later chapters in this book will testify, the setting has an impact on the leading characters in a text. Each character has to exist within his or her own cultural context. To take an earlier example, in *Romeo and Juliet* the violent world of Verona is a hostile place for a blossoming romance between the two lovers, on account of their parents' ongoing feud. In the *Merchant of Venice*, Shylock is forever perceived as a Jewish outsider in Venetian society.

- Do you have more sympathy with Romeo and Juliet because of the harsh world in which they live?
- Do you feel a little sorry for Shylock, even though he is the villain of the piece, because he is a Jew in a world hostile to his faith?

When we look at the exploits of an individual character, we need to consider the world in which they are compelled, in many cases, to operate. Understanding cultural context helps us to do that. It allows us to consider the background of the play, book or film.

Society changes all the time. More or fewer opportunities are opened up for people. It depends on where they live and the type of lifestyle afforded them. This is all part of the cultural context of a text.

- What is the setting of your text?
- Picture the world at the time of the text.
- What are the dominant issues for the characters who live in this culture?
- Are they supported by or do they rail against the society in which they live?
- What are the social circumstances of the central character in the text?
- What opportunities are opened up for him or her?
- How are the most disadvantaged people treated in this drama?
- Is the culture in any way oppressive for the main characters?

All characters exist within a social world. Stories create lifelike characters that readers or an audience come to like or dislike. Sometimes a harsh and unfeeling social environment compounds the psychological anguish and torment of a central character. The very examination of an issue can stir within any reader, audience or viewer the need to reassess the cultural restrictions of a particular society. Many texts lend themselves to a critique of society, for example *How Many Miles to Babylon?*, *Dancing at Lughnasa*, *Sive* and *The Constant Gardener*, to mention but a few.

Attitudes and values make up the fabric of our world. Social attitudes are uniform attitudes that are adopted by society as a whole. Society is defined as a community of people bound together by the same institutions, traditions and nationality. Over time, a society adopts certain principles and morals which are seen to be the norm, the most acceptable code of practice or behaviour for everyone in that society. Tess in Thomas Hardy's novel *Tess of the d'Urbervilles* suffers greatly on account of this.

The writer, playwright or director may not share these values. Their social critique may be communicated through the internal and external struggles endured by the central characters. The cultural context chapters highlight the importance of social attitudes and values in discussing many of the texts on the course.

The cultural context chapters outline aspects of the social world of the texts. These chapters explore, for example, class consciousness and the power of marriage and the family within the very fabric of society, as well as assessing the powerful vested interests that hold the strongest influences over the lives of many of the characters in a text. The 2009 examination paper referred to how 'the main character in a text is often in conflict with the world or culture they inhabit.'

Studying the comparative texts will set you on a journey of literary discovery. By the time you have finished this course, you will not read a novel, watch a play or view a film in quite the same way again!

2

Key moments

Key moments

This chapter will highlight and illustrate the importance of the key moments in the novels:

- Jennifer Johnston's *How Many Miles to Babylon?*
- Thomas Hardy's *Tess of the d'Urbervilles*
- Kazuo Ishiguro's *Never Let Me Go*
- Jane Austen's *Emma*

in the plays:

- John B. Keane's *Sive*
- Martin McDonagh's *The Lonesome West*
- Brian Friel's *Dancing at Lughnasa*
- Henrik Ibsen's *A Doll's House*
- Sophocles' *Oedipus the King*

and in the films:

- Michael Curtiz's *Casablanca*
- Fernando Meirelles' *The Constant Gardener*
- Damien O'Donnell's *Inside I'm Dancing*
- Marian Quinn's *32A*
- Kenneth Branagh's *As You Like It*.

Importance of key moments

Any explorer who is set to embark on a voyage of discovery needs to come equipped with the necessary tools for the journey. As you embark on your journey of literary discovery, you need to first choose the important key moments from each text, as these are your tools for the work ahead.

Key moments are pivotal to any text. As you progress through the course, you will discover that these moments can be used to explore the core modes of comparison in greater depth. This chapter is designed both as an introduction to the study of the texts and as a reference point to refresh your memory of the events in your chosen texts as you work through the course. The key moments will be examined in a chronological fashion.

How Many Miles to Babylon? BY JENNIFER Johnston

This novel tells the story of a forbidden friendship between Alec, the son of a landowning Anglo-Irish family, and Jerry, a Catholic from a poor family. Alec is emotionally blackmailed into joining the conflict of World War I by his mother, who wishes him to fight on behalf of king and country. His friendship with Jerry is the major flashpoint in the novel as both Alec's mother and Major Glendinning fail to realise its importance.

Alec awaiting execution

KEY moment

Alec awaits execution. He reiterates that he has the status of an officer and a gentleman. He is angry towards his mother. The other soldiers seem to believe that Alec is insane but his crime remains unclear. He describes the battlefield as a 'hundred yards of mournful earth.' The loneliness of the scene is reinforced by the fact that this place has become the centre of the world for 'tens of thousands of men.' Sadly, he predicts a tragic end for the 'heroes and cowards, the masters and the slaves.' The ugliness of this dismal scene is captured by the phrase, 'a thick and evil February rain' (pp. 1–2).

Alec's parents' disapproval of his friendship with Jerry

KEY moment

Alicia is taken aback by her son's knowledge of the international scene. Frederick euphemistically suggests that there are 'tensions,' but that these will be 'ironed out.' As he lights his match, he adds that the family seems 'so remote, so protected.' Alicia expresses her concern that her son has spoken to the servants. Alec is evasive. He replies, 'People. Around.' Alicia identifies

Jeremiah Crowe. She orders her son not to see him again. Alec protests. Even Frederick adopts a tougher stance and calls Alec's friendship with Jerry an 'unsuitable relationship.' He speaks of how his son has to pay attention to the 'responsibilities and limitations of the class' into which he was born.

Momentarily, they are interrupted by the parlour-maid. Alec is ordered to pour Frederick a glass of whiskey. He finds it very difficult to ascertain his mother's mood as he 'never had time to grasp her moods before they had changed.' Alicia is unimpressed by Frederick's lacklustre response, claiming that her husband is 'ineffective and old.' Frederick's hands are trembling as he takes up his glass and agrees with Alicia's assessment of him. Alec touches Frederick's knee. 'It was a brief gesture, as ineffective as one he might have made himself.' Frederick encourages Alec to obey his mother. Alec feels as if he has been dismissed: 'I felt that they had finished with me.' As he is about to leave, Alec is ordered not to befriend Jerry. Reluctantly, Alec promises to obey (pp. 29–30).

KEY moment Frederick's misery in his marriage to Alicia

Alec sits down beside the fire. There is silence. The fire burns in the room, but darkness descends upon them. Alec writes that their 'vulnerable faces' are 'hidden by the darkness.' Frederick claims that he adores Alicia, but hopes that Alec will 'never experience the humiliation of living with someone who is completely indifferent' to him. He reasons that Alicia is not sending Alec off to war for patriotic reasons, but because she hates her husband. They are both drinking. Frederick spends most of his days alone, explaining that he has not 'acquired the habit of talking with people.' Rather, he merely issues orders. Alec is well aware of his father's isolation. He realises that he will begin 'to speak to the shadows' when he leaves the room (pp. 43–44).

KEY moment Alicia's shock revelation

Alicia is unhappy about the prospect of Alec becoming more like Frederick. She urges him to join the war effort. Alec replies that he is deeply indifferent towards the cause. She accuses him of being a coward, claiming that 'cowards are not very nice people.' She refers to the importance of duty, love and obedience. Alec rejects this logic. He claims that his father needs him. She reminds him that she has sacrificed her life for him and that all the other boys in the locality have gone to join the war effort. Alec is scathing about them, calling them 'fools.' She labels them heroes. Alicia informs Alec that Frederick might not be his father. He is stunned and in these paragraphs it seems as if he is an observer watching events unfold. He is perturbed: 'Dispossessed in a sentence.' Alicia claims he is being melodramatic and leaves him as he struggles to come to terms with what she has just said. Looking around the room, Alec feels he can now 'escape the eyes of the ancestors on the walls' as he has become 'an intruder' to them (pp. 45–48).

Alec's final farewell

KEY **moment**

Alicia hopes her son is not 'sulking' when he refuses to eat. Alec detects an angry tone in his mother's voice. Frederick stirs restlessly as he reads his newspaper. Alec jokes about a condemned man not eating a good breakfast. He is eager to leave. He refers to his travel arrangements. Alicia is delighted and Alec observes his mother is triumphant. He writes that 'in spite of the petulance of her words, I was conscious of the radiance coming from her, a feeling of triumph.' Tentatively, Alec asks his father for some money, which Frederick is more than anxious to give. Frederick hides behind his paper, but Alec notices his hands are shaking. Alicia touches her son with a cold finger. Alec flicks it away as he would 'a fly.' Frederick remarks that his grandfather was a soldier. He offers Alec his gold watch. It seems that Alec is touched by this gesture. He writes, 'it was warm in my hand with the warmth of his body.' Frederick offers him more money and insists that he be kind to his mother. They shake hands and Alec leaves him standing there. Alicia hugs her son in a 'splendidly theatrical gesture.' Alec says he will never believe that Frederick is not his father. She laughs and urges her son to write (pp. 66–69).

A simple lack of choice

KEY **moment**

After Jerry has been found, Alec is taken to see Major Glendinning, who strikes Alec with his cane. Glendinning insists that he dislikes physical violence as much as Alec but laments that Alec will not listen to reason. Alec argues that he has contrary views on what reason means. Major Glendinning is keen to urge Alec to submit to army discipline and is shaking as he speaks, but continues to assert that such lack of discipline will not be tolerated. He adds that the charges against Jerry are very serious but Alec responds that this is the case on paper only. Glendinning is preoccupied with the war effort and with the impending attack: 'It might win the war. It must succeed, and for it to succeed there must be no flaw in the machinery.' Privately, Alec claims that World War I is the major's war: 'Outside, his war was shaking the world.' Glendinning makes it known that he is continually irritated by these 'pointless schoolboy discussions.' Alec closes his eye, labelling it comically a 'glorious war wound, even more ignominious than Bennett's flu.' He notes the patterns that 'weave and unweave themselves through life and history.' He terms these 'eternal recurrences' (pp. 147–49).

KEY moment — Alec's hopeless pleas on Jerry's behalf

'Let them give it a hero's grave'

Alec is immediately struck by Major Glendinning's aloofness: 'Cold disapproval, a nod, the papers, the pens, the neatly folded hands.' Glendinning informs Alec that Jerry is to be sentenced to death. Alec is aghast at the prospect and claims that there must have been some mistake. The major insists that experienced men have reached this decision. He notes Alec's refusal to 'be guided.' Alec wonders what would happen if he refused to carry out the order. Glendinning says that he would have Alec's body shipped back to his parents. Chillingly, he remarks on Alec's possible end: 'Let them give it a hero's grave.' Alec wonders where Glendinning was taught to be so evil. Major Glendinning replies that the world has taught him. Alec asks if there is any hope for Jerry. The major is adamant that there is none. Alec appears to acquiesce and Glendinning softens his approach very slightly. He comes over to Alec, touches him lightly on the shoulder and orders him to tell his men to shoot straight. Alec 'shuddered' when Glendinning touched him (pp. 150–53).

KEY moment — Alec's shooting of Jerry and his wait for execution

Alec's last conversation with Jerry is very poignant. They think of happier times and jokingly talk about the horses that could have won at the races. Alec checks to see that his gun is in good working order but puts it away once he hears footsteps. Jerry is seated. Alec encourages Jerry to sing an Irish rebel song: 'At the siege of Ross did my father fall.' Outside, the voices fade. Jerry continues to sing: 'I bear no hate against living thing, But I love my country above my King.' Alec shuts his eyes and pulls the trigger. Jerry collapses. Alec hears his chair fall. He hears footsteps but his eyes are still shut. The very force of the gunshot reverberates in his ears, even after the event. Alec is taken away to await his execution (pp. 153–55).

Tess of the d'Urbervilles BY THOMAS Hardy

Tess's father discovers that his family is linked to the illustrious d'Urbervilles. He is drunk and unable to drive the horse to market after celebrating this good news so Tess takes this responsibility on herself, but it results in a terrible accident that leads to the death of the horse. A contrite Tess returns to her family and feels compelled to seek out the blind Mrs d'Urberville, who is not the distant relative she assumes. Alec d'Urberville has a lustful eye on Tess. Tess becomes pregnant, but her tiny infant, whom she christens Sorrow, dies shortly after birth.

Tess then finds employment at Talbothays. It is here that she develops a strong relationship with Angel Clare, but she is unable to confess to her new lover the truth about Alec and Sorrow. Angel and Tess marry. Tess takes her opportunity after he confesses to a youthful transgression. Angel is horrified to discover the truth, believing her not to be the same woman he thought he had married. He gives her money and leaves for Brazil. Tess spends Angel's money on renovating the house and finds employment in Flintcomb-Ash.

A desperate Tess seeks out Angel's family, but leaves before making their acquaintance after she overhears them speaking disparagingly about the marriage. The situation becomes desperate when Tess's father passes away and her family face eviction. She is thrown helplessly towards Alec.

She is living with Alec in Sandbourne when Angel arrives. Tess is distraught because she feels Alec had deceived her when he claimed Angel would never return. Her anger boils over and she murders Alec in his bed. She spends one week with Angel until she is finally found, arrested and hanged for the murder of Alec.

Tess is portrayed as a complex character who fails to fit into the stereotype of a murderer or a victim.

KEY **moment** Tess's father meets the parson

Jack Durbeyfield asks the parson why he called him 'Sir John' one market day. At first, the parson is reluctant to explain. He introduces himself as Parson Tringham who researched the new county history. He explains to Jack that he is related to the 'ancient and knightly family of the d'Urbervilles.' He explains that if knighthoods were hereditary, like a baronetcy, then he would be called Sir John now. Jack is astonished by the news, previously believing he was the 'commonest feller in the parish.' He questions the parson further, but he learns that the line is now extinct and all lands have been lost. The parson continues to explain that 'there are several families among the cottagers of this county of almost equal lustre.' Jack offers him drink but the parson refuses as he observes that Jack is already drunk (The Maiden, Ch. 1).

KEY **moment** The tragic death of Prince and Tess's isolation

Tess agrees to take the horse, Prince, to market. She is accompanied by her brother, Abraham. Abraham talks continuously, asking his older sister searching questings. He asks her if she wants to marry a gentleman. She dismisses the idea that they possess a great relative, but as Abraham chats insistently, he begins to reflect on the advantage of wealth.

Abraham is interested in Tess's idea that the stars in the sky are worlds. Tess explains that most stars are splendid but some are blighted. Abraham wants to know if they live on a blighted or splendid star. Tess says it is a blighted one. Abraham falls asleep as Tess drives Prince along, but Tess also nods off. She is suddenly jolted from her imaginings when a light is shone in her face. A horrified Tess discovers that her horse is dead and that her carriage has strayed across to the other side of the road. Abraham contends that their family is on 'a blighted star, and not a sound one.' The atmosphere changes, nature goes quiet and the lane's white features are likened to the paleness of Tess's skin. Her father refuses to send the remains of Prince to the knacker's yard and buries him at home. The horse was the source of income for the household. 'The breadwinner had been taken away from them: what would they do?' (The Maiden, Ch. 4).

A dangerous moment?

KEY **moment**

Tess has to journey out with the workforce to Chaseborough. The Queen of Spades, Car Darch, is incensed to find a jar of treacle has been spilled down her back. Everyone laughs, including Tess, but it is the latter who is singled out for harsh treatment. The women encircle Tess. At this point, Alec appears and offers her a ride. Reluctantly, she rides off with him, pleased to have escaped the women. Car's mother says she is going 'out of the frying pan into the fire' (The Maiden, Ch. 10).

Alec's pursuit of Tess

KEY **moment**

Alec is determined to treat Tess like a lover, but she is reluctant. As much as she felt happy to be released from the women's clutches, she is uneasy in Alec's presence. She is unsettled when she realises how far they have strayed from the road and that they are in the wood. Tiredness descends upon her as she has been up since five o'clock. Alec places his arm around Tess but she brushes it away. He argues that he was only being kind. She is sorry. She explains she is leaving tomorrow. He declares his love for her, but she is horrified. Fog descends around them. Alec explains that because of the fog he is unsure of their exact location. He tells her he has given her father a new cab-horse and the children toys. She expresses her gratitude, but without enthusiasm, and is awkward in his company. She shivers in the cold. He places his light overcoat around her and explains that in September it gets colder in the evenings. He leaves her down amongst the leaves and pledges to return.

'Where was Tess's guardian angel?'

When he does return, he finds her sleeping amongst the leaves, just where he left her. A different narration takes over: 'Where was Tess's guardian angel?' The sexual impropriety of Tess's ancestors is briefly mentioned. The moment is critical for Tess's future development: 'An immeasurable social chasm was to divide our heroine's personality thereafter from that previous self of hers who stepped from her mother's door to try her fortune at Trantridge poultry-farm.' The implication is that Tess is raped by Alec (The Maiden, Ch. 11).

Tess
of the d'Urbervilles
Thomas Hardy

FIRST PUBLISHED:

Tess of the d'Urbervilles was serialised in 1889 by the illustrated weekly newspaper, *The Graphic*. Despite its later success as a defining work of literature, the novel was deemed too controversial for Victorian tastes and was censored, taking out all mention of Alec's seduction of Tess and her love child, Sorrow.

ABOUT THE AUTHOR:

Thomas Hardy (1840–1928) was born in Dorset, England, and regarded himself primarily as a poet who wrote novels mainly for financial gain. Works such as *Tess* and *Far from the Madding Crowd* earned him a reputation as a great novelist. The bulk of his fictional works explore tragic characters struggling against their passions and social circumstances.

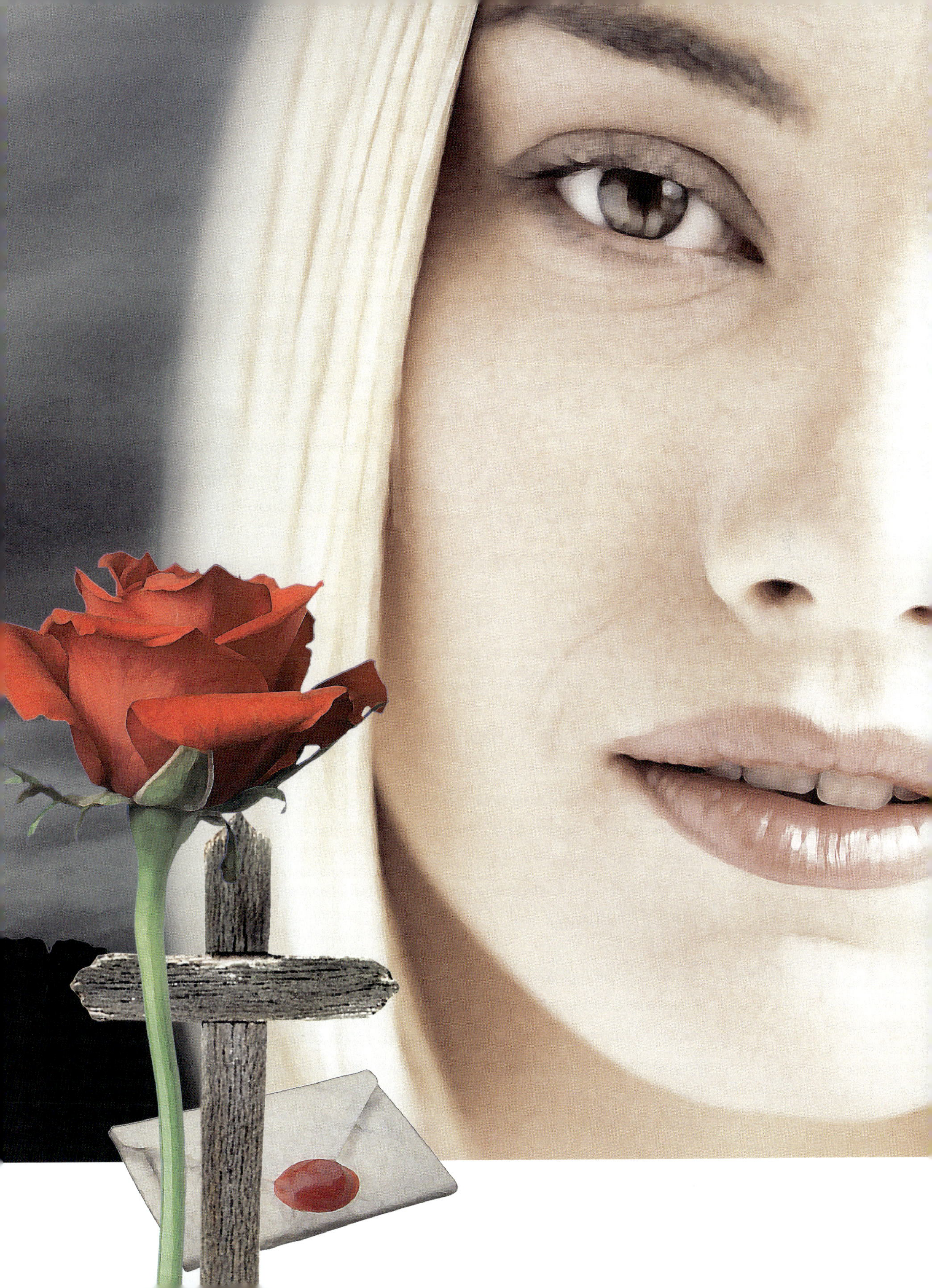

KEY moment Tess's distress

Tess explains to Alec that she is leaving, as he lights a cigar. Silence ensues. A few tears well up in her eyes. She answers him in monosyllables. He asks her why she is crying. She explains that she was born there. He retorts that everyone is born somewhere. Tess expresses a wish that she had never been born. She explains to a bewildered Alec that she did not understand his intentions towards her. Alec dismisses this as a mere excuse often used by many women, but Tess turns on him, saying: 'Did it never strike your mind that what every woman says some women may feel?' He says he is sorry and promises to provide for her in future. She asks him to leave her under the clump of trees. He wishes to give her a kiss but a stone-faced Tess merely offers her cheek by turning her head from side to side as she would for a portrait artist or hairdresser. He reasons that she will never love him. Tess calls him her 'four months' cousin' and he leaves her there to walk dispiritedly along the 'crooked lane' (Maiden No More, Ch. 12).

> *'Did it never strike your mind that what every woman says some women may feel?'*

KEY moment Tess as mother to her dying infant, Sorrow

Tess's newborn finds it difficult to breathe. Tess is concerned that the infant might die before he is baptised. She becomes her infant's parson and performs the ceremony by lighting candles and sprinkling water. She is watched by the children. Silence ensues.

Later, her child dies. He is buried in 'that shabby corner of God's allotment' (Maiden No More, Ch. 14).

KEY moment Tess's revelation to Angel

Angel is stunned to learn that his wife had a child by another man. He pokes at the fire, trying to come to terms with this revelation. She pleads with Angel to forgive her for her transgressions, but Angel is deeply reluctant. He reasons that Tess is not the woman he married. She is unsettled by his response and pleads her cause. Harshly, he looks upon her as an 'impostor; a guilty woman in the guise of an innocent one.' She is seized by the terrifying implications of his rejection of her, though his cutting sarcasm is lost on her. She begs his forgiveness. He admits that she is 'more sinned against than sinning,' but derides her ancestry, claiming that there is a link between the decline of her family's greatness and her 'want of firmness.' He re-examines his assessment of her as a 'new-sprung child of nature' and degrades her as a 'belated seedling of an effete aristocracy.' Tess thinks of drowning herself in the river but Angel dissuades her. However, Tess's history with Alec has poisoned her relationship with Angel. Angel adopts a rigid moralistic position and all but disowns her. He gives her money and flees to Brazil (The Woman Pays, Ch. 35).

Tess's murder of Alec

KEY moment

Mrs Brooks listens intently at the door after Tess ascends the stairs in her nightgown to Alec's room. She has just discovered that a contrite Angel was searching for her after his return from Brazil. As she goes into the room, Mrs Brooks listens to the unfolding argument between Tess and Alec. Alec is aware of the change in her composure. Tess's torment and distress is being communicated here. She explains how he has effectively manipulated the situation to his advantage and reasons that her hope for reconciliation with Angel is now lost. Words appear to fail her. Mrs Brooks notices her lips are bleeding. As Tess appears to move closer to the doorway, Mrs Brooks fears she will be found there, listening, so retreats down the stairs.

Afterwards, Tess appears, fully dressed, running down the stairs. She does not say goodbye. Silence ensues. There is a dripping sound. Fearing the worst, Mrs Brooks calls one of the workmen. She and the man make their way up to Alec's lodgings where they find an empty room. The breakfast is untouched, but the carving knife is missing. Mrs Brooks asks the man to go through to the adjoining room. Shocked, the man returns: 'My good God, the gentleman in bed is dead. I think he has been hurt with a knife – a lot of blood has run down upon the floor' (Fulfilment, Ch. 56).

Tess's arrest and tragic end

KEY moment

Tess and Angel spend one blissfully happy week together, but during their final hours together the police encircle Stonehenge. Tess asks Angel to look after her younger sister, Liza Lu, who has 'all the best of me without the bad.'

Tess is sleeping when the police find her. Angel asks for a few moments' respite. They relent. Tess awakens and, passively, she accepts the inevitability of her fate.

Later, Angel and Liza-Lu watch as the flag signalling an execution is raised. This marks the end of Hardy's heroine.

Never Let Me Go
BY KAZUO **Ishiguro**

A group of 'students,' Kathy, Tommy and Ruth, grow up together in what at first seems to be an ordinary boarding school in Hailsham. The narrator, Kathy H, now thirty-one, struggles to come to terms with her childhood and the dark reasons behind her very existence. As the story unfolds, it becomes clear that this is not a typical school; neither are Kathy, Tommy and Ruth mere ordinary students.

KEY **moment** Kathy's life as a carer

Kathy is proud of her accomplishments as a carer. Her donors tend to do much better than expected. She is happy to be offered the opportunity to choose her donors but it soon appears that the freedom to choose is meaningless as there are 'fewer and fewer donors left who I remember' (p. 4). She always chooses donors from Hailsham. She speaks to one of the donors, who is giving his third donation, and realises that he must be aware that 'he wasn't going to make it.' He asks her about Hailsham, anxious to hear her memory of it. As she talks to him, she is aware of the blurring of the distinction between her memories and his. However, as she reminisces about her life at Hailsham she considers how 'lucky' she has been (p. 5).

KEY **moment** Ruth's deception and a craving for love

One of the 'students' in Hailsham spreads the rumour that Ruth has been given the gift of a pencil case. Ruth lets everyone think it is from Guardian Geraldine. Kathy soon uncovers her deception.

One day Kathy admits she scanned the register, noticing who bought certain objects. Ruth snaps that it is a 'boring sort of thing to look at.' Kathy disagrees – it provides interesting information: it records those who bought certain items. Ruth is visibly upset but tries to hold back the tears. Kathy is unsettled that she has upset her 'dearest friend.' She quickly realises the reason for Ruth's deception: they all crave love. 'Didn't we all dream from time to time about one guardian or other bending the rules and doing something special for us? A spontaneous hug, secret letter, a gift?' Kathy tries to ameliorate the situation. Silence ensues. Ruth walks away (pp. 59–60).

Denied the chance to be a mother KEY moment

Kathy takes a particular liking to Judy Bridgewater's song 'Never Let Me Go.' She creates a story surrounding this song. Kathy imagines that the song is about a woman who is told she cannot have children but then, miraculously, gives birth. She is delighted but is also fearful that the child will become 'ill or be taken away from her.' Kathy realises that her story does not fit in with the rest of the lyrics but this does not perturb her.

One very bright, sunny day in the dormitory, she plays the song at a higher volume than before. She takes up a pillow and uses it to hold an imaginary baby in her arms, closing her eyes in concentration. Then, she notices Madame at the doorway peering in at her. She says that she 'froze in shock' but notices that there are tears in Madame's eyes. She expects to be reprimanded but Madame is silent. Kathy is conscious of Madame's look: 'But she just went on standing out there, sobbing and sobbing, staring at me through the doorway with that same look in her eyes she always had when she looked at us, like she was seeing something that gave her the creeps.' Kathy detects there is more to her look: 'Except this time there was something else, something extra in that look I couldn't fathom.' Madame turns away but Kathy still hears her crying as her footsteps fade along the dormitory corridor. Later, she confides in Tommy, who offers his own explanation: 'So when she saw you dancing like that, holding your baby, she thought it was really tragic, how you couldn't have babies' (pp. 70–73).

Miss Lucy's outburst and the truth KEY moment

Miss Lucy refers to the culture of secrecy that prevails at Hailsham. The extent of the deception becomes clear during Miss Lucy's outburst.

All the students are gathered in the pavilion. Kathy is distracted by Laura's joke until she notices that Miss Lucy is addressing the students. Miss Lucy asks Peter to repeat what he has just been saying to a fellow student. Peter is surprised by Miss Lucy's question but she summarises what he has said. She vocalises Peter's intention to go to America to be an actor. She reiterates her point about the difference between what the students have been 'told' and 'not told.' Miss Lucy refutes the idea that any one of them will be actors or work in supermarkets. She explains that their lives are 'set out.' When they are adults, they will be required to donate their 'vital organs.' 'That's what each of you was created to do.' She underscores their separateness: 'You're not like the actors you watch on your videos, you're not even like me' (pp. 79–81).

> KEY **moment**

Miss Emily's chilling truths

Kathy and Tommy meet Miss Emily, who says that she is unable to entertain them for long because she is waiting for the men to arrive with her bedside cabinet. Kathy asks her about the rumour to defer. Miss Emily says that it was 'something for them to dream about, a little fantasy.' Kathy is calm at this point even though this revelation 'should have crushed' her. Miss Emily explains that deferrals do not exist. Tommy wonders if deferrals had been true in the past, but Miss Emily denies it. He also asks if there ever was a gallery. Miss Emily replies in the affirmative. Kathy asks why all the art lessons were necessary given that their purpose for existing is to donate their vital organs and then die. Miss Emily acknowledges this question. She explains that it was to prove to the higher authorities, on whose sponsorship Hailsham depended, that the students had souls. Kathy and Tommy look at each other, puzzled by Miss Emily's reply. Miss Emily refers to how other students are brought up in appalling conditions that are very different from the privileged environment in Hailsham. She refers to this 'dream of yours, this dream of being able to defer.' Miss Emily says that she has no power to grant this.

She continues that before Hailsham, students or clones existed to supply medical science: 'In the early days, after the war, that's largely all you were to most people. Shadowy objects in test tubes.' Kathy questions why students should be badly treated. Miss Emily refers to the necessity for donations to be constantly available: 'There was no way to reverse the process.' Miss Emily explains that the primary concern was for the human population: 'However uncomfortable people were about your existence their overwhelming concern was that their own children, their spouses, their parents, their friends, did not die from cancer, motor neurone disease, heart disease.' As long as the world requires donations, Miss Emily argues, there will always be a 'barrier' to recognising Kathy and Tommy as fully human.

Kathy enquires about the Morningate Scandal. Miss Emily explains that a scientist had tried to produce children who were 'demonstrably *superior* to the rest of us?' She continues, saying that this superiority frightened people and so the funding for Hailsham simply dried up. The situation is hopeless: 'Your life must run the course that's been set for it.' She realises that this means they are 'pawns' but she tries to sweeten it by suggesting that they were 'lucky pawns.' Miss Emily continues to speak of the trends that come and go, but Kathy explains, 'it's our life.'

> *'In the early days, after the war, that's largely all you were to most people. Shadowy objects in test tubes'*

They ask her about Miss Lucy. Miss Emily describes her as a 'peripheral figure' and emphasises the importance of 'sheltering' the students in Hailsham. Kathy asks her why Madame appeared to be afraid of them, the way people are 'afraid of spiders and things.' Miss Emily is not irritated by the question; rather she explains that Madame did her very best for them. She admits that all the guardians were afraid of them. She admits that she feels 'such revulsion' towards them but that she fights against her feelings in order to do her job at Hailsham (pp. 252–64).

Kathy's conversation with Madame

KEY moment

Kathy meets Madame. She asks her if she remembers the incident in the dormitory. Madame admits that she does remember that day. Kathy explains the story surrounding the song. Madame has an 'altogether different reason.' She thought Kathy was holding the 'old kind world' to her heart knowing that it would 'not remain.' She looks at Kathy and at Tommy. She calls them 'Poor creatures.' Her eyes well up with tears (pp. 266–67).

KEY **moment** Kathy's farewell

Kathy explains that they 'didn't do any big farewell number that day.' Tommy comes down the stairs and they walk around the deserted square together. Tommy explains to her that when he scored a goal in Hailsham he would simply put his hands in the air. He tells her that he imagines that he is simply splashing in the water. Playfully, Kathy calls him a 'crazy kid.' They share a kiss. Then Kathy drives away in her car. She spots him smiling and waving to her. Still raising his hand, he turns away (p. 280).

KEY **moment** Kathy's memories

When Kathy hears that Tommy has 'completed,' she drives up to Norfolk. She looks into a field. She notices the rubbish that is entangled in the fence and the plastic carrier bags that are caught in the trees. She compares this to the 'debris' along the seashore. She is lost in thought. She expresses the hope that everything that was lost has 'washed up' in Norfolk. Then she imagines the faint figures of Tommy and Ruth calling out to her. She refuses to let them come any closer as the tears roll down her face. Then, she drives off to 'wherever it was I was supposed to be' (p. 282).

Emma
BY JANE **Austen**

Emma is the youngest daughter of her indulgent father, Mr Woodhouse. Both lament the loss of Miss Taylor, Emma's governess and good family friend, when she marries Mr Weston. Emma is in full command of the family household. She takes it upon herself to arrange marriages for couples in the neighbourhood, most notably Harriet to Mr Elton. As the story progresses, her impulse to do this has disastrous consequences. Despite her interest in love affairs, she is unaware of her growing love for Mr Knightley and that provides much of the excitement in the latter stages of the book.

KEY **moment** Life in Highbury

The novel begins with a description of Emma's character. She is twenty-one years old and enjoys a privileged life. Her life has been filled 'with very little to distress or vex her.' Her mother died when she was very young. Miss Taylor is important in Emma's life. When Miss Taylor marries, Emma misses her company.

Now Emma and her father are alone at dinner and both feel the absence of Miss Taylor in their lives. Emma is convinced that she encouraged the match between Miss Taylor and Mr Weston, though at heart, she considers it a 'black morning's work.'

Emma's older sister, Isabella, is married and lives in London. Emma wishes Christmas will bring her back 'to fill the house and give her pleasant society again.' Her father cannot fill the void as he is 'much older in ways than in years.' These opening pages capture the quiet solitude in Highbury (Ch. 1).

Mr Knightley at Highbury

KEY **moment**

Mr Knightley is described as an 'old and intimate friend of the family.' He is the older brother of Isabella's husband. He is made very welcome. Emma thanks him for his kind attention. She expresses concern that he has walked all the way to their house. Mr Knightley asks her about Miss Taylor's wedding. He views it as a positive development for it is better for Miss Taylor not to have 'two persons to please; she will now have but one. The chances are that she must be a gainer.' Mr Woodhouse argues that Emma must be very unhappy to lose Miss Taylor's delightful company. Emma turns away at this point 'divided between tears and smiles.' Mr Knightley takes a different view: 'Every friend of Miss Taylor must be glad to have her so happily married.' Emma continues that she contrived the marriage herself but Mr Knightley doubts this, saying that she only made a 'lucky guess.' Emma insists on her part in the match, claiming that she was instrumental in encouraging the union. He argues that Miss Taylor is more than capable of taking charge of her own concerns. Mr Woodhouse laments the change as Miss Taylor's marriage means the breaking up of 'one's family circle grievously.' Emma resolves to find a husband for Mr Elton but Mr Knightley asserts that he can more than 'take care of himself' (Ch. 1).

> Mr Woodhouse laments the change as Miss Taylor's marriage means the breaking up of 'one's family circle grievously'

KEY moment ## Mr Elton's rejection of Miss Smith in favour of Miss Woodhouse

Mr Elton reveals his interest in Emma. A stunned Emma Woodhouse explains that she will only deliver messages to Miss Smith. Mr Elton is unconcerned for the welfare of Miss Smith and compares her unfavourably to Emma. Mr Elton is dismissive of Harriet Smith, claiming that there could be some men 'who might not object to – Everybody has their level.' He argues he is not 'quite so much at a loss.' Mr Elton is quite enraged at this point after his frank exchange of views with Emma: 'If there had not been so much anger, there would have been desperate awkwardness; but their straight-forward emotions left no room for the little zigzags of embarrassment' (Ch. 15).

KEY moment ## Mrs Weston's observation

Mrs Weston confides in Emma the attention Mr Knightley has paid Jane Fairfax. He delivered the carriage for her so that she would not have to walk out in the night. Emma intimates that Mr Knightley is 'really good natured, useful, considerate or benevolent' and is not surprised by his action. Mrs Weston starts to speak of a possible union between Mr Knightley and Miss Fairfax. Emma is startled by this and refutes the idea that Mr Knightley has any intention of marrying. She adds that she 'cannot at all consent to Mr Knightley marrying.' Emma is horrified at the thought of his partner being Jane Fairfax: 'every feeling revolts' (Ch. 26).

KEY moment ## Harriet's love for Mr Knightley

Emma is concerned about Harriet's reaction when she learns about the secret engagement between Frank Churchill and Miss Fairfax. Emma is struck by her friend's odd behaviour. In her conversation with Emma, Harriet refutes the idea that she ever had an interest in Frank Churchill. Her voice is described as being as excitable as Emma's. Emma claims that Harriet was grateful to Frank Churchill for saving her from the gypsies, but Harriet discloses that Mr Knightley is superior to 'every other being upon earth.' A shaken Emma wonders if there has been some mistake. Harriet hopes that her good-natured friend will not put 'difficulties in the way.' Emma merely asks about Mr Knightley's intentions towards her. Harriet insists that he feels the same way.

Emma asks her about Mr Martin but Harriet replies that she knows 'better now, than to care for Mr Martin, or to be suspected of it.' Emma is shocked by Harriet's revelation: 'She was bewildered amidst the confusion of all that had rushed on her within the last few hours.'

Emma is condescending towards Harriet. Her jealousy becomes obvious when she thinks of Harriet and Knightley: 'Mr Knightley and Harriet Smith! – Such an elevation on her side! Such a debasement on his! It was horrible to Emma to think how it must sink him in the general opinion, to foresee the smiles, the sneers, the merriment it would prompt at his expense; the mortification and disdain of his brother, the thousand inconveniences to herself.' Emma's true feelings come to the surface: 'She had no hope, nothing to deserve the name of hope, that he could have that sort of affection for herself, which was now in question; but there is a hope (at times a slight one, at times much stronger) that Harriet might have deceived herself, and be overrating his regard for *her*.' Now Emma realises that she never cared for Mr Churchill at all (Chs 47, 48).

Mr Knightley's feeling for Emma

KEY **moment**

Mr Knightley admits that he envied Frank Churchill. Uncharacteristically, he lacks confidence. His words stumble out: 'If I loved you less, I might be able to talk about it more.' Emma is delighted. She is contrite about Harriet and about leading her friend 'astray.' Mr Knightley admits that he came to see how Emma would greet the news of Frank Churchill's engagement to Miss Fairfax. When he judges that she is indifferent, this gives 'birth to a hope, that, in time, he might gain her affections himself.' Mr Knightley's jealousy of Frank Churchill is unfounded, especially when he realises that Emma is indifferent to the prospect of Frank marrying Jane. 'She was his own Emma' (Ch. 49).

> *'If I loved you less, I might be able to talk about it more'*

Emma's marriage to Mr Knightley

KEY **moment**

Emma is concerned about her father's unhappiness over her marriage to Mr Knightley. She 'could not bear to see him suffering.' Mr Woodhouse's attitude changes when Mrs Weston's poultry house is robbed. Mr Woodhouse is very fearful and is happy to depend upon the protection of Mr Knightley. Emma marries Mr Knightley without pomp or ceremony. While Mrs Elton is scathing about the ceremony, her friends are joyful for the happy couple (Ch. 55).

BY JOHN B. Keane Sive

Sive is a young girl with dreams, whose life is destroyed by her menacing aunt-in-law, Mena. Mena insists that she marries Seán Dóta, a rich old farmer, for financial reasons. Sive's own family circumstances leave her open to old rural prejudice. Her mother died when she was a baby. Her father drowned before he could marry her mother. Sive is an illegitimate child. Such unfavourable family circumstances bring shame and prejudice. Sive's main supporter is her Nanna. Mike is a hesitant figure who fails to control his overbearing, greedy wife. Liam Scuab is in love with Sive, but their love for each other is a source of tension in the Glavin household. The result of such social pressures drives Sive to choose the most heart-rending end.

KEY moment Bad blood

Nanna is sitting by the fire smoking a pipe. Furtively, she hides the pipe when Mena enters. Mena is preoccupied with household chores. There is a bad-tempered exchange between them. Nanna laments the day her son took her for a wife. Nanna is dismissive of Mena and is critical of her upbringing and family circumstances.

KEY moment Careful plotting

Thomasheen emerges at the doorway of the Glavin home. His voice is described as having a 'rasp-like quality.' He asks Mena if she is alone and goes over to the fire. Mena dismisses the matchmaking idea at first. Thomasheen says that a man has spotted Sive cycling to school in the village. Thomasheen continues that this man is 'greatly taken' by Sive: 'He have the mouth half-open when he do be talking about her.' Mena explains that Sive was born out of wedlock but Thomasheen explains that '''Tis the youth, blast you, that the old men do be after. 'Tis the heat before death that plays upon them.' Thomasheen compares Sive to a pony and continues the image by suggesting that Sive's potential suitor 'will buy well and lose all to have her. He have a wish for the girl.'

When Mena learns his name, she is startled and exclaims that he is as 'old as the hills.' Thomasheen broaches the lucrative advantages of such a match and tells her that she will be given two hundred sovereigns if Sive will consent. Mena asks what Thomasheen will receive and he admits he will receive a hundred pounds. Mena suggests that Sive will scorn Seán Dóta for she has 'high notions.' He mentions that Sive is a 'bye-child.' Mena says that Sive is as 'flighty like a colt.' Mena is annoyed: 'Good money going on her because her fool of a mother begged on the death-bed to educate her.' Thomasheen sees this as a 'mortal sin.' Mena emphasises that ''tis against nature. She'll have her eyes opened.' Thomasheen rubs his hands gleefully at this point. He advises her to keep the two hundred sovereigns in her mind. Nanna interrupts their meeting and there is an angry exchange between Nanna and Mena. Nanna makes unfavourable comments about Thomasheen. When she leaves, Thomasheen sees the advantages of marrying Sive and of being 'rid of that oul' devil.' Mena notes Mike's weakness for money (Act 1, Scene 1).

> *'Good money going on her because her fool of a mother begged on the death-bed to educate her'*

Driving Liam and Sive apart

KEY moment

Sive is very much in love with Liam. However, Sive's uncle, Mike, does not accept their relationship. They meet furtively. Sive worries what will happen if her Uncle Mike finds Liam in her home. Liam is unconcerned. Sive is startled when Liam informs her that Thomasheen has been visiting the house. Liam declares his love for her and arranges a meeting place. Mike catches them together. He is angry but Sive claims that Liam was just passing by. Mike disagrees and says that Liam is like 'a rat' when he sees the 'nest empty.' He is ordered away (Act 1, Scene 1).

KEY moment ## Seán Dóta's lust for Sive

Mena asks Sive to go to Seamus Dónal's cottage to borrow a rail. Mena comments that Sive has a 'gift for obliging.' Thomasheen encourages Seán Dóta to accompany her on the road. Seán emphasises his power: 'There will no one cross her path with Seán Dóta walking by her side.' Sive protests that she is unafraid of the dark but Thomasheen describes her as a 'hare' on the lonely road. Seán and Sive leave together and Thomasheen is delighted: 'The seed is sown; the flower will blossom.'

Later that evening, Sive returns home. She meets Nanna and explains that she had been asked to go down to Dónal for a rail. Sive relates what happened when Seán Dóta accompanied her on the road: 'He nearly tore the coat off me. I ran into Dónal's kitchen but he made no attempt to follow' (Act 1, Scene 2). Nanna tells her that some men are like this.

KEY moment ## Nanna's isolation in her own home

When Pats and Carthalawn leave, the atmosphere becomes all the more menacing. Thomasheen accuses Nanna of broadcasting his affairs around the whole countryside. He says she is 'a lone woman' since her husband passed away. Thomasheen tells how old women are left in county homes, scrambling for a few potatoes. Mena is heartless: 'Walking the road she should be like the rest of her equals.' Mena even opens the door and shows her the world beyond. Nanna is angered: 'There is a hatchery of sin in this house.' She is defeated. Nanna stings Mena when she castigates her for being childless. Mena is enraged at this point and aims to strike her but she is held back by Thomasheen. Nanna finally rises and retires to her room. Mena looks towards Nanna's room with 'murderous intent.' Thomasheen claims that Nanna is 'tiring' (Act 1, Scene 3).

KEY moment ## Sive's growing isolation within her family

Sive enters with her satchel of books in her hand. Tentatively, she speaks to Mena about the puncture in her tyre and how she had to walk home. Thomasheen leaves. Sive is startled when Mena fusses over her meal. She tells Sive that there will be no more school. After some hesitation, Sive replies that she could never live with an old man, but her protests are angrily dismissed by Mena. Mena judges the situation well here. Sive stares beyond Mena towards the audience. Mena spells out the advantages of being driven while ordinary people walk. Sive is unconvinced, citing the possible adverse reaction amongst her peers. Sive's interest is gained when Mena mentions her family. Sive is eager to know more but her hopes are quickly dashed when Mena calls her a 'bye-child, a common bye-child – a bastard.' Sive tries to leave at this point but Mena takes her roughly by the arm, flinging her satchel across the room. Sive is forced to listen to the story of Mena's poverty-stricken life. Mena emphasises the importance of marrying a man of property in order to escape from poverty (Act 1, Scene 3).

> Mena emphasises the importance of marrying a man of property in order to escape from poverty

The only hope

KEY moment

Pats comes in furtively. Nanna comments, 'there's a great air of trickery about you.' Pats devises a plan but Nanna wonders if it is now too late. She emphasises Sive's distress. Pats declares that Liam loves Sive. Nanna explains that Sive is almost a prisoner in her own home. Pats' plan involves Sive creeping out of the house. They hear the sound of footsteps but Nanna allays Pats' fears. He continues to explain that Seán Dóta has 'no love for her. 'Tis the flesh of her he do be doting after.' Nanna gives him a coin and thanks him for his work. He gives her Liam's letter for Sive. Nanna hopes God will reward him. Pats admits he is a sinful man. Mike appears and Nanna conceals Liam's letter. Pats exchanges a few words with Mike and then departs (Act 2, Scene 2).

A dispirited Sive

KEY moment

Sive stands there totally unhappy in her new clothes. She takes off her high-heeled shoes and rubs her feet whilst holding on to the table. Slowly, she takes off her coat and hat and places them in her room. She emerges again with her flat shoes. She sits 'holding her hands in her lap awkwardly.' Mena places her hand on Sive's shoulder, asking her if she would like anything to eat, but she refuses. She seems totally dispirited. She refuses the drink Mike offers. Mena wonders if there is anything she would like. There is constant activity surrounding Sive but she seems oblivious to it, totally lost in her own thoughts.

She says that she will go to bed. She is described as rising 'slowly, wearily.' Thomasheen wonders if there is anything wrong, but Mena reassures him (Act 2, Scene 2).

KEY moment — The most heart-rending of ends

At first, all are frantic when they realise that Sive has disappeared. They stand back when Liam enters with Sive's lifeless body. Water drips from Liam and Sive. Thomasheen sneaks off at this point. Seán Dóta notices this and begins backing cowardly towards the door. Liam tells the tale of Sive's final minutes. He says that he saw her running towards the bog with 'only the little frock against the cold of the night.' Her cries could be heard in the night air. Mena wonders if she is dead. Liam crossly turns on her, accusing her of 'polluting the pure spirit of the child' with her nearness. Mike is deeply troubled and pleads with Liam to accompany him: 'There's no luck in going for a priest alone.' Liam leaves with Mike. Sive's body is left with Pats and Carthalawn. The scene ends with the pitiful image of a distressed Nanna crying over Sive's body (Act 2, Scene 2).

The Lonesome West
BY MARTIN McDonagh

This play depicts the lives of two brothers who live in a rural location in County Galway. Valene and Coleman often come to blows over the most trivial of subjects. The local priest, Fr Welsh, tries in vain to mediate between the warring brothers. Girleen Kelleher is a seventeen-year-old girl. She is in love with the priest. The weary priest writes a note to the brothers before he commits suicide. His words influence the brothers' subsequent behaviour.

KEY moment — Fr Welsh's conversation with Coleman

The opening exchanges between the priest, Fr Welsh, and Coleman suggest that there is a good deal of conflict in the family home. The scene occurs on the day that Valene and Coleman's father is buried. Fr Welsh reprimands Coleman for swearing. He comments on the good turnout, but Coleman claims that the congregation was made up of 'vultures only coming nosing.' Coleman also explains that his brother, Valene, is tight with money. Fr Welsh asks Coleman to admit that he is saddened by the death of his father, but he is reluctant to do so. He calls Fr Welsh the 'world's authority on lonesome' (Scene 1).

Coleman and Valene's argumentative relationship   KEY **moment**

Valene proudly carries in a number of figurines and carefully arranges them on the shelf. Fr Welsh remarks that Tom Hanlon was at the funeral. Coleman explains that he had his father arrested on a number of occasions for screaming at nuns. Valene expresses his hatred for the Hanlon family, as he blames them for the death of his dog. Coleman interjects that Valene has no evidence. Valene comments that he expects his brother to take the opposite view. Coleman remarks that the dog was always barking. Valene retorts that the dog did not deserve such cruel treatment and adds that it is natural for dogs to bark. Sarcastically, Coleman comments that the dog would have won the 'world's fecking barking record.'

Reflectively, Fr Welsh remarks that there is enough hatred in the world without Valene adding more. Coleman says that his cupboards are bare. Valene comments on Coleman's poverty: 'Never unbare are your cupboards.' Fr Welsh corrects Valene's grammar, insisting that there is no such word as 'unbare.' Coleman laughs, but Valene fails to see the humorous side. He says he noticed Fr Welsh communicating with Mick and Maureen at the funeral. Valene argues: 'a great parish it is you run, one of them murdered his missus, an axe through her head, the other her mammy, a poker took her brains out.' Fr Welsh agrees that God has no authority in this parish (Scene 1).

Fr Welsh's crisis of faith   KEY **moment**

Fr Welsh suggests that Coleman sees the 'good in people,' unlike himself, who is often at the 'head of the queue to be pegging the first stone.' Valene comments that this is yet another sign of his crisis of faith. Coleman concurs. Fr Welsh continues that he feels he has nothing to offer his parish at all. Coleman reports on his recent success in coaching the girls for the Connaught semi-finals, but the priest is quick to interject that this 'isn't enough to restore your faith.' He disagrees that the team was skilful as they cheated continuously (Scene 1).

KEY moment ## Who owns the house?
Coleman is sitting down reading *Woman's Own* magazine when Valene comes in carrying a bag. He places his hand on the stove to see if it is hot. Coleman claims he has not touched the stove. Valene asserts it is his stove as he paid three hundred pounds for it. He gloats at the prospect of the stove, gun and table being his and orders Coleman not to touch them without his express permission. Valene is the beneficiary of his father's will. He takes out his Tayto crisps and lays them on the table. Coleman offers his opinion on the superior taste of McCoy crisps. Valene claims Coleman drank some of his poteen, but his brother denies it. Then, Valene wonders if Coleman has squandered his insurance money, but Coleman insists he paid it. Frantically, Valene searches for his insurance book. He is not sure if it is O'Duffy's signature. Coleman claims Girleen fancies him and would provide him with free drinks. Valene scoffs at such a suggestion. Coleman starts to eat a bag of crisps. Valene insists he should pay for it. Coleman takes out twenty pence from his pocket and slams it on the table, saying that Valene can keep the change. Valene asserts he has 'no need of charity.' He gives him three pence change. Coleman throws the coins back at his brother. They scuffle on the floor. Fr Welsh interrupts to inform them that Tom Hanlon has committed suicide (Scene 2).

KEY moment ## The murder of Coleman and Valene's father
Valene is incensed that his brother has melted all his figurines in the stove. He vows to kill his brother. He walks around the room dazed and takes the gun down. Fr Welsh tries to intervene. Valene claims that one of his figurines was blessed by the Pope, but Fr Welsh says he cannot be provoked to violence over 'inanimate objects.' Valene is angry, but the priest argues that 'your own flesh and blood this is you're thinking of murdering.' Valene interjects that Coleman is responsible for the death of their father. The horrified priest says their father's death was an accident. Valene discloses that Coleman shot his father in the head, 'the same as he'd been promising to do since the age of eight and da trod on his Scalectrix.'

Coleman enters at this point, claiming he loved his Scalectrix as it had 'glow in the dark headlamps.' Valene turns the gun on his brother. Coleman is unperturbed and sits down. Fr Welsh tries to insist he did not kill his father deliberately. Valene is more concerned about the melting of his figurines. Coleman claims he did kill his father deliberately, as he was annoyed when his father made an unfavourable comment about his hair being 'like a drunken child's.' He insists it 'can never be excused.' Valene continues to lament the melting of his figurines. Coleman asserts there is another crime against God. He tells the shaken priest that Valene made him sign over his half-share of the property to him. Valene points the gun at Coleman. He pulls the trigger, but there are no bullets in the gun. Coleman produces the bullets. They scuffle on the floor. Fr Welsh is shocked by the brothers' violent behaviour. He distracts them by placing his fists into the bowl of steaming plastic. The brothers hear his screams and stop fighting. He rushes out. They agree he is 'outright mad' (Scene 3).

> Valene points the gun at Coleman. He pulls the trigger, but there are no bullets in the gun. Coleman produces the bullets

Fr Welsh's letter

KEY moment

Fr Welsh contends that the brothers really care for each other. They have lived together all their lives. Fr Welsh describes it as a 'lonesome existence' as both men are bachelors. He believes his greatest achievement as a priest would be to see them 'becoming true brothers again.' Based on prior experience, it is easy to see why the priest would have seen this hope as 'bordering on the miraculous' and jokes that he might be 'canonised after.' Despite their history of violence, Fr Welsh writes that he has faith in them (Scene 5).

Coleman and Valene's reaction to Fr Welsh's suicide

KEY moment

In a moment of revenge, Valene makes a dive for Coleman's neck in an effort to take the Tayto crisps from him. They scuffle on the floor. Coleman is determined to crush the crisps. Girleen stands there dismayed until, finally, she goes to the drawer, takes out a knife and pulls Coleman back by the hair. Valene pleads for his brother and both brothers break up the fight immediately. Girleen lets go of her grip of Coleman and places Fr Welsh's letter on the table

THE LONESOME WEST

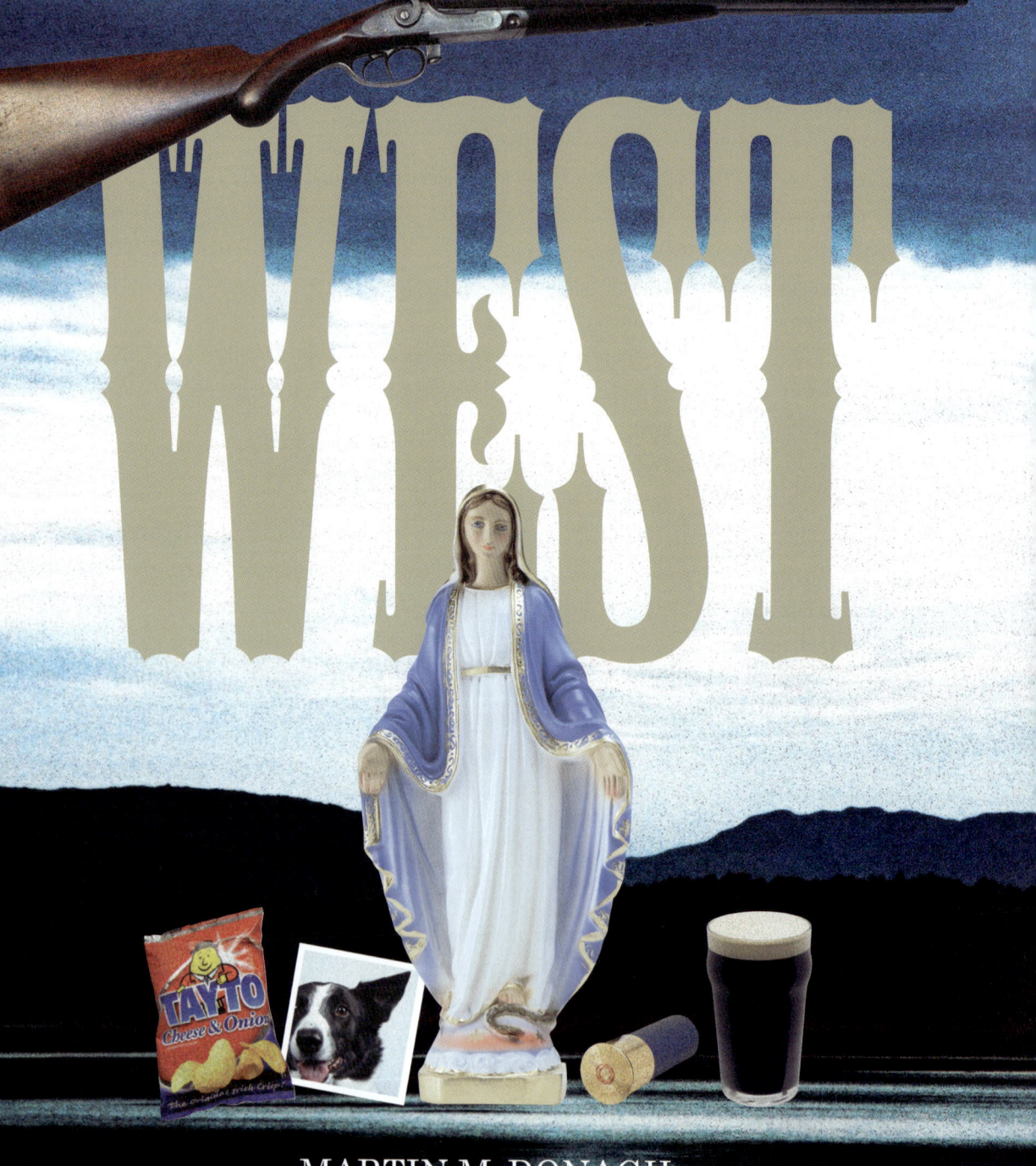

~ MARTIN McDONAGH ~

FIRST PERFORMED:
1997, Druid Theatre company and Royal Court co-production, Town Hall, Galway. It went on to win the Alfréd Radok Award for Best Play and was nominated for the Tony Award for Best Play in its first year.

ABOUT THE AUTHOR:
Martin McDonagh was born to Irish parents in Camberwell, London, in 1970. As a child, he spent nearly every summer in Connemara, where he became acquainted with the local dialect that features in his plays. His dramatic works to date include two dark comedic trilogies, *The Galway Trilogy* and *The Aran Islands Trilogy,* for which he has won numerous awards. McDonagh is also passionate about film, and following the success of *Six Shooter,* for which he won an Academy Award for Best Live Action Short Film in 2006, he wrote and directed his first full-length feature, *In Bruges.*

in front of them. She urges the brothers to read it. She summarises the contents: 'All about the two of ye loving each other as brothers it is.' Valene reads the part of the letter which relates to Coleman's murder of his father. Coleman laughs. At this point, Girleen sets about breaking her chain with a knife. She explains that for four months she had been saving her poteen money to buy the chain to give to Fr Welsh. Coleman tries to discourage her from cutting the chain whilst Valene argues that it is worth a tidy sum. Coleman says that he has never seen the point of letter writing.

Girleen asks if they liked the part of the priest's letter which referred to linking the priest's salvation with their reconciliation. Valene admits that he failed to understand that part. Girleen explains that the priest drowned in the lake in the same spot as Tom Hanlon. She pleads with the brothers to be reconciled: 'His soul in hell he's talking about, that only ye can save for him.' A horrified Coleman re-reads the letter. Valene offers her pendant back to her. She is visibly upset and leaves abruptly. Valene pledges to return the pendant to Girleen. Valene and Coleman admit that they are saddened to hear of the priest's death. Valene admits that 'Fr Welsh going topping himself does put arging o'er Taytos into perspective anyways.' Both reiterate this point clearly. When they realise that the priest's first name was Roderick they are on the brink of laughter, but stop themselves (Scene 6).

> *'His soul in hell he's talking about, that only ye can save for him'*

KEY **moment** A tenuous reconciliation?

An angry Valene is upset that Coleman has broken his stove and his figurines. He approaches his brother with a knife. Coleman takes up the gun. It is unclear to Valene or the audience whether Coleman has actually loaded the gun. A very tense stand-off ensues. Coleman explains that he wants to see Valene's stove and figurines destroyed before he dies. Valene expresses his desire to kill Coleman. Coleman replies: 'Try so.' Valene stares at him and then goes to return the knife to the drawer. He touches Fr Welsh's letter. He thinks about Fr Welsh: 'Fr Welsh is burning in hell, now, because of our fighting.' Coleman contends that he did not ask the priest to gamble his soul on their possible reconciliation and argues that five pounds would have been too great a stake, never mind a soul. He extols the virtues of fighting but admits that killing his father and Valene's dog went too far. Coleman apologises for these ghastly acts and says that he will repair the smashed figurines with superglue. Both agree that Fr Welsh was a '*middling* fella.' Valene is startled to discover that Coleman stole the insurance money. Valene seizes the knife in a rage but Coleman runs out of the door.

A tearful Valene discovers that Coleman had loaded the cartridges in the gun. He throws the gun away and takes out Fr Welsh's letter. He begins to light a match. He re-examines the impact of Fr Welsh's suicide: 'Do I need your soul hovering o'er me the rest of me fecking life?' He does not damage the letter: he has a change of heart. Instead he smoothes the letter out and places it back with Girleen's chain. He adds that he does not have to buy Fr Welsh a drink now. Sadly, he looks at the letter and the crucifix. Then he leaves. The light remains focused on the priest's letter and the crucifix for a half second longer (Scene 7).

Dancing at Lughnasa BY BRIAN Friel

This is the heartbreaking tale of the Mundy family, who struggle to survive on a small farm in Ballybeg in the 1930s. Kate, the eldest sister, tries to dominate the family. Jack arrives home from his time as a missionary priest amongst the lepers in Africa. Chris, the youngest sister, has an illegitimate son, Michael, who narrates the play from his earliest memory to the poignant end of the play. The play also describes young Michael's first meeting with his father, Gerry. The sisters gather together to protect Rose, but Agnes takes special care of her. Maggie is the cook and keeps the family together. The sisters love dancing and music, which transform their mundane lives. A number of unfortunate events conspire to break up the Mundy family.

Foreboding

KEY **moment**

The opening scene has two elements. Michael narrates while all the characters form a tableau, after which the sisters engage in animated conversation.

The sisters love to dance. Michael tells the audience that Kate insists that the wireless is called 'Marconi.' Maggie's whimsical name 'Lugh' is viewed as too pagan for the religious Kate. Michael speaks about the earlier arrival of Fr Jack from the leper colony. Instead of being the hero that Michael imagined him to be, he is described as a 'forlorn figure' who is 'shuffling from room to room as if he were searching for something but couldn't remember what.' Change is seen as a negative force: 'And even though I was only a child of seven at the time, I know I had a sense of unease, some awareness of a widening breach between what seemed to be and what was, of things changing too quickly before my eyes, of becoming what they ought not to be' (Act 1).

> Maggie's whimsical name 'Lugh' is viewed as too pagan for the religious Kate

KEY moment Family togetherness

Some of the Mundy sisters set about their daily chores. Maggie is making a mash for the hens and Agnes is busily knitting gloves. Rose carries in a basket of turf and Chris is ironing. Their activities come to an abrupt end when Chris begins to stare at herself in the cracked mirror. She wonders why it is still hanging on the wall. Maggie insists that it keeps out bad luck. Agnes ponders on her deepening wrinkles. Chris thinks she will start wearing lipstick. Maggie comments humorously that tomorrow it will be the gin bottle. Agnes alludes to Kate's stern approach when she repeats her words: 'Do you want to make a pagan of yourself?' Chris holds up the surplice suggesting that it would make a nice dress while Rose spontaneously bursts into song: 'Will you come to Abyssinia, will you come?' She dances around the room. Maggie is just about to light a cigarette. She commends Rose's performance. They both dance around the room. Rose switches on the wireless and they all hear a few seconds of music entitled 'The British Grenadiers.' The music stops abruptly (Act 1).

KEY moment Family arguments and the arrival of Gerry

Kate and Maggie watch at the window as Chris dances with Gerry. Kate comments on Chris's relationship with Gerry. Agnes snaps at Maggie: 'I'm busy! For God's sake can't you see I'm busy.' Maggie is surprised by her reaction.

The spotlight turns to Gerry and Chris, who are dancing together. Outside, Gerry pledges his love for Chris, but she knows he is unreliable. Inside, Kate constantly refers to Gerry as the 'creature.' Agnes reminds Kate that he has a Christian name. Meanwhile, Kate is annoyed that 'the creature has no sense of ordinary duty.' She wonders if Gerry even realises how Chris has to work to provide for her son, Michael. Agnes rises and is about to leave through the back door. Kate continues to admonish Gerry, arguing that 'the beasts of the field have more concern for their young than that creature has.' Agnes is infuriated at this point, insulted by Kate's constant reference to Gerry as 'the creature.' Agnes retorts that his name is Gerry and repeats it earnestly. She calls her a 'damned righteous bitch.' Agnes is on the verge of tears and leaves. Kate is aghast at Agnes's outburst but Maggie offers her no suggestions as to the cause of their sister's displeasure. Maggie just claims that Agnes is concerned also for Chris's welfare. Kate is annoyed that Gerry's presence 'suddenly poisons the atmosphere in the whole house.' Maggie just starts to sing and Kate comments on the way she knows the 'aul pagan songs' better than she does her Christian prayers. Kate has a change of heart, realising that she is being self-righteous (Act 1).

> *'... the beasts of the field have more concern for their young than that creature has'*

'It's all about to collapse'

KEY moment

Kate worries about the future. She feels that all her work is in vain. She believes in responsibility, obligation and good order. Now she notices that 'hair cracks' are 'appearing everywhere; that control is slipping away.' She is also fearful that the 'whole thing is so fragile it can't be held together much longer. It's all about to collapse.' Kate is worried that Chris will relapse into one of her depressions when Gerry is gone. She fears for the future, especially for Rose. She realises that she may not have a job in September and suspects that the parish priest is lying to her about the falling numbers of students attending her school. Maggie tries to reassure her that nothing is about to collapse. It is a touching scene as Kate falls into her arms for comfort. She holds on to a fragile hope (Act 1).

KEY **moment**   Jack's different view on the family

Jack asks about Michael's whereabouts. Chris replies that he is busy making kites. Jack then enquires about Chris's husband. Kate answers that she is unmarried and that Michael's father is Welsh. Maggie takes up the point that all the 'sisters are in the same boat, Jack. We are hoping that you'll hunt about and get men for all of us.' Jack then calls Michael a 'love-child.' Chris agrees. Jack is proud of Michael, claiming that Chris is lucky to have him. Agnes argues that they are all lucky. Jack then goes on to say that Ryangan women are always anxious to have 'love-children,' as children bestow fortune upon the household. He asks the other sisters if they have love-children but Kate reacts angrily at this point, adding that in Ballybeg love-children are 'not exactly the norm.' Kate then urges her brother to take some exercise and his medicine (Act 1).

Michael narrates that Kate had been right about Jack. She would lose her job in the local school because of Jack's wayward beliefs. Kate's fears about Rose were also to be realised. The family was soon to break up before their very eyes.

KEY **moment**   Rose's disappearance

When Rose goes missing, the sisters are frantic. In different ways, they are concerned for her. Rose's disability is more obvious in this scene. The audience is invited to share the sisters' concern. They argue about the possible choice of response until Maggie co-ordinates their efforts. However, very soon, an easily distracted Rose arrives home having placed a fistful of berries in her mouth. Agnes rushes over to her, wanting to hug her but instead she 'catches her arm.' Agnes merely asks her if she is better now. Rose reassures her. Maggie is more than willing to change the subject to food while Agnes promises Rose that they will go bilberry picking the following Sunday. She then enquires about the cans. Rose explains that she has left the cans behind the quarry wall and that she will collect them in the evening. She asks for her overall.

Kate has been quiet up to now. Just as Rose is about to walk to her room, Kate questions her further. Rose informs Kate that she has been in Lough Anna. Kate asks her to repeat her answer. Chris tries to intervene at this point. Rose admits that she has spent the afternoon with Danny Bradley on his father's boat and that she had brought along chocolate biscuits and a bottle of milk. She retorts that the Sweeney boy is not dying as Kate had earlier claimed. Kate is concerned about Rose's liaison with Danny Bradley and the shame that it might bring on the family (Act 2).

The real crisis of Rose and Agnes' departure
KEY **moment**

Michael narrates that one morning the family awoke to find that Agnes had left a note saying that she and Rose are departing for England. Her handwriting is described as 'resolute.' This emphasises Agnes's determination to leave home. Rose accompanied her. Despite their best efforts, the other Mundy sisters fail to find them (Act 2).

The last scene of the Mundy family together and Michael's narration
KEY **moment**

It is a sunny day and the family is in the garden. Jack is wearing his army uniform, but it does not fit him. There is a ceremonial exchange of hats between Jack and Gerry. Jack reiterates that he was an army chaplain in the Great War. Gerry does a Charlie Chaplin impression. There is talk about the wireless. Agnes explains that Gerry fixed the wireless, but it is broken again. Chris comments it is 'possessed.' Kate says that September is her favourite month. Agnes promises Rose that they will go bilberry picking the following Sunday. Gerry is proud of the artwork on Michael's kite. Kate agrees that Chris has a 'very talented son.' Towards the end, Maggie tries to share her joke about the gramophone, but forgets the essentials of the joke.

> The sisters adopt the same positions they had at the beginning of the play with a few changes

The sisters adopt the same positions they had at the beginning of the play with a few changes. Agnes and Gerry are on the garden seat. Jack is dressed in his old army uniform beside Agnes. Rose is positioned upstage left. Maggie is at the kitchen window. Kate cries. Michael narrates.

Michael explains that Fr Jack died of a heart attack. He says Agnes and Rose's departure left a deep void amongst the remaining sisters. Kate obtains a job teaching Austin Morgan's children. Chris works in the knitting factory. Maggie behaves as if 'nothing had changed.' The play ends with the song 'It's

Time to Say Goodnight.' There is an air of nostalgia while Michael shares his memories of the Lughnasa weeks of 1936. Dance, a 'wordless ceremony,' has a powerful effect on the sisters.

A Doll's House
BY HENRIK Ibsen

Nora is married to Torvald Helmer, a bank manager. Nora has a childish, dependent relationship with her status-conscious husband. Out of love for her husband, Nora commits a transgression. Anxious to save her husband's life, she borrows money from Krogstad using her father's forged signature as guarantor for a loan. Her deception is uncovered and she finds herself blackmailed by Krogstad. Helmer soon discovers the truth and reprimands his wife severely. At this point, the dynamics in their relationship change and Nora engages in her first mature conversation with her husband in eight years of marriage.

KEY moment Nora's relationship with her husband, Helmer

Nora returns in festive cheer and furtively listens at her husband's door. Helmer is in his study. He calls her 'my skylark.' She pops a few macaroons into her mouth. Excitedly, Nora wants to show her husband what she has bought. Helmer is startled by the word 'bought.' He opens his study door. He asks her if she has been overspending again. Nora delights in Helmer's new position. She pleads for more money at Christmas. She wonders why he does not just borrow money, now that he has a secure position in the bank. Helmer is determined that he will not borrow: 'A home that is founded on debts and borrowing can never be a place of freedom and beauty.' He hands her some money for the Christmas season and asks her what she would like for a Christmas present. She simply pleads for more money. He describes her as an 'expensive pet.' Nora accepts his definition of her: 'If you only knew how many expenses we larks and squirrels have.' He fears that his wife has inherited her

> *'A home that is founded on debts and borrowing can never be a place of freedom and beauty'*

father's spendthrift qualities and asks her if she spent money in the pastry shop. She denies it, though it is clear to the audience that she is lying (Act 1).

Krogstad's menace
KEY moment

Nora plays happily with her children until Krogstad appears at the doorway. Nora is unnerved by his presence and quickly ushers the children away. She is concerned that he should arrive on Christmas Eve. Krogstad coldly suggests that her happiness over the festive season depends on her. He asks about Mrs Linde's new position. Nora claims she had some influence over her husband. He enquires if Nora would help him. At this point, she denies that she has any sway over her husband's decisions. He mentions the loan she took out. In particular, he refers to the IOU which her father signed. He cross-examines her and during the questioning she unwittingly admits that her father died on the twenty-ninth of September. Krogstad realises Nora's deception immediately as the date on the IOU suggests that her father had been alive three days later. Nora is silent. Then, defiantly, she acknowledges that she forged her father's signature. Krogstad is aware of the legal implications of Nora's admission. Nora states her reasons, but Krogstad is quick to interject that the law does not concern itself with motives. He threatens her. Nora is left deeply distressed. When he leaves, the delighted children return, but a troubled Nora shepherds them away (Act 1).

Nora's monologue
KEY moment

Nora is deeply unsettled by Helmer's words. Helmer claims that lies and deception poison the environment in the home. Nora is concerned for her children. When Helmer exits, Nora's distress is evident:

Nora: (Pale with fear) Corrupt my little children–! Poison my home! (Short pause. She throws back her head) It isn't true! It *couldn't* be true! (Act 1)

Nora's worst fears realised
KEY moment

Nora is deeply troubled by Krogstad's presence in her house as she is fearful that Helmer will uncover the truth. She walks over and bolts Helmer's study door. Krogstad is wearing an overcoat, heavy boots and a fur cap. At first, Krogstad feigns sympathy, claiming that the problem can be settled quite amicably. Then he produces the letter disclosing everything to her husband. He makes even more demands. He anticipates that Helmer will be compelled 'to create a new job' for him. He paints a terrifying image of those who have drowned in the 'cold, black water.' Krogstad delights in his prospective triumph over Helmer: 'I've got him in my pocket' (Act 2).

KEY moment — Time is running out

Helmer sits at the piano while Nora seizes the tambourine. She wraps a shawl around herself and dances the tarantella while Helmer plays the piano. He urges her to dance slowly but Nora is behaving frantically. Helmer stops abruptly. Dr Rank offers to play for Nora. Mrs Linde interrupts while Helmer notes that Nora is dancing as if her 'life depended upon it.' Nora agrees. He asks her to stop, disappointed that she has forgotten the steps he had taught her. She places her tambourine aside. Nora is passive here: 'You must show me every step of the way.' She pleads with him not to open the post and Helmer's suspicions are aroused. Dr Rank encourages him to give in to his wife and Helmer concedes. Nora is left alone with Mrs Linde, who reports that Krogstad has left town. Nora sits there 'waiting for the miracle to happen.' Mrs Linde wonders what miracle she expects. Mrs Linde leaves, while Nora simply counts the hours before Helmer opens Krogstad's letter (Act 2).

> Mrs Linde leaves, while Nora simply counts the hours before Helmer opens Krogstad's letter

KEY moment — Krogstad's and Mrs Linde's isolation

The Helmers' music is being played upstairs. Mrs Linde is anxiously awaiting Krogstad's arrival. She lets him in. He refers to her note. She pours out her heart to him. He is unsettled by her revelation that she married a man merely for the security of money. He clenches his fists. She pleads that she was in a precarious financial situation with her ill mother and young brothers to support. Krogstad expresses his hurt over her betrayal and his grief over losing her. He aptly describes himself as a 'shipwrecked man, clinging to a spar.' She tries to console him, but his suspicions are aroused, thinking she is trying to save her friend, Nora. Mrs Linde shares her own story of loneliness and expresses a hope that 'two shipwrecked souls could join hands.' She hopes she can be a mother to his children. Krogstad plans to ask for his damning letter back but Mrs Linde claims that Helmer needs to know the truth. Krogstad is blissfully happy (Act 3).

Helmer's horror at Nora's deception

KEY **moment**

Helmer is shocked to read the contents of Krogstad's letter. He questions Nora about it. Nora anticipates a miracle: 'You're not going to suffer for my sake. I won't let you!' Helmer is angry, castigating her as a 'hypocrite, a liar – worse, worse – a criminal.' He draws a parallel between her behaviour and that of her father: 'I repeat, all your father's recklessness and instability he has handed on to you!' He rebukes her for her lack of morality. Helmer contends that now Krogstad has power over him. He orders her to take off her shawl. Nora is silent while her husband declares that their relationship is over, except for public appearances. He is startled when the doorbell rings: 'Hide yourself, Nora.' Nora stands there motionless. The maid arrives with Krogstad's second letter. In it, Krogstad absolves Nora from all blame by returning the IOU. Helmer is delighted by his sudden reversal in fortunes. Nora goes to take off her fancy dress (Act 3).

A new Nora?

KEY **moment**

Nora emerges in her new clothes. She launches into her first direct and frank communication with her husband in eight years of marriage. She compares Helmer's treatment of her to that of her father. She likens her life with him to a playroom. She argues that her children have been her 'dolls.' She expresses the need to assert herself and discover her unique role in the world. Helmer is horrified that his wife intends to leave him. He protests that she has 'sacred duties,' but she insists that her first duty is to herself. Helmer calls on religion as an 'infallible guide in such matters.' Nora reacts to this. She no longer believes that something is true because it is written in books. Helmer is shocked by her answer and wonders how a young woman can have such thoughts.

Helmer is hurt by Nora's assertion that she no longer loves him, despite his kindness to her. Now she sees Helmer in a new light. She says she had expected Helmer to take full responsibility but was fearful of the consequences. This miracle failed to materialise. Nora explains that she had expected her husband to sacrifice himself for her. Helmer dismisses the idea: 'But no man can be expected to sacrifice his honour, even for the person he loves.' Nora retorts that many women sacrifice themselves. She claims that she can no longer stay in the house with a 'complete stranger.' Helmer is troubled by the prospect of his wife leaving him. Nora tells him that he is free of any obligation towards her. They exchange rings. She wonders how she could ever have thought that life with Helmer 'could become a marriage.' Then she walks out of the door. A fleeting moment of hope strikes Helmer only to be dashed when he hears the door slam behind her (Act 3).

Oedipus the King
BY Sophocles

This is the shockingly tragic tale of one man's search for his identity. Oedipus is a competent king of Thebes, who previously saved the Greek state from destruction by solving the riddle of the Sphinx. A delighted city state made him king. Now, the city's inhabitants are dying from a plague and they have come to their king for assistance. In this deeply religious society, Oedipus consults the oracle. He is informed that the previous king's murder has never been solved. He is determined to find the murderer, unaware that the murderer is himself. Horrified, Oedipus discovers that he has, unwittingly, killed his father and married his mother.

KEY moment The plague of Thebes

King Oedipus, concerned, listens as a despondent priest talks about the distress suffered by the people of Thebes. Oedipus is proud of his past achievements as king and is willing to assist his people in their present predicament. The priest vividly describes the state of the city: 'A blight on the fresh crops / and the rich pastures, cattle sicken and die / and the women die in labour, children stillborn.' He praises the king as the 'first of men.' Oedipus expresses his concern for his people, explaining that he swiftly sent his brother-in-law, Creon, to the oracle of Apollo at Delphi to ask assistance in deciding what course of action to follow. He is determined to carry out the oracle's pronouncements. He says he would be a traitor if he did not 'do all the god makes clear.'

Creon arrives. Oedipus prays: 'Lord Apollo, / let him come with a lucky word of rescue, shining like his eyes!' Spirits rise. Oedipus is determined that Creon should report the oracle's message publicly. Creon refers to the unsolved murder of King Laius. Ironically, Oedipus says that he 'never saw the man.' Creon informs Oedipus that Laius went to consult the oracle but never returned. He claims the king was killed by a band of robbers. Oedipus is dismayed to learn that his murder was left unsolved but Creon explains that they were distracted when the city was plagued by the Sphinx. Oedipus pledges to defend Apollo's interests: 'Whoever killed the king may decide to kill me too, with the same violent hand – by avenging Laius I defend myself' (1–160).

Seeing the truth

KEY **moment**

Oedipus is determined to uncover the truth. Tiresias, a blind prophet, is escorted by a boy into the palace. The prophet utters his grim prediction, 'How terrible – to see the truth / when the truth is the only pain to him who sees!' He pleads with the king to be sent home, but Oedipus presses him further, pleading with him not to leave. Oedipus is dismayed by the pessimism of the seer's words, but fails to appreciate their true meaning. Tiresias prefers to remain silent, but this response enrages Oedipus, who is verbally abusive towards him: 'Nothing! You, you scum of the earth, you'd enrage a heart of stone.' Tiresias expresses pity for the angry king, explaining that the insults he flings at him will come back to haunt him. The tension mounts and Tiresias finally answers Oedipus's accusation, claiming that the truth will reveal itself even if he remains silent. Oedipus then accuses the blind man of being implicated in Laius's murder. However, Tiresias labels Oedipus the 'curse and the corruption of the land.' Oedipus hurls abuse at the old man, mocking his blindness: 'You've lost your power, stone-blind, stone-deaf, senses, eyes blind as stone!' Tiresias insists that Creon is not the cause of his downfall; rather it is by his own hand. Triumphantly, Oedipus expresses his pride in solving the riddle of the Sphinx. Tiresias refers to a self-perception that Oedipus lacks. Rich corruption imagery is evoked: 'No man will ever / be rooted from the earth as brutally as you.' Tiresias refers to the dichotomy of Oedipus's life; the stranger who is really Theban-born and the horror of the revelation of his real identity. He predicts his future blindness. Oedipus ushers him out of his palace, banishing him from the court, enraged by his words (338–525).

KEY moment   Oedipus's accusation

Creon is deeply distraught to discover that Oedipus is accusing him of jointly conspiring to usurp him from the throne of Thebes. He feels the humiliation of being 'branded a traitor in the city.' Oedipus arrives, incensed to find Creon in the palace. He takes on the role of inquisitor, asking why Tiresias did not accuse him of Laius's murder until now. Creon says that he does not want the trappings of power. He pleads not to be convicted on flimsy evidence. The chorus plead Creon's case but Oedipus calls him his 'mortal enemy.' Jocasta arrives and tries desperately to appease the warring parties. The chorus continues to plead Creon's case in the light of his previous good character and expresses the hope that Oedipus will not 'cast him out – disgraced.' Oedipus is moved by the chorus's pleas and so relents, but his anger at Creon remains (573–750).

KEY moment   The messenger arrives

A messenger arrives to inform Oedipus that Polybus is dead. In a way, Oedipus is relieved as he feared that the horrific deed foretold by the oracle would come true. Jocasta is equally reassured that Oedipus's fears were groundless. He is concerned that his mother lives. Jocasta urges her husband to take pride in the present moment, to live as if 'there's no tomorrow.' The messenger enquires further. Oedipus shares his agony of exile. The messenger reassures the king that 'Polybus is nothing' to him as he is not his father by blood.

The messenger explains that Oedipus had been found by a shepherd on Mount Cithaeron with his feet tied. He explains that he, the messenger, took Oedipus as an infant to the childless king and queen of Corinth, who were delighted to receive him. Jocasta tries to dissuade Oedipus from investigating further, saying that he is doomed and expressing the hope that he will never discover his identity. She flees from the court in deep turmoil. Oedipus thinks she is unsettled at the prospect of discovering he is a mere commoner. The chorus is dismayed by her 'wild grief' and fears the outcome. Oedipus is determined to continue his search and to uncover his identity (998–1214).

The unspeakable truth
KEY moment

At first, the shepherd feigns a poor memory, but Oedipus is easily enraged by the shepherd's reluctance to tell the truth. Happily, the messenger informs the shepherd that the little boy he gave him to adopt is now king, but an angry shepherd rebukes him. Enraged further, Oedipus reprimands the shepherd and threatens him with torture if he does not willingly volunteer the truth. The fearful shepherd is treated roughly by the guards. Reluctantly, the shepherd relates how Jocasta gave him the child to kill. He says that, instead, he handed him over to the messenger. It is a moment of horrific revelation for Oedipus: 'O god – all come true, all burst to light!' He flees from the court, in contrast to the shepherd and messenger's slow departure (1231–1310).

Casablanca
DIRECTED BY MICHAEL Curtiz

Victor Laszlo is a Czech resistance fighter who, accompanied by his wife, Ilsa, has made his way to Casablanca in the expectation of securing a safe passage to America. Ilsa had a romantic relationship with Rick in Paris just before the Germans invaded the city in 1940. Rick now owns a nightclub in Casablanca, where Ilsa and he meet up again. The true reason why Ilsa left him in Paris, vowing never to see him again, is revealed. Ilsa is determined that Rick gives the letters of safe passage to Victor and vows not to leave him again. While Ilsa's love for Rick is evident, at the end of the film Rick lies to Victor about their relationship. Rick and Ilsa part for a second time.

Ilsa meets Rick
KEY moment

Ilsa goes over to the piano where Sam is playing. Instantly, he recognises her as the woman who broke Rick's heart all those years ago in Paris. She urges him to play their song, 'As Time Goes By.' Sam relents. Rick hears the music and goes over to Sam. He is startled to discover that Ilsa is there.

Later, Rick meets her husband, Victor Laszlo. Ilsa recalls the day she met Rick in Paris. Rick remembers that the 'Germans wore grey, you wore blue.' Ilsa comments that when the Germans march out, she will wear that dress again. The chief of police good-humouredly reminds them of the curfew restrictions.

KEY moment Rick's precious moments with Ilsa

This key moment is told in flashback. Rick and Ilsa drink together by the piano. They look out the window as it is announced that the Germans are invading. He utters the line, 'Here's looking at you, kid.' Sam softly plays 'As Time Goes By.' Ilsa comments that the whole world is 'crumbling' as they are falling in love. Rick remarks on the bad timing. He asks her where she was ten years ago. She says she was at the dentist. They hear heavy gunfire and Ilsa admits her heart is pounding. It is clear that the Germans are approaching. He wants to marry her, but she is reluctant. They arrange to meet at the station. She pledges her love for Rick but claims that in this 'crazy world anything can happen.' She urges him to kiss her 'as if it were the last time.' They kiss passionately.

'Here's looking at you, kid'

KEY moment Rick and Ilsa's love

Rick admits to her that he possesses the letters of transit. He claims that with the letters he will 'never be lonely.' Ilsa realises how Rick feels about her but suggests to him that Victor's life is more important. She mentions Paris but Rick claims that this is 'poor salesmanship.' He says that she will say anything now to get what she wants. She accuses him of wanting revenge, of being cowardly and weak, and says that he is their 'last hope.' Then she points a gun at Rick and orders him to hand over the letters. He urges her to shoot but tears well up in her eyes. She says that she tried to stay away: 'If you knew how much I loved you, how much I still love you.' They kiss passionately.

Ilsa explains that she discovered just before she left Paris that Victor, whom she presumed dead, was in fact alive. She explains that she had to tend to her husband. Rick comments that this is 'a story without an ending.' Ilsa declares her love for Rick and that she can never leave him again. He replies: 'Here's looking at you, kid.'

A surprise ending?

KEY **moment**

At the airport, Rick hands the letters of transit to Victor. Captain Louis Renault of the police is temporarily held prisoner by Rick, who has a gun in his pocket. Rick claims that Ilsa only pretended to love him in order to obtain the letters of transit. There are tears in her eyes as Rick speaks. Victor expresses gratitude to Rick for his assistance. Victor and Ilsa set off towards the plane.

The chief of police says that Ilsa knew that Rick was lying about her feelings for him. Major Strasser arrives and is told that Victor is about to leave by plane. Hurriedly, he goes to the phone to request assistance, but Rick shoots him. Other policemen arrive and Captain Renault comments that the major has been shot, so they should 'round up the usual suspects.' Rick and the policeman walk off together. Rick comments that this is the 'beginning of a beautiful friendship.'

The Constant Gardener
DIRECTED BY FERNANDO **Meirelles**

Tessa is an aid worker in Africa. She is also a committed political activist who is concerned for the lives of the poor in Kenya. She works with a Belgian doctor, Dr Arnold. Together they uncover the scandal surrounding the piloting of a new drug called Dypraxa. This drug has unknown side-effects but it is more economical for the pharmaceutical company to test it on African people rather than go through the more expensive conventional medical trials. Tessa and Arnold are murdered. A grief-stricken Justin, Tessa's husband, continues to search for the truth, which implicates officials in the high commission where he works.

There are minor characters whose actions serve to darken the text. Sir Bernard Pellegrin is Justin's boss at the high commission. He is a villain who acts to pursue the business interests of the Swiss–Canadian pharmaceutical company KDS in Africa. Sandy Woodrow is Justin's friend. However, he attempts

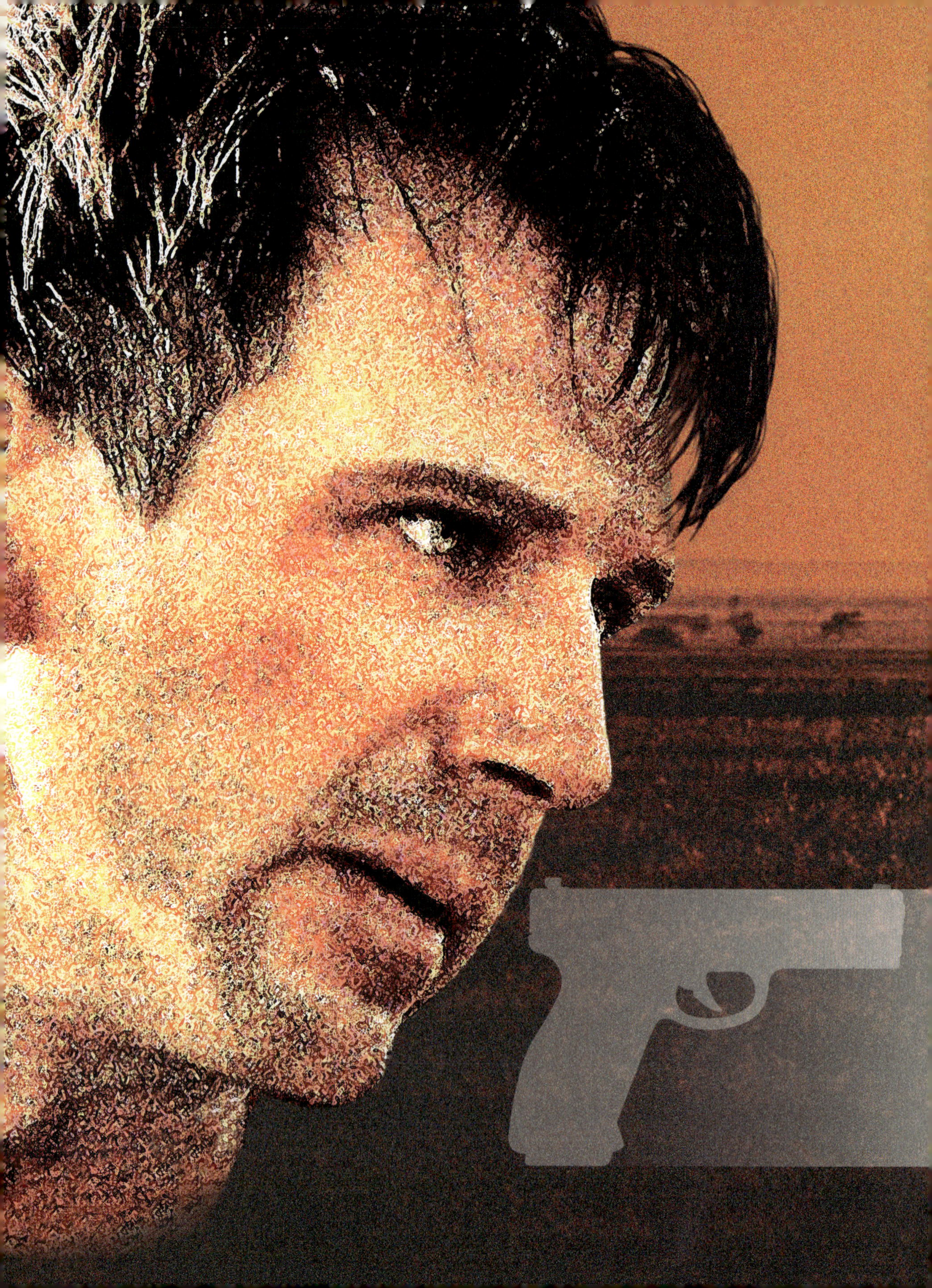

RELEASED:
2005

STARRING:
Ralph Fiennes as Justin Quayle and Rachel Weisz as Tessa Quayle.

STORY BY:
John le Carré, based on his novel of the same name.

AWARDS:
The film received four Academy Award nominations, ten BAFTA nominations, and three Golden Globe nominations. Weisz won both an Oscar and Golden Globe for her performance.

ABOUT THE DIRECTOR:
Fernando Meirelles was born in 1955 in São Paulo, Brazil. He studied architecture at university but, passionate about film-making, he set up an independent production company producing experimental videos and TV programmes. His breakthrough movie, *City of God*, was a hard-hitting film set in the slums of Rio de Janeiro, and earned him an Oscar nomination for best director. His biggest budget movie to date, *Blindness*, was released in 2008.

THE CONSTANT GARDENER

to instigate an illicit affair with Tessa, but his feelings are not reciprocated. Tessa confides in him, mistakenly believing he can be trusted, but he betrays Tessa by informing Sir Bernard of her whereabouts. He justifies his actions on the grounds that the company provides much-needed employment in a deprived region. Curtiss is a businessman who falls out of favour. When he becomes bankrupt, he discloses to Justin the truth about the company's clandestine activities.

KEY moment Justin's final farewell to Tessa

Arnold and Tessa are just about to get on a plane. Tessa says a fond farewell to her husband, Justin. Arnold offers to carry her bag. The scene gradually fades and Justin is left standing alone.

KEY moment Justin's first meeting with Tessa

Justin is delivering a lecture. He emphasises the importance of diplomacy in the foreign service. Tessa asks a question about British involvement in Iraq and terms it 'Vietnam: the sequel.' Justin replies that, as a diplomat, he goes where he is sent. She remarks that 'so do labradors.' There is commotion. She is against certain aspects of British foreign policy. He acknowledges her argument. Eventually, all the people depart and the room is deserted except for Justin and Tessa. He goes over to her and she apologises for her outburst. She is struck by his willingness to try to protect her. They walk off together.

KEY moment The treatment of Wanza

Tessa loses her baby in an African hospital. When Sandy arrives, Tessa is nursing a black baby beside Justin and Arnold. The baby's mother, Wanza, is fifteen years old and dying. Her child has been named 'Blessing.' Tessa tells the heart-rending tale of Wanza's brother, Kioko, who travels miles just to keep the flies off his terminally ill sister. She comments that this is the blessing. Her death is due to a side-effect of the drug Dypraxa. Taking advantage of Justin's momentary absence, Tessa asks Sandy to investigate as she concludes that Wanza has 'been murdered.' Sandy insists that she should stop involving herself in matters that do not concern her, mentioning that it would not serve her career. Tessa explains that Justin is unaware of much of the work she does.

Sandy remarks that such an admission does not surprise him. Tessa refers to what she has discovered and expresses a hope that he will act on her information. Sandy makes a promise to her, 'within reason.' Wanza dies in the bed next to Tessa. Near by, a white doctor is being urged to stop testing this new drug on people.

The lack of choice for the sick

KEY **moment**

Justin turns up at the medical centre. He is looking for Wanza's brother, Kioko. Finally, after much searching, he finds him in the queue. A woman becomes very irritated as she leaves. A doctor spots Justin. A series of mobile phone calls are made by different people. The doctor goes over to Justin to ask him about his reason for being there. He enquires after the woman. The doctor argues that she was refusing treatment. The doctor also remarks that he does not see any of Justin's countrymen there.

> Justin makes the point that ordinary people 'are not even informed that they are testing a new drug'

Justin believes that she requested treatment. He stares at Kioko's card and asks what the initials I.C. mean. The doctor explains that they have consented to the treatment. Justin concludes that the people there are denied access to general medical care if they refuse to take the new drug. Justin makes the point that ordinary people 'are not even informed that they are testing a new drug.' The doctor comments that he does 'not make the rules.' Policemen arrive and arrest Justin and little Kioko.

Sandy's revelation to Justin

KEY **moment**

Justin produces Sandy's letter to Tessa asking for Sir Bernard's letter to be returned. He alludes to this in his initial comments to Sandy. He calls KDH, the Swiss–Canadian company, part of an 'axis of evil.' Sandy, however, asks him to think more about British interests and the advantage of 1,500 jobs for a depressed area. Sandy explains that to stop the test would have involved a three-year delay, which would have cost 'millions of dollars.' He claims that it did not involve killing 'people who wouldn't be dead otherwise. Look at the death rate. Not that anybody's counting.' Sandy admits that he loved Tessa but that he betrayed her when he informed Sir Bernard of her whereabouts. Justin hands him back his letter and storms off.

Later that evening, Curtiss asks to speak to Justin. Justin is suspicious of his intentions at first, but as the banks are closing in on his debts, Curtiss has decided to declare all to Justin. He takes him to a remote area where Wanza and sixty-two others are buried in unmarked graves, claiming that they 'never officially existed.'

KEY moment One little girl and the dangers of Africa

Justin's search brings him to a medical doctor who is working in a war-torn region of Sudan. As they are speaking about Tessa, they are interrupted by bandits on horseback who raid the village. People are frantic and children run to and fro. The bandits fire indiscriminately into the crowd, killing many people, and take the cattle. They also burn down the homes. Many violent men take screaming children. One dazed man looks around at the destruction of his home. A woman is shot as the doctor and Justin run amidst the chaos. Eventually, they manage to get to the plane where a little girl patiently waits for them. She smiles when she sees them. Frantically, they stumble onto the plane but the pilot refuses to take the little girl as only aid workers are allowed. Justin produces money but the pilot refuses, claiming that there are millions in a similarly desperate situation. Justin argues forcefully that this is 'a child's life. There are no rules to cover that.' Suddenly, the girl runs off. Justin calls after her. The plane leaves and they watch as the little girl continues to run. Justin asks what will happen to her. He is told that if she is lucky she will make it to a refugee camp.

> The plane leaves and they watch as the little girl continues to run

KEY moment The truth revealed at Justin's funeral

Sir Bernard calls Justin a 'true gentleman' and emphasises that he committed suicide, highlighting his 'tormented state of mind.' Tessa's cousin reads Sir Bernard's letter of reply to Sandy. In the letter, he displays his annoyance at Tessa's report and orders Sandy to keep a check on her. Sir Bernard wants to keep hidden that they closed their 'eyes to the deaths.' Sir Bernard absconds amidst a throng of media reporters. Tessa's cousin highlights the corruption in the pharmaceutical company and high commission and continues to say that

Justin was murdered by 'persons unknown.' He claims that it is easy to test this new drug in Africa: there are 'no murders in Africa, only regrettable deaths.' He says the benefits of civilisation are derived from African deaths, as their lives are 'bought so cheaply.'

The final word
KEY moment

Justin sits in the location where his beloved Tessa was brutally murdered. He imagines Tessa beckoning him there and calling him home. At that moment, he hears soldiers marching towards him. One calls out his name. He turns around and then looks out at the water. He closes his eyes and softly speaks her name.

Inside I'm Dancing
DIRECTED BY DAMIEN O'Donnell

This film follows the lives of two young men, Rory O'Shea and Michael Connolly, who want to move from Carrigmore, a care home, to live independently. Rory has muscular dystrophy. Michael has cerebral palsy. They employ a headstrong but conscientious young woman, Siobhán, to care for them. At first, it appears that the boys have succeeded, but trouble looms when Michael falls in love with Siobhán.

Rory and Michael are isolated from the rest of the community on account of their disabilities. Rory has only a short while to live, while Michael is unable to communicate with the world around him. They want to engage with the world but their disabilities hinder them.

The isolation of Michael Connolly in Carrigmore
KEY moment

The cleaner sets about vacuuming the floor. The residents, whose faces are expressionless, sit around the television, which is showing a children's programme. Michael is staring into space but notices a trailing electric cable. He tries to warn the cleaner of a possible accident as the cable gets caught in one of the wheelchairs. He attracts the attention of the manager of the home, who wonders if he wants to go to mass. She points to his alphabet. Another care worker comes in with a bunch of flowers and trips over the cable.

KEY moment Rory and Michael talk about their families

Rory's father arrives at the care home. He brings drinks for his son. A tense conversation follows. His father comments that it is better than the last place, but Rory interjects that all these places are the same. His father says that he can return home, but Rory refuses. When his father leaves, Rory comments that his father can barely look after himself. He asks about Michael's parents. Michael produces a folder which contains newspaper cuttings of his father, who is a barrister. Rory asks if he ever comes to see him but Michael shakes his head. Rory comments that he 'dumped' Michael. His mother is dead. Rory dryly wonders if his father knows about the 'secret fan club.'

KEY moment Fergus Connolly's history of isolating his son

Michael and Rory arrive at the courthouse. They are taken to Fergus Connolly's secretary. She does not know Michael. She asks about the date of his appointment with her boss. Rory jokes that it was 1981, but then passes off the comment by saying something about the traffic. The secretary is close to dismissing them. They hear voices inside Fergus's office. Rory shouts out that it is a 'blatant case of criminal neglect.' Fergus Connolly sees his son. His embarrassment is well shown as he ushers his associates away. He allows Rory and Michael inside. He asks them what they want, but Rory urges him to speak to Michael. Michael notices a picture of his father smiling at his other son's graduation. Fergus tries to hide the photograph by positioning himself in front of it. Rory comments unfavourably on Fergus's reaction. Michael is deeply troubled and cannot speak to his father. Rory tries to fill in the gaps, saying that Michael is 'shy and proud.' He adds that it is 'demeaning' for him to be here and that he was deeply reluctant to come. Fergus wonders what they need from him. Rory tells him of their need for accommodation. Fergus then asks: 'What then?' Rory implies that this is all they require.

KEY moment Siobhán's rejection of Michael's love

There is silence at the kitchen table. Siobhán introduces their new carer, who is fully qualified. Michael is deeply upset when Siobhán informs them that she is leaving. She retorts that she deserves some respect, too, and takes Rory to task for his attitude. She also says that a woman has a right to say no even to a man in a wheelchair, referring to the awkwardness at the party when Michael clung to her while they were dancing. Rory insults her further and she reacts strongly and leaves. Tearfully, Michael goes after her but, failing to catch up with her, goes out by himself in the rain. Rory follows him. He asks Michael if he is going back to Carrigmore. They meet at the lit-up bridge, in the evening. Rory tells the distraught Michael that he shares his love. He claims that Michael, unlike him, has a future. He urges him never to give up this gift. Michael says that the bridge railing is too high to fall in. Rory tries to make light of the situation by offering to complain to Dublin Corporation on the grounds of discrimination against those in wheelchairs. There is a slight change of mood. The boys whirl around in their wheelchairs.

The loss of a friend
KEY **moment**

At Rory's bedside, Michael claims that he still needs his friend, but Rory insists that Michael is independent. Michael takes him by the hand and they both look at each other. Tears trickle down their faces.

Michael reapplies for independent living on his friend's behalf. He is successful. Sadly, he has no opportunity to tell him of his success, as Rory dies in hospital. A tearful Michael hugs Rory's father and Siobhán sheds tears.

Michael on his own
KEY **moment**

Michael is given some support from Siobhán. He thanks her for her kindness. At that point, she leaves. He stays in the room and stares at Rory's absent chair. He hears Rory's voice in his head urging him to go out. He goes out, on his own, into the bustling streets.

32A
DIRECTED BY MARIAN Quinn

This film tells the story of friendship and coming of age in Dublin in the late 1970s. Maeve and Ruth are the main characters. Family plays a big part in the film, as do burgeoning sexuality and the social issues of the day, including drugs and the 'generation gap.' The youth culture of the era is well explored, especially through the music of the time. Seen through predominantly female eyes, this film presents a picture of life in Ireland that in some ways is quite alien to us now, but in others remains steadfastly the same.

KEY moment ## A quiet dinner table
Silence prevails at the dinner table. Maeve arrives and greets everyone. No one responds to her as she sits down at the table. It is a conflict-ridden home as a small bag of drugs has been found in Dessie's pocket. Maeve laughs but her mother is furious.

KEY moment ## Maeve's deception
Maeve has already left the family home when two of her friends call around for her. Maeve's mother expresses her surprise as she explains that she thought Maeve was 'going to the pictures with you.' Her friends' embarrassment is obvious, but instantly they admit there must be some confusion over meeting arrangements. They leave Maeve's mother looking bewildered.

KEY moment ## Ruth waits for her father
Ruth waits with her friends just outside the cinema. Maeve is noticeably absent. Time ticks on. Ruth's father fails to arrive.

Unknown to Ruth, her movements have been closely watched by the taxi driver. Later, it transpires that he is Ruth's father. He observes his daughter going to the cinema to watch *Saturday Night Fever* with her friends. Later that evening the three chase after a bus and laugh amongst themselves when they fail to catch it. A taxi stops beside them. One of the girls comments that she thinks her aunt has given her five pounds. In the taxi, Ruth puts on a performance claiming that the driver is her mother's chauffeur. It is an awkward moment for Ruth's father.

KEY moment ## Ruth comes face to face with her father
Ruth's father drives her home. Ruth and her friends are astonished that the taxi driver knows where she lives. It is the moment of recognition for Ruth. Ruth's composure changes and she runs frantically from the car. She orders her father to get away from her. It is quiet and dark. Her father faces her while Ruth's

friends rush to her side. He asks her to go for a drive, but she refuses. Ruth's father calls her a 'lovely girl' and explains he is going to England for six months and gives her an address, which her friend takes. Her hurt spills over and she shouts angrily at him. He leaves a deeply distraught Ruth standing there, but her friends circle around her.

Maeve's punishment   KEY **moment**

Her mother is in hospital and Maeve is busily serving the dinner. The atmosphere is friendly until the father arrives and asks to speak to Maeve in private. He has been speaking to the local shopkeeper, who is portrayed as a gossip. Maeve's younger sibling, jokingly, makes a remark about her being in trouble. Maeve is ordered by her angry father to clean out the garage. He returns to check that she is still working.

Ruth's mother uncovers Ruth's deception   KEY **moment**

Ruth's mother is irate when she discovers Ruth had arranged furtively to meet her father. In a dismissive fashion, she throws his letter on the bed. Ruth explains that her father gave her a lift in his taxi and that he has gone back to England for a while. She produces the photograph, insisting that it is hers. Her mother orders her never to let him venture into the house.

> Ruth asks why her father left. Her mother says she is well aware of the reason for his departure

Ruth asks why her father left. Her mother says she is well aware of the reason for his departure. Ruth says she likes him, but her mother responds sarcastically: 'Good for you.' She storms off. Later, a more contrite Ruth ventures into her mother's bedroom and puts her arm around her.

Maeve's mother arrives home   KEY **moment**

Maeve's mother arrives home from hospital. The children begin to argue with one another until the father asks if they would give their mother some peace. Maeve watches in silence. All the children are ushered out. Her younger sister asks why Maeve does not have to leave. Sharply, Maeve answers it is because she is fourteen years old. Her mother tastes one of Maeve's fairy cakes. Her father leaves her alone with her mother. Her mother makes a conciliatory

32A

RELEASED:
2007

STARRING:
Ailish McCarthy as Maeve Brennan, Sophie Jo Wasson as Ruth Murray, and Orla Long as Orla Kennedy

STORY BY:
Marian Quinn

AWARDS:
Tiernan McBride Screenwriting Award, Galway Film Fleadh Best First Feature and an IFTA for cinematography

REVIEWS:
'Sweet and brightly lit coming of ager. Quinn makes a strong impression'
– *Variety Magazine*

'Refreshingly simple, a coming of age drama laced with easy charm and a touch of class'
– *Sunday Tribune*

ABOUT THE DIRECTOR:
Marian Quinn was born in Illinois in 1964 into an Irish-American family that has become synonymous with the screen. She, along with her four brothers, including Aidan, who plays Maeve's father, have all forged successful careers in theatre and film. After studying English in Dublin, Marian trained as an actress in Chicago and worked on both stage and screen. Her first foray into writing and directing was a short film entitled *Come To*, which was well received internationally. Together with Tom Weir she set up Janey Pictures, which is based in Dromahair, Co. Leitrim. *32A* is their first full-length feature.

maeve ♥ brian

move. She comments that Maeve has 'the place lovely' and then wonders where her friends have gone. At this, Maeve bursts into tears and seeks comfort from her mother.

KEY moment ## Maeve's birthday

It is Maeve's birthday and the family is in good humour. Maeve shows off her new 'drainpipes' and her mother remarks that old fashions are returning. Dessie gives his sister a present which she opens excitedly, only to find it is a shirt. She thanks him. Her father emerges, wishing Maeve a happy birthday, but then says that she forgot to defrost the freezer. A startled Maeve obeys, only to discover that her friends are there to wish her a happy birthday. Her family stays at the doorway, demonstrating their togetherness.

DIRECTED BY KENNETH Branagh
As You Like It

This film is an adaptation of Shakespeare's romantic comedy about four couples, Orlando and Rosalind, Celia and Jaques, Phoebe and the Shepherd, the Fool and Audrey. While primarily a light-hearted romance, it is also a darker tale of the banishment of the duke by his power-hungry and paranoid brother, Frederick. Jaques and Orlando have a troublesome relationship which results in Orlando leaving for the Forest of Arden. Rosalind is banished by Frederick. Celia, Frederick's daughter, is unsettled by her father's treatment of her cousin and tells her vengeful father she cannot live without Rosalind. Celia and Rosalind leave for the Forest of Arden in disguise. Frederick is left alone in the palace as many flee his régime.

KEY moment ## A siege in progress

The duke, his daughter, Rosalind, Celia, his niece, and other courtiers and attendants enjoy a performance by a Japanese woman. It is nightfall. Food is being served while Jaques stands furtively by the doorway. The duke speaks lovingly to Rosalind, as the guests enjoy the performance.

Outside, an invasion is about to commence. A group of soldiers is submerged in the water waiting for the opportune moment to attack. The soldiers storm around the court and invade the building. Chaos ensues. Frederick, armed and dressed in black, meets his brother face to face. The duke is to be banished and Rosalind is taken away by one of the soldiers. The duke and all the courtiers flee the scene in haste to the Forest of Arden.

The rivalry between brothers

KEY **moment**

One night in the pouring rain, Orlando accosts his elder brother, Jaques, about his dismissive and unfair treatment of him. He argues that Jaques has not honoured his father's will, which stated he was to provide him with a proper education. A dangerous stand-off follows. They tussle in the pouring rain, watched by a loyal servant. Orlando proclaims his father's spirit 'grows strong' in him. Orlando leaves. Jaques dismisses his servant by calling him a 'dog.' The incensed servant contrasts his treatment now to the kindness shown by his late father, Sir Royland de Boys. He leaves his master's company.

Maliciously, Jaques maligns Orlando's character. He has serious misgivings about this but he does not let these thoughts hold sway.

Rosalind's banishment

KEY **moment**

Rosalind confides in Celia that she loves Orlando. This conversation is interrupted when an angry Frederick bursts in to inform a startled Rosalind that she is to be banished. He goes on to say that if she is found within a twenty-mile radius, she will die. Rosalind, horrified but defiant, asks her paranoid uncle the nature of the crime she has committed. He replies that he does not trust her. Cleverly, she argues that his mistrust of her cannot make her a traitor. He

> He goes on to say that if she is found within a twenty-mile radius, she will die

takes Celia into his confidence by explaining that Rosalind's presence in the court makes her the focal point of sympathy amongst the people. He argues that Rosalind is 'too subtle.' Celia's love for her cousin is stronger and she contends that she cannot stay in the court without Rosalind. She orders her father to 'pronounce that sentence' of exile on her. Frederick bows his head and returns to Rosalind. Aggressively, he takes her by the throat and threatens her. He then leaves.

KEY moment   Orlando's false perception of Arden

Orlando meets the former duke and his courtiers, who are encamped in the Forest of Arden. One of the lords, also named Jaques, is about to eat an apple. Orlando steals up to the gathering with his sword in hand. He orders them to eat nothing. Jaques raises the apple to his mouth in defiance, but Orlando claims he will die. The duke asserts there is no need as he is welcome to eat at the table. A shameful Orlando puts his sword away, saying: 'I thought that all things had been savage here.' He explains that his loyal servant has collapsed due to the twin evils of 'age and hunger.' He pleads with them not to eat anything until he returns with his servant. The duke promises willingly, adding 'we are not all alone unhappy.' Quickly, Orlando goes in search of his servant.

KEY moment   Orlando's and Jaques' reconciliation

Orlando comes upon his badly beaten brother. He looks disdainfully upon him, but does not touch him. As he walks away, he hears a lion growling in the undergrowth. He pushes his brother, Jaques, away and bravely faces the lion. A weary Jaques strikes out at the violent creature. He goes over to his badly injured brother, Orlando. They clasp each other's hands as Orlando calls out for his love, Rosalind.

KEY moment   Frederick's loneliness

A distraught Frederick clutches his daughter's fan as he sits alone at court. In a deserted room, he is informed that many have fled to the Forest of Arden in support of the usurped duke. There they live like Robin Hood's merry men and 'flee time carelessly' as they did in the Golden Age.

KEY moment   The wedding day

Rosalind is no longer in disguise. It is a very emotional reunion between father and daughter. Orlando is delighted to have the opportunity to marry his true love. The older shepherd marries three happy couples: Celia and Jaques, Rosalind and Orlando, Phoebe and the younger shepherd.

    The middle son of Sir Royland de Boys returns with good news. Frederick has had a change of heart. He informs them that Frederick had ventured out with his soldiers to kill his elder brother, but on his travels he encountered a religious man who brought about his conversion. Now he has relinquished power and returned everything to his elder brother. The people are delighted and everyone, except one lord, dances merrily together around the Forest of Arden and then as they return to the duke's castle.

Later, Frederick is sitting beside a tree when his daughter, Celia, finds him. She kisses him and departs. He smiles lovingly at her.

In disguise, Rosalind delivers her final address. In it, she ventures out of the world of the film. She speaks of the love that women 'bear to men' and of the love men have for women, for 'none of you hate them.' Playfully, she retires into her dressing-room. The door is closed.

CLASSROOM
activities

1. **Which key moment tells you most about the restrictions or freedoms offered in society? Choose one key moment from one text in formulating your answer.**

2. **Choose a key moment that highlights your chosen theme best. Justify your choice.**

3. **Which is the happiest or saddest point in each of your texts? Explain your choice.**

3

Theme or Issue:
isolation

Theme or Issue: isolation

Isolation means separation from others, either through choice or without one's consent. People can become segregated from others for a range of reasons, which can have social, political or emotional causes. The key idea is being set apart, or setting oneself apart, from one's family, friends and the wider community.

The way the story is told in each of these texts evokes a sense of alienation from the social community. Some of the central characters are pariah figures while others make efforts to find their voice in what are often lonely worlds.

This chapter will explore the theme of isolation as it is developed in:
- Jennifer Johnston's *How Many Miles to Babylon?*
- John B. Keane's *Sive*
- Henrik Ibsen's *A Doll's House*
- Michael Curtiz's *Casablanca*
- Damien O'Donnell's *Inside I'm Dancing*.

In attempting to show how the theme of isolation is presented in each text, you should:
- Clearly explain the term 'isolation'
- Show how the theme is first presented in each of your three texts
- Identify pivotal moments when the isolation of a central character reaches its peak
- Determine how the theme of isolation is resolved.

How Many Miles to Babylon?   THEME: isolation

Alec is an isolated figure whose separation from his social community is evident from the first pages of the novel. He claims he does not love any 'living person' (p. 1). He describes vividly the loneliness of his childhood. Class and education are depicted as 'barriers' rather than privileges. Our sense of Alec's isolation is compounded by descriptions of the big cold house in County Wicklow where authoritarian family traditions and Alicia's volatility stifle personal communication.

Alec lives in perpetual isolation. Re-read the key moment entitled 'Alec's Parents' Disapproval of His Friendship with Jerry' outlined in Chapter 2. Notice Alicia's dominance. Alec is conscious of his mother's passive aggression: 'She drew her lips together, tightly, angrily before she spoke.' A series of imperatives are used: 'You are never to see him again.' Alec's father, Frederick, feels cut off from the international scene; his world is a parochial one. He claims that they are 'so remote, so protected' (pp. 29–30). This is a self-imposed isolation.

'She drew her lips together, tightly, angrily before she spoke'

Alec tries to protest that Jerry is his friend, but his protests are in vain. Neither parent understands the importance of Alec's friendship with Jerry. Here, he reluctantly acquiesces to their demands, increasing his isolation further.

Frederick suffers in a similar vein to Alec, who is aware of his father's isolation from Alicia. Re-read the key moment entitled 'Frederick's Misery in His Marriage to Alicia.' The atmosphere is dark and dispiriting. Frederick is conscious of Alicia's contempt for him and of the failure of their marriage. The word he uses is 'indifferent,' which suggests he is lonely and ignored.

There are moments of tenderness between Alec and Frederick, and Alec's empathy with his father has not gone unnoticed by Alicia. Re-read the key moment entitled 'Alicia's Shock Revelation.' In a pivotal moment, she informs her son that Frederick might not be his father. Alec now perceives the world in a new light. He feels separated from Frederick's ancestral heritage:

'Dispossessed in a sentence' (pp. 47–48). Alicia's revelation exacerbates Alec's sense of isolation and has the desired effect of sending her son off to war. Characteristically, the self-absorbed Alicia ignores her son's feelings.

Alec's isolation from his fellow officers is self-imposed. His refusal to mix with them is noted by Major Glendinning. Characteristically, Glendinning views Alec's distance from the other officers negatively, implying that Alec sees himself as superior to them. He urges him to mix. It is clear that, like Alicia and Frederick, the major disapproves of Alec's friendship with Jerry. His aggressive tone takes Alec by surprise: 'Let it be understood once and for all that I will have no talking between the men and the officers. Talking' (p. 92). Alec finds it difficult to voice an objection, compounding his isolation further: 'My voice was hard to find' (p. 92). While his introverted character makes it difficult for him to move towards others, his isolation as an officer is also due to his preferential treatment of Jerry and his general view of the soldiers under his command; he sees them as human beings, in direct conflict with the establishment view.

Jerry's friendly presence helps to combat Alec's isolation, but the loneliest moment of all is when it becomes clear that his best friend is to face the firing squad for deserting the army to find his father. Alec's desperation is highlighted in his conversations with his military superior. In the key moment 'Alec's Hopeless Pleas on Jerry's Behalf,' notice the way Alec constantly pleads on his friend's behalf and how Major Glendinning is not prepared to listen. Glendinning is essentially an establishment figure whose superiority also makes him an isolated figure, though his isolation is self-imposed. The major feels closer to Alec once he believes he is prepared to carry out the order and he places his hand on Alec's shoulder, but Alec resents this gesture and his body gives an involuntary shudder. Even this unconscious action embodies Alec's isolation from his fellow officers.

Nothing exemplifies Alec's isolation more than the shooting of his best friend. Re-read the key moment entitled 'Alec's Shooting of Jerry and His Wait for Execution.' This is a very poignant moment. Alec is friendless and alone in a harsh, conflict-ridden world.

Overall, isolation is well conveyed throughout the novel. The reader is conscious of Alec's isolation as a son from his mother, as a member of the gentry from the local people at home in Wicklow, and as an Irishman in the

British army in war-torn Flanders. While Alec's societal privilege is a contributory factor in his isolation, the twin evils of Alicia and Major Glendinning conspire to make Alec's life a very lonely one.

CLASSROOM activities

1. How does the writer's treatment of Alec's early childhood explore the theme of isolation?

2. How is Jerry instrumental in introducing Alec into a broader social world?

3. In the key moment 'Alec's Parents' Disapproval of His Friendship with Jerry,' describe the importance of Alec's conversation with his parents about Jerry in light of Alec's need for a friend.

4. Is Alec merely a victim of the class-conscious society in which he lives? Explain your answer.

5. In what way is the key moment 'Alicia's Shock Revelation' an isolating moment for Alec?

6. Re-read the key moment entitled 'Frederick's Misery in His Marriage to Alicia.' Are Alec and Frederick alike?

7. Describe the levels of isolation conveyed in the key moment 'Alec's Hopeless Pleas on Jerry's Behalf.'

Sive

THEME: isolation

Isolation is a central concern in John B. Keane's tragedy, *Sive*. Initially, the main protagonist's isolation is not deeply felt as she is a supported figure within the Glavin family. However, this is to change. Mike's meddling in Sive's blossoming relationship with Liam is suggestive of troubles to come. Re-read the key moment entitled 'Driving Liam and Sive Apart' outlined in Chapter 2. From the outset, they meet furtively. Sive comments that it is 'cold and lonely waiting in the dark,' while Liam suggests it is 'cold and lonely, too, at home' (Act 1, Scene 1). Mike is angered to find Liam with Sive. He castigates him and orders him to leave. It is an isolating moment for both Liam and Sive.

Sive is not the only isolated figure in this text. Nanna's isolation is deeply felt. She is viciously and mercilessly castigated on account of her age. Re-read the key moment entitled 'Nanna's Isolation in Her Own Home.' Nanna's vulnerability is evident in this scene. Her protests are meek in comparison to Thomasheen and Mena's verbal onslaught. Thomasheen paints a bleak picture of old women left forlorn in the county home, scrambling around for a few potatoes. Nanna becomes an almost dejected figure in this scene.

Mena and Thomasheen attempt to isolate and torment Sive further. In the key moment 'Sive's Growing Isolation within Her Family,' Sive's dreams for the future are cruelly dashed as Mena flings her schoolbag across the room, signalling an end to her school friendships and her education. Instead of protecting Sive, her vicious aunt-in-law callously supports the marriage arrangement with Seán Dóta. She compounds Sive's isolation from the social community by referring to the manner of her birth. She reiterates that Sive has no name, that her 'father was nothing' and that she needs a husband to give her a name. She labels her a 'bye-child, a common bye-child – a bastard,' thus separating her from the rest of the respectable community (Act 1, Scene 3). Sive feels this deeply and wants to get away from her, but Mena takes her roughly by the arm and forces her to listen to Mena's own family history. This is a very isolating and demeaning moment for Sive.

> She labels her a 'bye-child, a common bye-child – a bastard,' thus separating her from the rest of the respectable community

Sive's isolation is increased by Mike's agreement to the prospect of Sive marrying Seán Dóta, thus effectively sealing her fate. Her isolation is exacerbated also by Nanna's inability to follow through on a plan of escape, leaving Sive in deep torment towards the end of the play. Tragically, Sive remains unaware that Nanna, Pats and Carthalawn are attempting to support her. (They are thwarted by Liam's love letter being intercepted by Thomasheen.) In the key moment 'A Dispirited Sive,' the dreaded wedding day is looming and Sive is deeply unhappy at the prospect of marrying Seán Dóta. She is awkward in her new adult clothes and takes off her high-heeled shoes to rub her feet. She is deeply troubled and dispirited and leaves the company: 'I think I'll go to bed instead. My head is on fire' (Act 2, Scene 2). Her slow, lethargic responses are contrasted with the life and enthusiasm that surrounds her. She does not share Mike, Thomasheen or Mena's excitement. Their financial gain is at the expense of her future.

Mena, Thomasheen and Seán Dóta's evil practices lead to Sive being driven to the most isolating of all acts: to take her own life. The key moment 'The Most Heart-rending of Ends' details Sive's last moments in all her desperation and loneliness. The prevailing mood is one of sadness. Yet with Sive's death the roles are reversed. Mena's power has been broken. Thomasheen, Seán Dóta and Mena now become isolated figures. Thomasheen and Seán sneak cowardly away, ending their input in the final moments of the play. Mena is quite unable to deal with the situation. Mike is fearful at the prospect of having to face the priest by himself. Nanna is alone in her grief. She cries over Sive's lifeless body. Isolation is well represented in the final moments of the play.

In this play the darker forces are well represented by Thomasheen, Seán and Mena and their triumph for most of the play leads to Sive's tragic isolation. The importance of class in this society leaves Sive vulnerable to Seán Dóta's lustful exploitation and subsequent misery and isolation. Sive becomes a prisoner in her home. Mercilessly, she is left bereft and alone. Most tragic of all, Sive is unaware of the support she has received from Nanna, Liam, Pats and Carthalawn. Such support could have helped her overcome her isolation but Sive, nonetheless, is left all alone in her final harrowing hours.

CLASSROOM activities

1. Re-read the key moment 'Driving Liam and Sive Apart.' Describe the isolating aspects of this key moment.

2. To what extent is Sive an isolated figure in the Glavin household before the arrival of Thomasheen?

3. With reference to the key moment 'Nanna's Isolation within Her Own Home,' answer the following:
   (a) How is Nanna sidelined by Thomasheen and Mena?
   (b) 'Prejudice towards the elderly has horrific consequences.' Discuss.
   (c) How do Thomasheen and Mena present themselves as superior to Nanna?

4. How does Mena isolate Sive in the key moment 'Sive's Growing Isolation within Her Family'?

5. Thomasheen intercepted Liam's letter. To what extent does this make him responsible for Sive's ongoing agony and her eventual suicide?

6. Re-read the key moment entitled 'A Dispirited Sive.'
   (a) How is Sive set apart from the other characters in this scene?
   (b) Examine the responses of the other characters towards Sive. Why do you think none of them is aware of her ongoing turmoil and distress?

7. Who is the most isolated figure in the key moment entitled 'The Most Heart-rending of Ends'? Explain your choice.

THEME: isolation — A Doll's House

The play opens with Nora as the central character. The apartment is a hive of activity. However, all is not as it might at first appear. Re-read the key moment entitled 'Nora's Relationship with Her Husband, Helmer' detailed in Chapter 2. The tenor of communication between them is like that between an adult and child. Notice how Helmer describes Nora as 'squander-bird' and 'skylark.' She behaves accordingly, accepting her pet names, often sulking and playing with her coat buttons. Nora and Helmer appear united, albeit superficially. Nora, however, has a secret, which she relates to Mrs Linde; she borrowed money in order to save her husband's life but claimed that the money had been given to her in her father's will. Soon it becomes clear to the audience that Nora and Helmer inhabit different worlds. Helmer is socially conscious and financially cautious while Nora is generous and self-effacing.

Nora's isolation deepens as the play progresses. The villainous Krogstad defeats her at every level. In the key moment 'Krogstad's Menace,' Nora is at the heart of the family home playing with her children, but when Krogstad appears at the doorway she becomes unsettled and quickly ushers the children away. Krogstad adopts a courtroom-style approach, which isolates Nora in her own home. In the cross-examination, she discloses that her father died on the twenty-ninth of September. This is a dangerous admission as Krogstad realises that he could not have signed the IOU because it is dated three days later. Nora is overwhelmed by the situation. She acts defensively, but Krogstad cruelly interjects that the law does not concern itself with motives. She is so totally dejected and bewildered that she cannot continue the game she had been playing with her children. Nora's growing isolation is a triumph for Krogstad.

Nora and Helmer are separated from each other at this point. She cannot disclose to him her deception and Krogstad's bribery. This heightens the tension further. Re-read the key moment entitled 'Nora's Monologue.' This is a dark time for Nora. She is made anxious by Helmer's comments about the corruption of the young. Helmer is determined to blame mothers for all of society's ills. Nora is deeply unsettled by his words, and takes them to heart. In this key moment, Nora's isolation reaches a new pitch.

Greater problems emerge during Krogstad's second visit. Refer to the key moment entitled 'Nora's Worst Fears Realised.' Here, Krogstad's authority is shown. Initially, Krogstad feigns good will, giving Nora a false sense of security. His dark motive becomes clear when he produces a letter for Helmer. He is triumphant at the thought of Helmer being subject to him: 'I've got him in my pocket' (Act 2). To add to Nora's isolation, he paints a frightening and graphic image of those who have drowned in the 'cold, black water.' Suicide is the most isolating moment of all. Nora admits she has had suicidal thoughts, suggesting her increasing isolation. The gravity of the situation becomes apparent when Krogstad drops the letter for Helmer in the letter box.

> Krogstad has lived a lonely life and aptly describes his isolation with the powerful image of a 'shipwrecked man, clinging to a spar'

Nora is not the only isolated figure in this play. Mrs Linde's and Krogstad's isolation becomes evident in the middle of the play. Re-read the key moment entitled 'Krogstad's and Mrs Linde's Isolation.' Krogstad has lived a lonely life and aptly describes his isolation with the powerful image of a 'shipwrecked man, clinging to a spar.' Mrs Linde explains her unhappiness in her marriage, her concern to support her mother and brothers. She is childless and expresses a hope that 'two shipwrecked souls could join hands' (Act 3). She first appears as an isolated figure, but has now found a place at the heart of Krogstad's life and home. Nora is to find herself on a different journey.

At this moment, Nora and Helmer's marriage is about to fall apart. In the key moment 'Helmer's Horror at Nora's Deception,' Helmer's actions effectively isolate him from his wife. He admonishes her in a derogatory fashion and declares their relationship is in shreds except for mere public appearances. His pride is stung at the thought of Krogstad having power over him. The illusion is gone; Nora sees her husband in a new light. By word and action, he has distanced himself from his wife.

In the key moment 'A New Nora?', Nora takes off her fancy dress and emerges in her ordinary clothes. She launches into her first adult-to-adult conversation with her husband in eight years of marriage. Nora, resolute, explains she is leaving Helmer and tells him he has no responsibility for her once she leaves the family home. They exchange rings and Helmer is left disconsolate. It is a deeply isolating moment for the status-conscious Helmer. He is defeated.

Nora's act of leaving him will bring shame on the family. She argues that too much divides them, and that she needs to find an independent role for herself in the world. Her future survival is not certain, but it is clear that her isolation is self-imposed. Helmer, distraught, tries in vain to salvage the situation by trying to convince Nora of his ability to change. He fails. Krogstad's meddling highlights that there has never really been a point of connection between Nora and Helmer. Despite his faults, Helmer loves Nora. He communicates his defeat by sinking down into the chair and burying his face in his hands. A fleeting hope strikes him but then he hears the front door slam. It is the point of no return.

> A fleeting hope strikes him but then he hears the front door slam. It is the point of no return

The theme of isolation is intrinsic to *A Doll's House*. At the beginning of the play, Helmer and Nora appear to be a loving couple. As the play unfolds, they become different people. At first, Nora grapples with her secret which she fears will be exposed by Krogstad. This isolates her from her family. Her inner turmoil is conveyed by the playwright. A horrified Helmer isolates his wife by his melodramatic and selfish response to Krogstad's letter. This enables Nora to see her husband in a new light and to reassess their relationship. The most isolating moment of all comes at the very end. Helmer faces the future without his wife while Nora struggles to find her identity, which is a lonely experience. Isolation is well explored in the play, which highlights the primary importance of the individual over the family.

CLASSROOM **activities**

1. Re-read the key moment entitled 'Nora's Relationship with Her Husband, Helmer.'
   (a) Describe Nora and Helmer's relationship.
   (b) How different are they?

2. In the key moment 'Krogstad's Menace,' how does Krogstad isolate Nora in this scene?

3. To what extent is Nora's isolation self-imposed?

4. Refer to the key moment entitled 'Nora's Worst Fears Realised.'
   (a) How is this one of the darkest hours for Nora?
   (b) How successful is Krogstad as a villain?

5. Explain Mrs Linde's and Krogstad's isolation.

6. Describe Helmer's reaction to Nora's deception. What does this tell us about his character?

7. 'Helmer is a tragic figure, destined to be alone.' To what extent do you agree with this statement? Give reasons for your answer.

Casablanca — THEME: isolation

At the beginning of the film *Casablanca*, Rick personifies the isolated figure. His club, Rick's Café Américain, is a hive of activity but he distances himself from it. He rarely socialises and confides in no one. To intensify the situation, Casablanca is a place of desperation as refugees try, often in vain, to escape from war-torn Europe. Betrayals await at every turn. Rick is bitter for another reason; he has lost the woman he loves. This bitterness has changed him.

Ilsa's arrival is a shock for Rick. She is with her husband, Victor Laszlo, suggesting that Rick is destined to be alone. Look again at the key moment entitled 'Ilsa Meets Rick' highlighted in Chapter 2. Rick is in the midst of a social gathering. Though having a social drink, he appears to be apart from the others. Tensions run high, especially when Captain Renault refers to the curfew. It is a difficult moment for Ilsa and Rick. Victor's prominence in the Czech resistance movement creates further tension and suspense.

Ilsa's arrival reminds a grief-stricken Rick of her rejection of him in Paris. In the key moment 'Rick's Precious Moments with Ilsa,' he relives their final

RELEASED:
1942

STARRING:
Humphrey Bogart as Rick Blaine, Ingrid Bergman as Ilsa Lund Laszlo and Paul Henreid as Victor Laszlo.

STORY BY:
Murray Burnett and Joan Alison, based on their unproduced play *Everybody Comes to Rick's*.

AWARDS:
Casablanca was nominated for eight Academy Awards and won three: Best Picture, Best Director and Best Screenplay. In 1998 the American Film Institute voted it number one in their 100 Greatest American Movies list. In 2005 it was named in *Time* magazine's 100 Greatest Films and the following year the Writers Guild of America voted the screenplay the best of all time.

CASABLANCA

ABOUT THE DIRECTOR:
Michael Curtiz (1888–1962) was born Manó Kertész Kaminer to a Jewish family in Budapest, Hungary. After graduating from the Royal Academy of Theatre in his native city in 1912, he began acting in and then directing films. He worked all over Europe, refining his craft, and in 1926 moved to the USA to work for Warner Brothers in Hollywood. He enjoyed a long career at the WB studios, where Curtiz (his adopted anglicised name) directed the features that made him a filmmaker of international renown. His films encompass nearly every genre imaginable and some, including *Casablanca*, *Mildred Pierce* and *Yankee Doodle Dandy*, are regarded as classics. He is widely acknowledged as one of the most versatile, prolific and successful Hollywood directors.

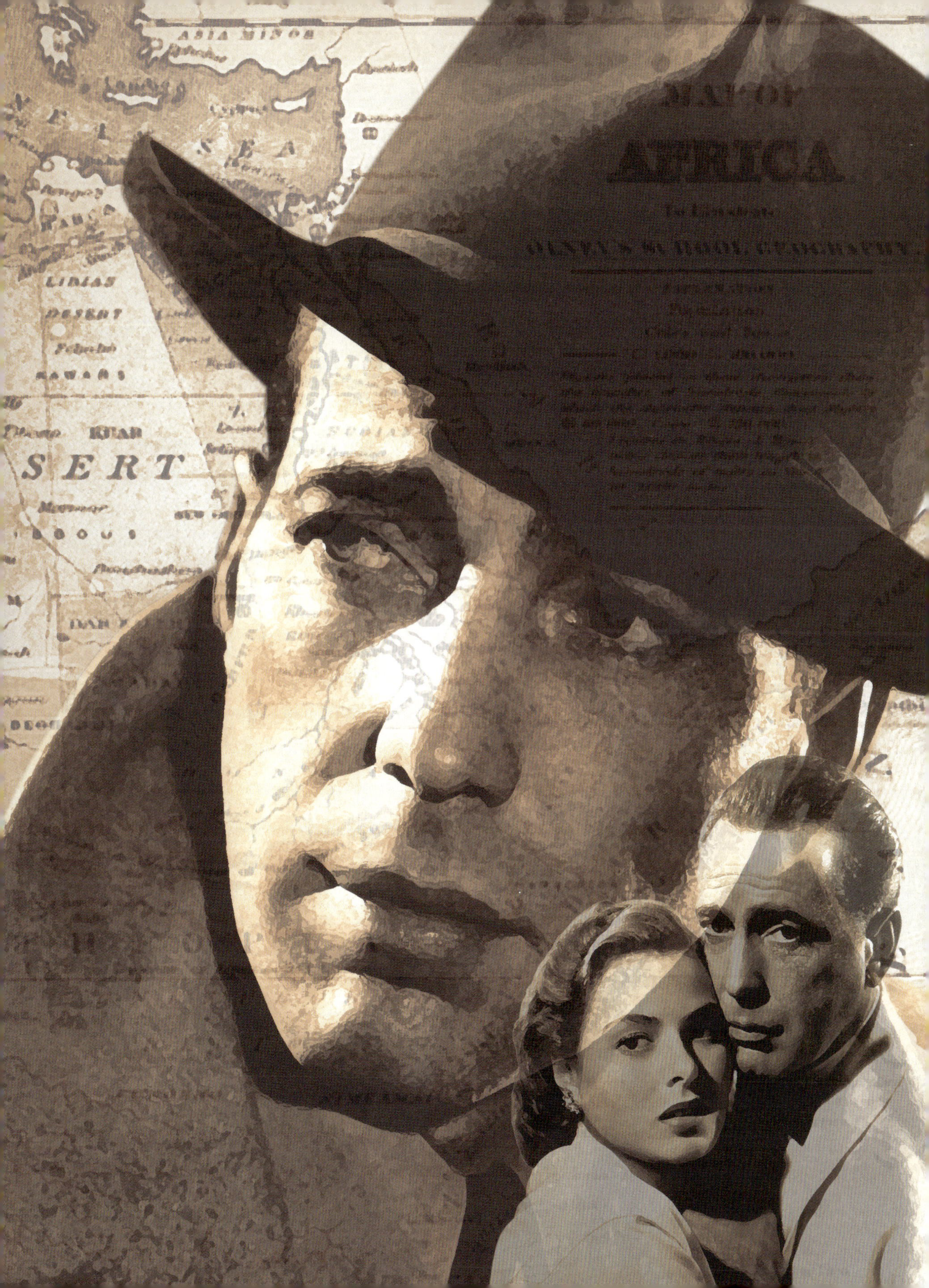
ASIA MINOR
AFRICA
SERT

moments together. In this flashback scene, a happy, free-spirited Rick delights in Ilsa's company. A sense of nostalgia is created with the song 'As Time Goes By.' However, it is a dangerous and violent moment and Ilsa is distressed at the thought of the approaching German army. They hear gunfire and Ilsa admits her heart is pounding. Her words have a ring of finality, but Rick is too much in love to notice. Later, a hurt Rick reads the contents of Ilsa's letter on a wet station platform in Paris. The German army is marching into Paris and people are frantic to escape the city. Rick has lost the woman of his dreams. It is a dark and lonely moment.

Rick is deeply isolated. Look again at the key moment 'Rick and Ilsa's Love.' Rick is startled to find Ilsa in his quarters. There is tension in the air as Ilsa asks for the letters of transit. Rick is distant, and keeps her apart from him with biting sarcasm. He seems to take pride in his isolated status and disputes any interest in political causes: 'I am the only cause I'm interested in.' She reminds him of Paris, but he distances himself from her overture by claiming that talk of Paris is just 'poor salesmanship.' Ilsa is emotionally stung by his coldness, claiming that he is their 'last hope.' She turns the gun on him. This is a deeply isolating moment for the two former lovers. She orders him to give her the letters but he moves closer to her, urging her to shoot: 'Go ahead and shoot. You're doing me a favour.' This heightens the tension and the isolation of the moment. Ilsa turns away from the brink and buries herself in his arms. She relates her torment in Paris when she was torn between her love for Rick and her duty to her husband. She relates how she believed her husband had died trying to escape and describes it as a deeply distressing and isolating time. She says she was lonely, devoid of hope until she met Rick in Paris. The lovers are effectively reunited, but it is a partial victory, as the fear for Victor's life remains.

> *'I am the only cause I'm interested in'*

Look again at the key moment entitled 'A Surprise Ending?' outlined in Chapter 2. In the closing scenes Rick holds Captain Renault hostage, as he hands a delighted Victor the letters of transit giving him safe passage from Casablanca. He lies to Victor, claiming that his relationship with Ilsa is over. There is an unspoken assertion that the Allied cause is more important. Rick claims Ilsa pretended to love him in order to obtain the letters of transit. Ilsa's eyes well up with tears as she walks to the plane with her husband. It is Paris all over again.

This deeply isolating moment, like Paris, is another parting for Rick and Ilsa, this time forever. Rick faces the prospect of imprisonment when the Germans find that Major Strasser has been shot. Rick is as isolated a figure as he was when the film began, surrounded by the forces of the Vichy régime, the effective puppet government of Hitler's forces. However, Captain Renault offers him the hand of friendship in his darkest hour. His true feelings for the régime become apparent when he throws the Vichy water into the bin. Rick and Captain Renault leave together, to continue their resistance work, thus reducing Rick's isolation. Rick pledges himself to the anti-fascist cause and Captain Renault calls him not only a 'sentimentalist' but also a 'patriot.' Rick acts both out of love for Ilsa and hate for the Nazis.

> Rick acts both out of love for Ilsa and hate for the Nazis

The theme of isolation is well explored in the film *Casablanca*. The life of the refugee is fraught with many dangers in the harsh and unfriendly environment of occupied Casablanca. Gambling is the preferred pastime as the desperate endeavour to win enough money to secure safe passage to a new life. Rick emerges as a lonely character who becomes bitter after losing the woman of his dreams. Ilsa's presence rekindles his love for her, but much of Rick's isolation is self-imposed. Ilsa highlights her own lonely journey when she reveals her love for Rick. There comes a point when a happy ending seems possible, but Rick acts to save Victor. This surprise ending leaves Ilsa and Rick separated from each other for ever.

CLASSROOM activities

1. Describe the setting of *Casablanca*.

2. What is your initial impression of Rick?

3. Consider the key moment entitled 'Ilsa Meets Rick.' How is this an isolating moment for both of them?

4. Look again at the key moment 'Rick's Precious Moments with Ilsa.'
   (a) Why is it an unfortunate time to fall in love?
   (b) Describe Rick's response when he reads Ilsa's farewell letter.

5. Describe the isolating elements in the key moment entitled 'Rick and Ilsa's Love.'

6. 'The ending of Casablanca leaves two lonely people.' To what extent is this statement true? Give reasons for your answer.

THEME: isolation — Inside I'm Dancing

In the opening scene of the film, 'The Isolation of Michael Connolly in Carrigmore,' we get an insight into Michael's deeply isolated existence. There is a very clear divide between the careworkers and the patients. The manager of the home is unable to see beyond Michael's disability. We can see that Michael is far more capable than is thought, but he is demeaned in this scene by being presented with a child's alphabet to help explain himself. Michael's isolation is captured on many levels. His frustration is etched on his face. His inability to communicate is the root cause of his isolation.

Michael's friendship with the rebellious Rory reduces his isolation. First and foremost, Rory translates for him. This enables him to be understood and brightens his approach to the world. Michael has been institutionalised all his life and is unaware of the world beyond Carrigmore. Michael's father's history of ostracising his son is well explored, but Michael's desire to connect with his father is also evident. He has carefully kept newspaper cuttings of his father's successful legal career. Rory is accurate in claiming that Michael's father effectively 'dumped' him. He has no contact with his family, primarily as a result of the actions of his negligent father.

The key moment entitled 'Fergus Connolly's History of Isolating His Son' is a deeply isolating moment for Michael, in which he is depicted as being silent and unresponsive. He is unsettled by his father's presence. Years of neglect have distressed him. In order to attain their dream of living independently, both Rory and Michael require the financial resources of Michael's father, Fergus Connolly. Rory aptly calls it a case of 'criminal neglect.' Even the word 'neglect' assumes a denial of contact between father and son and the leaving of a child bereft and alone.

Fergus stands motionless at the desk while Michael is seated on the other side in his wheelchair. The division between father and son could not be more apparent. Magnifying Michael's torment, Fergus speaks in a cold and calculated way. His choice of formal language is unlikely to have the effect of establishing a positive relationship between father and son. Fergus appears dismissive of the need to reach out to his son, or he is possibly unable to do so. Emphasis is placed on the word 'home.' Michael has to create his own home since normal family life is denied him.

Michael faces further isolation when Siobhán rejects his love. Siobhán insists she saw Michael only in a caring capacity. The key moment 'Siobhán's Rejection of Michael's Love' relates an awkward and distressing scene. Michael's heart is broken and he reacts by going out in the pouring rain late at night. To support his friend in his darkest hour, Rory goes after him and they meet on the lit-up bridge. Many elements contribute to isolation in this scene. Michael suffers the psychological and emotional loss of Siobhán. The pouring rain and darkness mirror his distressed state of mind. The two friends refer to the most isolating moment of all, suicide. However, both turn away from the abyss. Light-hearted banter turns the negative element of this moment around. The atmosphere brightens at the end of the scene as the pair whirl around in their wheelchairs.

> The two friends refer to the most isolating moment of all, suicide. However, both turn away from the abyss

Michael's isolation deepens when he faces the prospect of losing his friend, Rory. It is a touching scene on many levels. Michael insists he still needs Rory's support, but Rory reaffirms his belief in the strength of his friend by arguing that he is self-supporting. The key moment entitled 'The Loss of a Friend' highlights the transience of close relationships. This scene emphasises that isolation is part of human experience.

In the key moment 'Michael on His Own,' Michael's complete isolation is depicted. His situation has changed dramatically throughout the film. The most negative aspect is that he is now on his own. Michael goes into town independently, but without Rory he faces a lonely future, which darkens the text considerably.

Isolation is well illustrated throughout the film, but with Rory for companionship, Michael does not feel so isolated. He becomes more independent and willing to engage with the outside world. However, Rory's and Michael's physical disabilities create an effective apartheid between them and the able-bodied members of the community. This division persists throughout the film, thus contributing to their overall isolation. In response, Michael and Rory are determined to embark on an independent course through life which, however lonely, appears inevitable.

CLASSROOM activities

1. How is Michael isolated at the beginning of this film?

2. Refer to the key moment entitled 'Fergus Connolly's History of Isolating His Son.' What aspects of this key moment make it an isolating one for Michael?

3. Is Rory correct to describe Fergus's attitude towards his son as a 'case of criminal neglect'? Give reasons for your answer.

4. Look again at the key moment entitled 'Siobhán's Rejection of Michael's Love.' Describe the elements in this scene which convey the theme of isolation.

5. How important is Rory and Michael's friendship?

6. Overall, how well do you consider the theme of isolation to be developed? Refer to the whole film in formulating your answer.

4

Theme or Issue:
exploitation

Theme or Issue: exploitation

exploitation is one of the core themes in many of the texts on the course. Exploitation usually involves the subjection of a person or group of people to unjust treatment.

This chapter will explore the theme of exploitation as it is developed in:

- Kazuo Ishiguro's *Never Let Me Go*
- John B. Keane's *Sive*
- Fernando Meirelles' *The Constant Gardener.*

In attempting to show how the theme of exploitation is presented in each text, you should:

- Clearly explain the term 'exploitation'
- Show how the theme is first presented in each of your three texts
- Identify pivotal moments when the exploitation of a central character reaches its peak
- Determine how the theme of exploitation is resolved.

THEME: exploitation — Never Let Me Go

At the heart of Kazuo Ishiguro's *Never Let Me Go* is the recurring theme of exploitation. Kathy's exploitation evokes great pathos throughout. The only reason for the existence of Kathy, Tommy and Ruth is to serve medical science in providing a pool of organs for the human population. Their lives are predetermined.

This ghastly reality does not become apparent until the middle of the novel.

The chilling exploitation of these three young people is graphically presented. On one level, Hailsham appears to be a privileged private boarding school, but as the story unfolds we begin to question this impression. An eerie atmosphere is created throughout the novel.

At first, it appears that Kathy is inventing a tragic story around a song. Refer to the key moment entitled 'Denied the Chance to Be a Mother' detailed in Chapter 2. This key moment evokes pathos on many levels. To use the word 'tragic' seems appropriate; 'tragic' suggests deep and unparalleled sadness. Tragedy is present throughout Kathy's life.

In this key moment, Madame's reaction is rather strange; she appears to see Kathy as different from her and only grudgingly accepts her humanity. On another level, this scene offers an introduction to the bizarre nature of Hailsham itself, though at this stage it leaves the reader with more questions than answers. Kathy and Tommy have no parents. A normal family life is denied them. A future family experience is equally beyond their reach; Kathy's life is blighted by never being able to become a mother. Her imaginings in relation to the song, which is also the title of the book, have powerful significance. Kathy imagines that the woman in the song is offered the miraculous chance of becoming a mother, but is fearful of the possibility that the child may be taken from her. This fictional woman's life is mirrored by Kathy's own experience; it is, effectively, a story within a story. Kathy's life, however, is more horrific than any fiction she could fabricate.

> *'But she was afraid of us in the same way someone might be afraid of spiders'*

As the story unfolds, it becomes clear that Madame and the guardians are overseers in a diabolical and inhuman project which involves the exploitation of Kathy, Tommy and Ruth to serve the interests of wider humanity. The guardians offer little parental support to the young people in their care. Their distance is unnerving. At an early point in the novel, Ruth observes how awkwardly Madame behaves in the students' company. Madame's fears become apparent: 'But she was afraid of us in the same way someone might be afraid of spiders' (p. 35). At a stroke, the students are compared to lowly insects, further confirming their powerlessness over their own lives. They are expected to retreat into the shadows.

Hailsham offers only the veneer of respectability; the ghastly, diabolical reality haunts the novel from Miss Lucy's speech onwards. Re-read the key moment entitled 'Miss Lucy's Outburst and the Truth' set out in Chapter 2. Miss Lucy's expression of truth is lost on most of the students. Her words do not provoke open rebellion as the students are unable to demonstrate much disquiet, given the secrecy of the project. A ghastly fatalism prevails as Kathy, Tommy and Ruth are effectively dehumanised in order to justify their exploitation in a medical project. Throughout Miss Lucy's speech she highlights their separateness from the rest of humanity. Her words are clinical and chilling, and evoke little feeling for their plight: 'Your lives are set out for you. You'll become adults, then before you're old, before you're even middle-aged, you'll start to donate your vital organs. That's what each of you was created to do' (p. 86). This happens while the students are sheltering from the rain. The turbulent weather prefigures the students' pessimistic future, highlighting the furtive exploitation underlying the novel. Even after Miss Lucy's speech, her optimism about the sun reappearing does not serve to dispel the overall gloom or diminish the pathos of the moment.

> A ghastly fatalism prevails as Kathy, Tommy and Ruth are effectively dehumanised in order to justify their exploitation in a medical project

Miss Emily's comments later are even starker and much less apologetic. Re-read the key moment entitled 'Miss Emily's Chilling Truths' summarised in Chapter 2. Her words are chilling, devoid of feeling. She claims that the most powerful in society want 'the students' to return to 'the shadows' (p. 259). 'The shadows' is reiterated, emphasising the students' sense of otherness and human ambiguity, thus justifying their exploitation. Miss Emily admits that she battles against her feelings of revulsion. Kathy and Tommy are clones; a human identity is effectively denied them. Only Kathy and Tommy search for the unpalatable truth; even the right to defer is denied them. It makes this moment pivotal in *Never Let Me Go*. By the end of the novel, the reader is aware that the lives of Kathy and Tommy are devoid of hope. Their lives have been predetermined, thus giving them no influence over their futures. The need for organs is greater than any disquiet about the use of 'clones' in the process.

Madame's conversation with Kathy and Tommy serves to highlight their exploitation further. In the key moment 'Kathy's Conversation with Madame,' we see that the predetermined and unaltered sequence of their lives is irrevocable. Miss Emily's matter-of-fact language accentuates Tommy and Kathy's hopeless predicament. Madame calls them 'poor creatures' and emphasises her inability to change their destinies.

What happens next is chilling. Kathy realises that after Tommy's fourth donation it will be the end: 'How maybe, after the fourth donation, even if you're technically completed, you're still conscious in some sort of way; how then you find there are more donations, plenty of them, on the other side of that line; how there are no more recovery centres, no carers, no friends, how there's nothing to do except watch your remaining donations until they switch you off' (p. 274). This is a graphic and startling image as it likens Tommy to a machine. Kathy's language demonstrates her inability to express her innermost feelings, which suggests that she is numbed by the whole experience.

As a consequence of this exploitation, Ruth and Tommy die. Kathy is denied the right to enjoy a long-term relationship with Tommy. All they can do is share a kiss in a deserted car park. Kathy is left alone at the end of the novel, with only her memories of Ruth and Tommy. She drives to Norfolk and looks into a field. She imagines that she sees the shadowy figures of Ruth and Tommy in the distance but she does not draw them closer. Readers can assume her future will follow Tommy's tragic path. This is inevitable.

The theme of exploitation could not be better described than it is in *Never Let Me Go*. The exploitation of the 'students' is relentless. The present and future are negatively conveyed. Almost every word or action described in the novel graphically depicts exploitation at its worst. Even the word 'tragic' does not fully capture the portrayal of the diabolical situation. Hailsham has been successful in conditioning the students to respond passively to their inescapable future.

CLASSROOM activities

1. **Assess the quality of Kathy's life.**

2. **What impression are you given of Kathy's adult life?**

3. Re-read the key moment entitled 'Miss Lucy's Outburst and the Truth.' Discuss the importance of Miss Lucy's outburst in the context of the whole novel.

4. In the key moment 'Miss Emily's Chilling Truths,' what is Kathy's response to her exploitation? What makes this key moment chilling?

5. Compare and contrast Madame and Miss Emily in the key moment 'Kathy's Conversation with Madame.'

6. To what extent is the ending of *Never Let Me Go* inevitable?

7. To what extent is the reader conscious of Kathy's humanity?

8. How effective is this text in examining the theme of exploitation?

THEME: exploitation — Sive

John B. Keane's play *Sive* involves the inevitable exploitation of the character Sive for the financial benefit of others. Mena's evil, exploitative machinations have the effect of isolating the young Sive from her own family. The merciless Mena, the lustful Seán Dóta and the mercenary Thomasheen conspire against young Sive for their own gain. Her marriage to Seán Dóta is deemed desirable on the grounds that it is a lucrative arrangement for many interested parties, making Sive a pawn.

In *Sive*, the theme of exploitation is powerfully treated. Sive is a girl whose dreams for the future are maliciously quashed by Mena and the matchmaker, Thomasheen. The dominance of Mena and Thomasheen ensures that Sive will be exploited. Re-read the key moment entitled 'Careful Plotting' detailed in Chapter 2. Effectively, Thomasheen sees Sive as a pony that Seán Dóta is willing to buy at the highest price. Sive is to be auctioned. Seán Dóta is the highest bidder. Sive's view on the subject is to be dismissed. Finance is the only consideration. The fact that Sive is a 'bye-child' – a child born outside wedlock – means that she is more vulnerable still.

Seán Dóta's intentions towards Sive are less than honourable. Seán is depicted as a lustful figure who wants Sive for her youth. He is asked to accompany Sive on the road and claims that 'there will no one cross her path with Seán Dóta walking by her side.' Sive protests that she is unafraid of the dark, but Thomasheen describes her as a 'hare' on the lonely road. Seán and Sive leave together while Thomasheen happily comments about the situation: 'The seed is sown; the flower will blossom' (Act 1, Scene 2). Later, Sive relates how Seán behaved towards her: 'He made a drive at me. He nearly tore the coat off me. I ran into Dónal's kitchen but he made no attempt to follow' (Act 1, Scene 2). Sive aptly describes him as a 'sick oul thing.' A mercenary view of Sive predominates.

Mena's evil machinations serve to isolate and demean Sive further. This is done in a phased fashion. In the key moment entitled 'Sive's Growing Isolation within Her Family,' we see at first how Mena tries to emphasise the social advantages of marrying Seán Dóta. Sive is not convinced and Mena becomes more desperate. Instead of protecting Sive, Mena is maliciously supporting the marriage arrangement. She is undaunted by Sive's deep-seated unhappiness at the prospect. She offers Sive advice: 'You will have no enemy when you have the name of money' (Act 1, Scene 3).

'You will have no enemy when you have the name of money'

Mena describes the poor people of Ireland in a horrendous fashion. Her attitude towards Sive is no less dismissive. She reiterates that Sive has no name, that her 'father was nothing' and that she needs a husband to give her a name. This suggests that she is different from the rest of the social community and exposes her to further victimisation and exploitation. She is identified purely in negative terms as being a 'bye-child, a common bye-child – a bastard' (Act 1, Scene 3). Mena sees Sive's task in life as satisfying a man's hunger: 'It is no more than a hunger.' Sive gets up to leave but Mena takes her roughly by the arm, flinging her satchel across the room. This suggests that her dream of finishing her education is deemed unimportant.

The darker forces represented by Thomasheen, Mena and Seán Dóta suffocate the very notion of love. Pats realises this when he confides in Nanna that Seán does not love Sive: ''Tis the flesh of her he do be doting over' (Act 2, Scene 1). The true self or soul of Sive is seen as worthless, underlining her exploitation all the more.

Sive

JOHN B. KEANE

FIRST PERFORMED:
1959, Listowel Drama Group. Despite being initially rejected by the Abbey Theatre, the Listowel Drama Group's performance of *Sive* went on to win first prize at the All-Ireland Amateur Drama Festival. Professional performances in Cork and Dublin followed and *Sive* was then broadcast twice on Radio Éireann – all before the end of its first year.

ABOUT THE AUTHOR:
John B. Keane (1928–2002) was born and educated in Listowel, Co. Kerry. The son of a primary school teacher, he developed a love of literature early in life. After a short time working in England, he returned to Kerry to run a small public house with his wife, Mary. The life of a publican provided him with valuable insights into people's behaviour, and he drew on these to become one of Ireland's most prolific literary figures in the second half of the 20th century. Keane wrote 18 plays and 32 works of prose and poetry, and was known as a man of wit, intelligence and learning.

All this leaves Sive in a very difficult position towards the end of the play. The dreaded wedding day is looming and she is deeply unhappy at the prospect of marrying Seán Dóta. She is even denied the right to choose her own clothes. Sive is awkward in her new clothes, taking off her high-heeled shoes and rubbing her feet. She takes off her coat and hat at a slow pace. Later, she holds her hands awkwardly while constant activity goes on around her. Her words convey her troubled state of mind: 'I think I'll go to bed instead. My head is on fire' (Act 2, Scene 2). Sive has now distanced herself from her family. It is her means of protest. Her lifeless responses contrast with Mena, Mike and Thomasheen's gaiety. There is talk of an approaching storm, prefiguring Sive's tragic end.

Mena, Thomasheen and Seán Dóta's evil practices lead desperate and victimised Sive to take her own life. Re-read the key moment entitled 'The Most Heart-rending of Ends.' Mena is vanquished as Liam rounds on her for 'polluting the pure spirit of the child' with her nearness. Thomasheen and Seán Dóta sneak away, silencing their input in the final moments of the play. Such a cowardly reaction is indicative of their characters. It is too late for a change of heart. Sive is now dead. The prevailing mood is one of sadness, encapsulated by Liam's description of Sive's final moments. Sive's exploitation has resulted in her untimely death.

Sive is the most victimised character in this play. As a young girl, she is compromised for financial gain by three notable adversaries, Mena, Thomasheen and Seán Dóta. The seeming triumph of these three leads to Sive's effective dehumanisation as she is not afforded the chance to choose a marital partner. Sive's tragic end is her resistance to such pressure. Her suicide defeats Mena, Seán and Thomasheen. However, this is a hollow victory as the audience is left with the heart-rending sight of Nanna crying over Sive's lifeless body.

CLASSROOM activities

1. Re-read the key moment entitled 'Careful Plotting.' Comment on Mena's view of Sive. What impression do you get of Thomasheen?

2. To what extent is Sive considered an object rather than a person? Support your answer with clear reference to this key moment.

3. Re-read the key moment entitled 'Sive's Growing Isolation within Her

Family.' What is your opinion of Mena? Support your answer with clear reference to this key moment.

4. In the key moment 'A Dispirited Sive,' how is Sive's defeat shown? To what extent is this scene imbued with a sense of foreboding?

5. In 'A Dispirited Sive,' how is Mena shown to be triumphant? How is Sive's exploitation presented here?

6. To what extent is Sive's suicide a desperate act to avoid her exploitation at the hands of Seán Dóta?

The Constant Gardener
THEME: **exploitation**

The Constant Gardener takes a global view of exploitation in its many guises. Poverty-stricken African populations are mercilessly targeted by a pharmaceutical company to take part unwittingly in a medical experiment. Their participation is manipulated because many are sick and in need of medical care. This cruel, vicious operation of Machiavellian proportions is designed so that the company can limit their costs and increase their profits. The British high commission and the Kenyan police force acquiesce in this practice.

The theme of exploitation is graphically highlighted throughout the film. The starving millions are afforded no voice. Life in Africa is a constant struggle. The key moment 'The Treatment of Wanza' introduces viewers to the theme of exploitation. A girl named Wanza lies dying in a busy and under-funded hospital in Africa. Tessa is trying to alert Sandy to a possible scandal and is busy searching for information. Wanza has been given a drug which has not been tested properly and the side-effects have led to her death. It is no exaggeration to say, as Tessa does, that Wanza has been murdered. Wanza represents the sick millions for whom day-to-day life is a constant struggle. The scene is filled with pathos.

Tessa's murder is an attempt to cover up the crimes of the pharmaceutical company and the collusion of the high commission and the Kenyan police. Justin embarks on a search to uncover the truth. He learns that Wanza's medical record has been erased, making it seem that she never existed. Her value as a person is deemed so little that she is not even afforded the dignity of a proper burial. This is further compounded when Justin goes in search of her younger brother, Kioko.

Look again at the key moment entitled 'The Lack of Choice for the Sick.' This key moment conveys the effective exploitation of the poor and the dying in Africa by the pharmaceutical company. The poor woman at the front of the queue is denied treatment because she will not consent to take the drug Dypraxa. This is exploitation at its most grotesque. The denial of proper treatment means the denial of the right to life. The medical centre, which should be saving lives, is engaged in the merciless exploitation of the sick and dying in Africa. A network of officials is involved in this exploitation. Kioko's protests go ignored. The police act swiftly and attempt to prevent Justin's search. Justin's very presence could jeopardise the whole project.

> The medical centre, which should be saving lives, is engaged in the merciless exploitation of the sick and dying in Africa

Justin's suspicions are confirmed when he has his last conversation with Sandy. Here, Justin aptly labels KDH an 'axis of evil.' In the key moment 'Sandy's Revelation to Justin,' Sandy's attitude demonstrates indifference to the high number of deaths in Africa. He is able to justify the project on the grounds that it serves British commercial interests well, as KDH could provide much-needed employment in a socially depressed region in the UK. He implies that the African sick are an expendable commodity since death is part of life for the continent's poor. This serves to dehumanise the poor and sick Africans for first-world commercial gain.

Later that evening Curtiss shows Justin the unmarked graves where Wanza and sixty-two others are buried. Their lives are seen to be worthless. Their deaths are concealed as if these people had never lived. It is a classic case of the exploitation of the masses for the benefit of the few, of the exploitation of Africans for the benefit of first-world countries.

KDH and the high commission are not the only ones engaged in a campaign of terror. This is graphically represented in the key moment entitled 'One Little Girl and the Dangers of Africa.' The raiders ransack a village and steal the children for further exploitation. A dazed man looks around at his burning village. People are just shot as if their lives are valueless. As Justin and the doctor clamber onto the plane, attention turns to the plight of one Sudanese child. Justin tries in vain to bring the girl with them, even to the point of bribery. He is unsuccessful. The little girl runs off into the wilderness. Her future is not certain. If she is lucky, she will make it to a refugee camp. However, she is exposed to the dangers of Africa. The raiders deliberately target children. The brutality of parts of Africa is well captured in this scene. Exploitation is part and parcel of everyday life for the poverty stricken. As the plane lifts off, the camera focuses on this little girl, who is almost a dot on the landscape, reflecting her helplessness in a harsh and unwelcoming world. The moment could not evoke greater pathos.

The scale of the exploitation becomes clear at Justin's funeral, in the final moments of the film. Tessa's cousin, Arthur 'Ham' Hammond, refers to the scandal that involved the collusion of Sir Bernard in the high commission, the Kenyan police force and KDH. Sir Bernard's career is ruined, but not before Justin becomes another casualty. Ham makes other fitting observations. He claims that it is easy to test this new drug in Africa as there are 'no murders in Africa, only regrettable deaths.' He argues that the lives of the African poor are 'bought so cheaply.' This suggests that different rules apply in Africa. Human life is expendable. As he speaks, shots appear of African children, smiling amidst rubbish dumps, and a grief-stricken Kioko, writing his older sister's name on a wall as if to preserve her memory. These children are the casualties of an inhumane policy.

There are many victims in the text. The volatile Tessa and the mild-mannered Dr Arnold Bluhm meet brutal ends in their laudable efforts to uncover the truth. The scale of exploitation is enormous but focus is given to two minor characters whose entrance and exit have powerful significance. The passive, kindly brother of Wanza, Kioko, is one of the many indirect victims of the Swiss–Canadian company, KDH. The fate of the little girl in Sudan is graphically illustrated in the scene where she runs through a sandy, barren landscape. Her chances of survival are slim. Exploitation is presented on many levels in the film.

The Constant Gardener emphasises the fragility and precariousness of human life. In this environment, exploitation is rife. The text emphasises how easy it is to exploit the poor and fragile for commercial gain. A racist and imperialist attitude predominates amongst the ruling classes represented in this film. This is most evident in the premeditated manner in which the needs of the African poor are easily disregarded so that the business interests of a first-world power can be served.

CLASSROOM activities

1. Look again at the key moment entitled 'The Treatment of Wanza.' Comment on the treatment of the girl in this scene.

2. Examine the role of the pharmaceutical company in the exploitation of Africans in the key moment 'The Lack of Choice for the Sick.'

3. The key moment 'The Lack of Choice for the Sick' highlights the theme of exploitation. In what way is this effectively shown?

4. Look again at the key moment entitled 'Sandy's Revelation to Justin' and comment on Sandy's attitude to the African people.

5. In the key moment entitled 'One Little Girl and the Dangers of Africa,' to what extent do the raiders exploit fellow Africans?

6. In your opinion, how well does the film convey the exploitation of Africans?

7. 'In Africa, different laws apply.' Discuss this statement in the context of the film.

5

Theme or Issue:
family relationships

Theme or Issue: family relationships

family is defined as a group of people who are related either by birth or by adoption. The diversity of family life is reflected in many of the texts on the comparative course.

This chapter will explore the theme of family relationships as it is developed in:

- Jennifer Johnston's *How Many Miles to Babylon?*
- Martin McDonagh's *The Lonesome West*
- Brian Friel's *Dancing at Lughnasa*
- *32A* directed by Marian Quinn.

In attempting to show how the theme of family relationships is presented in each text, you should:

- Clearly explain the term 'family relationships'
- Show how the theme is first presented in each of your three texts
- Identify pivotal moments when the central character's relationship with his or her family reaches a crisis point
- Determine how the theme of family relationships is resolved.

THEME: family relationships — How Many Miles to Babylon?

Dysfunctional family relationships predominate in *How Many Miles to Babylon?* An only child, Alec grows up without company and his loneliness is evident from the opening pages. His negative attitude towards his mother is obvious from the start: 'My heart doesn't bleed for her.' He describes his childhood as lonely and isolated: 'As a child I was alone' (p. 3). His relationship with his parents is virtually non-existent. His mother denies him the right to go to school and he is tutored privately. Frederick, his father, is powerless to exercise any influence over his wife and Alec feels isolated during his parents' arguments: 'Their words rolled past me up and down the polished length of the table' (p. 7). Characteristically, Alicia triumphs. His mother's voice is described as being 'north-north-east cold.' She demonstrates a callous attitude towards her son. In her view, Alec exists for his mother rather than as a person in his own right.

This negative impression of family life is maintained throughout the novel. Alec is discouraged from forming friendships with his peers in the neighbourhood on account of his privileged position. Re-read the key moment entitled 'Alec's Parents' Disapproval of His Friendship with Jerry' summarised in Chapter 2. Alicia is annoyed to discover that Alec has been friendly with Jerry. This is communicated through her non-verbal response: 'She drew her lips together, tightly, angrily before she spoke' (p. 28). Alicia cuts her son off from the rest of the community. She uses imperatives: 'You are never to see him again.' Frederick agrees with Alicia here. This further isolates Alec from his family. He reaches out to Frederick by touching his knee: 'It was a brief gesture, as ineffective as one he might have made himself' (p. 30). This could have become an important bonding moment between father and son, but Alicia's meddling prevents it. This is an important key moment as it describes the authoritarian atmosphere of the home in County Wicklow. Alicia's insane self-obsession is obvious. Alec feels as if he has been dismissed: 'I felt that they had finished with me.' Communication is suffocated by Alicia's menacing presence in the household.

A chance to develop a positive relationship with Frederick occurs afterwards. In the key moment 'Frederick's Misery in His Marriage to Alicia,' Alec is conscious that Frederick's vulnerability mirrors his own. He describes their 'vulnerable faces' being 'hidden by the darkness' (p. 41). Frederick opens up to Alec about his troubled relationship with his wife. His ability to communicate with Alec is hampered by the loneliness of his life. He explains that he has never 'acquired the habit of talking with people' (p. 43). Rather, he

Jennifer Johnston

How Many Miles to Babylon?

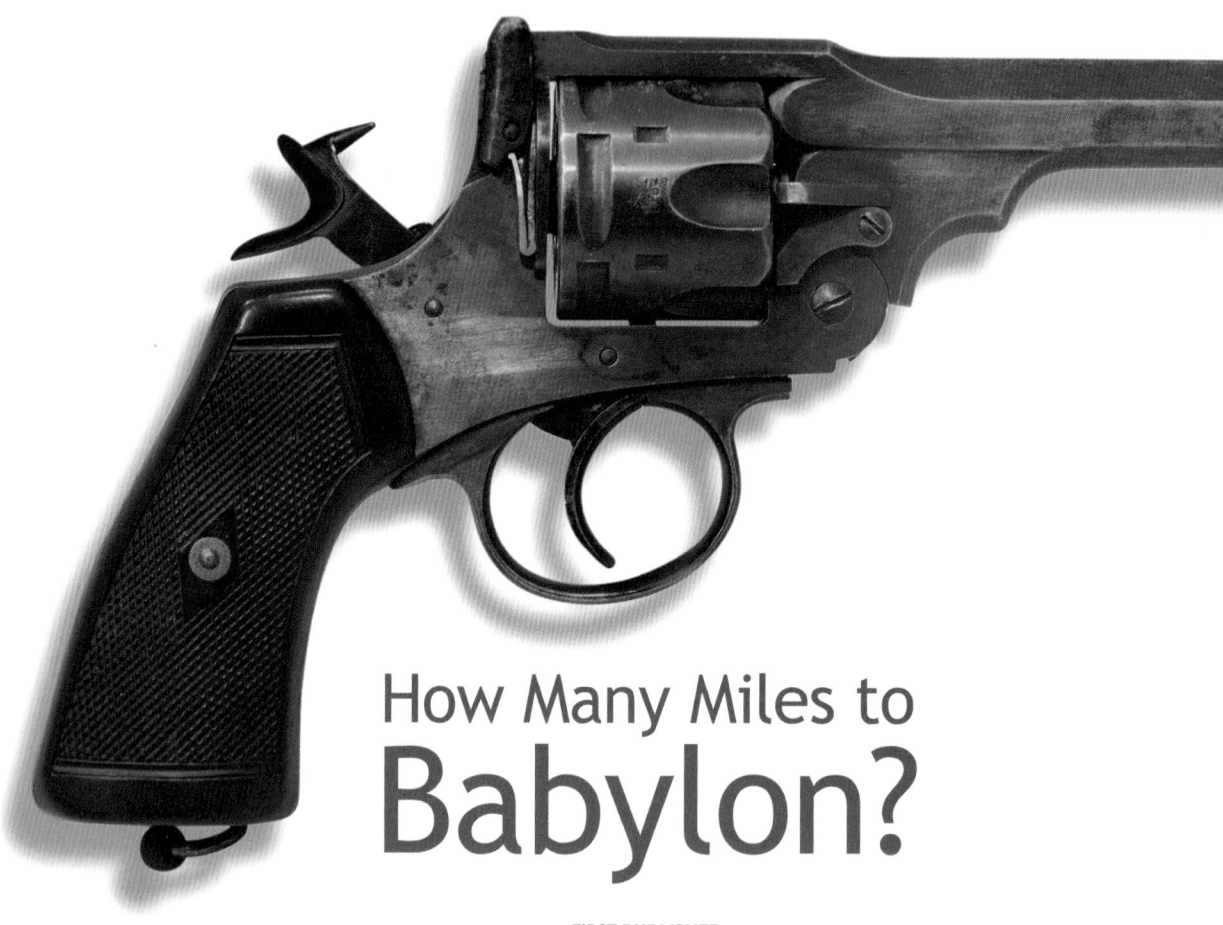

FIRST PUBLISHED:
1974 by Hamish Hamilton

ABOUT THE AUTHOR:
Jennifer Johnston was born in Dublin in 1930. Her novel *Shadows on Our Skin* was shortlisted for the Booker Prize in 1977 and in 1979 she won the Whitbread Book Award for *The Old Jest*. She lives in Derry.

ADAPTATION:
In 1982 *How Many Miles to Babylon?* was adapted for the BBC starring Daniel Day Lewis as Alec and Christopher Fairbank as Jerry.

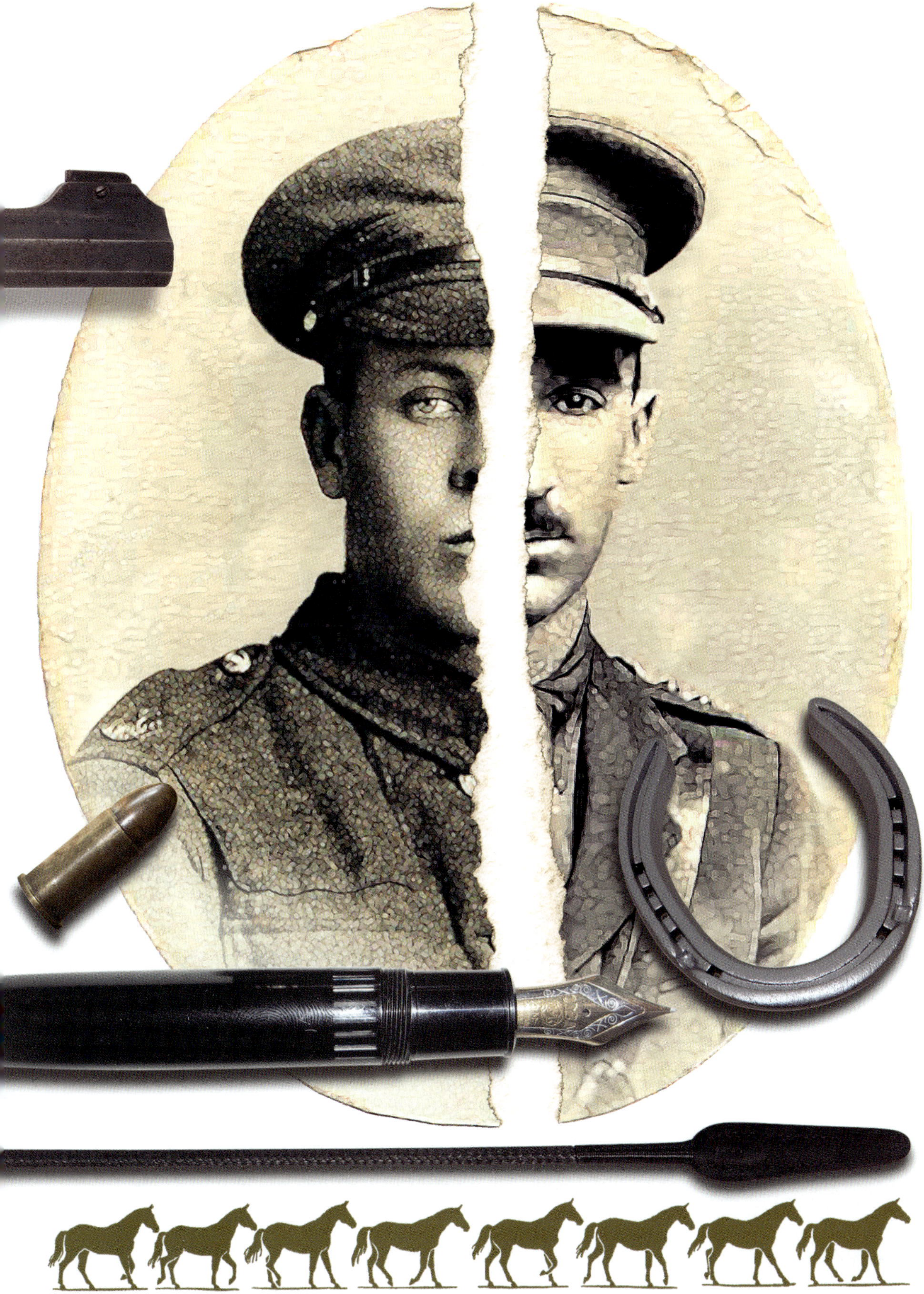

merely issues orders. It is dark. Frederick, lonely and dejected, is hiding away. Alec expects his father will talk to the shadows once he has closed the door.

Alicia's jealousy of Alec's sympathy towards Frederick is well depicted. Re-read the key moment entitled 'Alicia's Shock Revelation.' Alicia is fearful that Alec has become unduly influenced by Frederick, especially when he voices his cynicism about the war. Initially, she tries to persuade him to join the war effort by using emotional blackmail, but Alec responds by saying that his father needs him. At this point she resorts to desperate measures and informs her shocked son that Frederick might not be his father. Now Alec perceives the world in a new light. He sees the portraits of Frederick's ancestors in a different way; he feels apart from them, as if he were an 'intruder.' He becomes 'Dispossessed in a sentence' (p. 47). The shock has reverberated throughout his entire being. The family bond has been broken. The choice of the word 'escape' is interesting. It implies he has been spellbound by the ancestral gaze and now he can avert his eyes. Alicia's shocking revelation has the desired effect of encouraging her son to go to war.

> Now Alec perceives the world in a new light. He sees the portraits of Frederick's ancestors in a different way; he feels apart from them, as if he were an 'intruder'

The key moment 'Alec's Final Farewell' is the last time Alec will see either of his parents. Alicia's accomplishment is contrasted with Frederick's fear. Alec is aware that Alicia is triumphant: 'In spite of the petulance of her words, I was conscious of a radiance coming from her, a feeling of triumph' (p. 66). Her jubilation is shown in her response to Alec. He describes her hugging him as a 'splendidly theatrical gesture' (p. 69). It is, by its nature, superficial; Alicia fails to respond to her son beyond melodrama. Frederick's response is more humane. As he reads his paper, his hands are shaking. Alec is genuinely touched by Frederick's gift of his own gold watch, which had in turn been given to him by his father: 'It was warm in my hand with the warmth of his body' (p. 68). Again this stresses the bond between them. One can understand why Alec is disinclined to believe Alicia that Frederick is not his father.

Like Alec, Jerry is also encouraged by his mother to join the war effort. He refers to his mother talking about his wages, of which she leaves him a mere shilling. She hopes he will join the army because she will then have 'two envelopes arriving' (p. 16). However, she brings about the unfolding tragedy, by encouraging her son to give his family priority over his duty as a soldier. Jerry is willing to consent to his mother's request: 'If he's dead itself she'll get the pension. You'll ask won't you? If he's wounded maybe there'd be something I could do for him' (p. 130). Major Glendinning refuses Jerry's request but Jerry acts out of family loyalty, in contravention of army regulations. He pays the ultimate price for his disobedience.

Unlike Jerry, Alec is less loyal to his family. Frederick writes of Alec's 'contemptuous dismissal' of Alicia's feelings of concern, characteristically leaping to his estranged wife's defence. Alec harbours unresolved anger towards his mother and his painful experiences on the battlefield seem to have hardened his resolve against her. Later, when Major Glendinning threatens to have his body 'shipped home' to his parents if he refuses to comply with the order of execution against Jerry, Alec privately voices his indifference to his family: 'There was a very long silence while I thought of my parents' (p. 152). Such silence speaks volumes. Alec places his concern for Jerry's life beyond any duty towards his parents. Like Alicia, Major Glendinning is unaware that Alec's friendship with Jerry is the most important thing in his life. He urges his rebellious officer to think about his parents but is met with silence. This speaks volumes about Alec's relationship with them.

A deeply negative portrayal of family life during World War I is depicted throughout *How Many Miles to Babylon?* Alec's mother is responsible for deepening Alec's childhood isolation and leaving him ill-equipped, emotionally and socially, for the challenges of the battlefield. The resolution of the family conflict is impossible.

CLASSROOM activities

1. What is your initial impression of Alec's family background?

2. 'Alicia is so preoccupied with herself that she has no regard for Alec's welfare.' To what extent do you agree with this statement?

3. Refer to the key moment entitled 'Alec's Parents' Disapproval of His Friendship with Jerry.' What does this tell you about Alec's family life?

4. Re-read the key moment entitled 'Frederick's Misery in His Marriage to Alicia.' How does Alec offer Frederick sympathy in this scene? Is sympathy enough?

5. Refer to the key moment 'Alicia's Shock Revelation.' Describe Alec's reaction to her revelation. Do you believe Frederick is not Alec's father?

6. Look at the key moment 'Alec's Final Farewell,' and assess the strengths and/or weaknesses of Alec's home life.

7. Is the theme of family relationships resolved satisfactorily in the novel? Justify your answer.

THEME: family relationships — The Lonesome West

The Lonesome West highlights negative aspects of family life in a context where communication has broken down. From the outset of the play it is obvious that the brothers have a long history of arguments, backbiting and hostility in their family environment. Re-read the key moment entitled 'Coleman and Valene's Argumentative Relationship' detailed in Chapter 2. It is just after their father's funeral. No grief is shown. Instead, there is an argument over an unrelated topic. Valene is distressed over the death of his dog and vows revenge against the Hanlon family whom he considers responsible. Coleman shows no understanding and takes a contrary view to his brother. There has been a cycle of hostility; their father had been arrested by Tom Hanlon for screaming at nuns.

The brothers argue over the most trivial of issues. In the key moment entitled 'Who Owns the House?' Valene boasts that the gun, the stove and the table are his property and Coleman is forbidden to touch any of them without his 'express permission.' This infantile attitude contributes to the negative atmosphere in the family home. On the surface, the cause of the argument is that Coleman took a packet of crisps, which gives rise to a physical scuffle on the floor. Violence appears to be the only answer to their constant disputes. Both are intent on increasing the tension and exacerbating the pandemonium at home.

The crisis deepens. Re-read the key moment 'The Murder of Coleman and Valene's Father,' where Fr Welsh tries to act as peacemaker between the warring brothers. Valene is enraged to find his precious religious figurines have been melted in his stove. Coleman is the culprit and Valene vows to kill his brother. The peace-loving priest is horrified, claiming that no one should kill his 'own flesh and blood' because of 'inanimate objects' (Scene 3). This emphasises the importance of the family as the cornerstone of Irish life. The importance of family ties is easily dismissed by Valene, while Coleman confesses to murdering his father because he insulted him, saying that his hair was like a 'drunken child's.' Coleman had a deep-seated anger towards his father which eventually exploded, leading to a fatal shooting. Valene capitalised on the tragic situation by forcing Coleman to sign over his share of the family home. Neither Valene nor Coleman expresses any grief for their father. Valene is more concerned with the melting of his figurines than with his father's death. A tense stand-off ensues. Valene pulls the trigger, only to find that Coleman has the bullets in his hand. The history of conflict leads to certain flashpoints and this is one of many. Valene and Coleman find it difficult to co-exist in the same environment.

There is a complete lack of reference to Valene and Coleman's mother. Their loneliness is emphasised on a number of levels, not least because Valene and Coleman are bachelors. The priest is aware of the void in their lives: 'All it is is ye've lived in each other's pockets the entire of ye're lives, and a sad and lonesome existence it has been, with no women to enter the picture for either of ye to calm ye down' (Scene 5). While there is undue focus on the brutalities of life in this play, both domestic and against the self, the playwright highlights the dread of loneliness and the genuine human need for the company of others. Fr Welsh's death draws out the brothers' humanity. In the key moment 'Coleman and Valene's Reaction to Fr Welsh's Suicide,' the brothers are at first dismissive and laugh over the contents of Fr Welsh's letter. However, they are jolted out of their complacency when they hear the news of his death. Girleen impresses upon them the need to act more responsibly in order to save Fr Welsh's soul from an eternity in hell. The priest's letter acts as a catalyst for change as the brothers are forced to examine their subsequent behaviour. A sense of humanity is instilled in them. Valene gives expression to it: 'Fr Welsh going topping himself

> *'Fr Welsh going topping himself does put arging o'er Taytos into perspective anyways'*

does put arging o'er Taytos into perspective anyways' (Scene 6). This suggests that Fr Welsh has had reason to hope for them.

A further cause of conflict emerges at the end of the play. In the key moment 'A Tenuous Reconciliation?' the situation could easily have resulted in tragedy. Coleman has the gun while Valene holds a knife. Predictably, the feud is once again sparked over trivial issues: the damage to Valene's stove and figurines. However, the moment changes course when, uncharacteristically, Valene puts the knife back into the drawer. He is concerned for Fr Welsh's soul. Coleman highlights the importance of a good fight as a demonstration of concern, although he concedes that the murder of the dog and his father was a step too far. In a conciliatory fashion, Coleman offers to mend Valene's figurines with superglue. This is one essential step in mending their broken relationship. Girleen's summary of the priest's hopes for them echo throughout: 'All about the two of ye loving each other as brothers it is' (Scene 6). However, this moment of reconciliation is lost when a horrified Valene discovers that Coleman stole his insurance money. He reverts to his old behaviour when he seizes the knife but Coleman dashes out of the door. Valene is about to put a match to the priest's letter, but instead smoothes it out and places it beside Girleen's chain. This is an important symbolic act which suggests that redemption is forever possible, even in the most dysfunctional of relationships.

Family relationships undergo change throughout *The Lonesome West*. Initially, it appears that the brothers' dysfunctional behaviour towards each other is firmly entrenched, as the violence seems perpetual. Despite this, there is hope. Fr Welsh's letter to Valene and Coleman acts as a catalyst for change as it encourages them to re-examine their behaviour towards each other. Tentatively, the brothers begin to find a mechanism through which they can resolve their constant squabbles over trivial issues without having to resort to violence. In this way, the cycle of family conflict is broken.

CLASSROOM activities

1. Refer to the key moment entitled 'Coleman and Valene's Argumentative Relationship.' Comment on the conflicts that arise in this scene.

2. What is your initial impression of Valene and Coleman's attitude towards each other?

3. 'The family is in crisis.' Discuss this statement in the light of the key moment 'The Murder of Valene and Coleman's Father.'

4. How does the brothers' relationship undergo change throughout the play?

5. To what extent is Fr Welsh's letter instrumental in forcing Valene and Coleman to re-assess their attitudes towards one another?

6. Refer to the key moment entitled 'A Tenuous Reconciliation?' detailed in Chapter 2. What do you think are the crucial weaknesses in the brothers' relationship? Can the brothers' conflict be resolved?

7. How satisfactory is the ending of *The Lonesome West*? Give reasons for your answer.

Dancing at Lughnasa
THEME: family relationships

Family relationships form a central theme throughout *Dancing at Lughnasa*. Re-read the key moment entitled 'Family Togetherness' outlined in Chapter 2. This moment highlights the positive aspects of the sisters' relationships. Chris talks about improving her image as she looks in the cracked mirror. In the midst of the drudgery of household chores, the sisters find a moment to entertain one another. All share a love of dancing. This is an act within an act as Rose and later Maggie dance merrily around the room. The wireless only hums out a few notes, but this minor inconvenience does not prevent Rose and Maggie dancing. Their life and youthful enthusiasm are well captured in this scene. It is a moment of sweet family togetherness and humorous banter.

The atmosphere of the house abruptly changes when Gerry arrives. In the key moment 'Family Arguments and the Arrival of Gerry,' we see how Kate criticises Gerry for having 'no sense of ordinary duty.' Maggie is silent on the subject but Agnes's feelings for Gerry rise to the surface. This scene suggests that there are tensions in the house and that Kate's overbearing influence is resented. Agnes secretly harbours feelings for Gerry. Kate and Maggie are unaware of their sister's inner turmoil but Kate is conscious of a change in the family atmosphere.

Michael's relationship with his father is drawn upon throughout the play.

Michael is an illegitimate child looked after by five sisters and is well loved. He expresses an interest in getting to know Gerry, who has been an absent father to his young son. Michael is shy of him. At the beginning of the play, Michael records how his father was a stranger to him, thus making the Lughnasa weeks of 1936 momentous for him as it was his first opportunity to 'observe' his father (Act 1). Michael wishes to see him again: 'Is he coming back?' (Act 1). However, we find out later in the play that Michael will be disappointed. Gerry Evans lived parallel lives and had another family in Wales. His promises to Chris were false. On finding out the truth about his father, Michael's first thought is to protect his mother by keeping it from her.

We see different ideas of what family means in the key moment 'Jack's Different View on the Family.' Despite the social shame attached to having children outside wedlock, Fr Jack is pleased to have a child in the house. He is proud of Michael, and says that Chris is lucky to have him. He further claims that Ryangan woman are always anxious to have 'love children' as children bestow fortune upon a household. Kate is aware that this view runs contrary to prevailing Catholic thinking and argues that love children are 'not exactly the norm.' She urges her brother to take some exercise and his medicine. Fr Jack's generally easy-going temperament does not run to arguing with Kate, unlike Agnes in the earlier scene. Yet it is clear from the scene that Michael is welcomed into the very heart of family life, illustrating the Mundy family's support for one another.

Despite Kate's overt authority, her concerns for the family are genuine. She has a deep sense of foreboding about the future of the Mundy family. In the key moment 'It's All about to Collapse ...,' a softer side to Kate emerges. Roles are reversed as Maggie comforts her. Kate fears 'control is slipping away; that the whole thing is so fragile it can't be held together much longer. It's all about to collapse.' She is anxious that the family unit is about to break down and is overwhelmed by the difficulties in life, so much so that she seeks solace in her sister Maggie's arms.

Kate's fears appear to be realised when Rose disappears from the family home. During the key moment 'Rose's Disappearance,' a crisis develops. Maggie appears the most stable figure here and takes command of the situation. The sisters are frantic but are able to co-ordinate their efforts. All are delighted when a distracted Rose arrives home. Initially, Rose appears to have been able to keep her liaison with Danny Bradley a secret. However, a forthright Kate enquires about her whereabouts. Defiantly, Rose informs Kate that she saw Danny Bradley but will not disclose any further details about the afternoon. This suggests that Rose wishes to chart an independent course for herself. Kate's protectiveness suffocates the household and limits the other sisters' freedom to manoeuvre.

Despite this, it is external factors rather than a weakness from within that are instrumental in breaking the Mundy family apart. A new knitting factory is set up near by, thus diminishing the family resources further. Faced with the prospect of scant employment at home, Agnes and Rose emigrate to England. This is the crisis that leads to the eventual break-up of the five sisters. Fr Jack's death adds to the remaining sisters' woes. With the departure of Agnes and Rose, life is not the same. The saddest of ends is depicted when Michael, by then an adult, discovers Rose dying in a London hospice, but she does not recognise him.

> *Dancing at Lughnasa* represents the positive aspects of family life where each member acts to support one another

Family relationships are well explored in *Dancing at Lughnasa*. It is a non-traditional family, the core of which consists of five unmarried sisters who are forced to live unfulfilled lives. Fr Jack and Michael complete the family. They are under attack from outside forces and the play highlights how poverty can break up the family unit. Re-read the key moment entitled 'The Last Scene of the Mundy Family Together and Michael's Narration.' A deep sense of foreboding is created. It is largely a feature of Michael's nostalgic memory. The moment cannot last. Their family happiness is fleeting as Fr Jack is soon to die and Agnes and Rose will leave for ever. The closing moment gives a happy and contented view of family life, tinged with the sadness of change that we know will affect their lives forever.

Dancing at Lughnasa represents the positive aspects of family life where each member acts to support one another. Rose is protected and Michael is welcomed. Even Fr Jack's spiritual search is acknowledged by the strict Kate. The Mundy family exudes energy. For all the negativity that surrounds it, the family has a positive core.

CLASSROOM activities

1. Describe the positive aspects of family life depicted in the play.

2. Re-read the key moment entitled 'Family Togetherness.' How is the strength of the sisters' relationships conveyed?

3. In the key moment 'Family Arguments and the Arrival of Gerry,' describe what you see as the significance of Agnes's outburst.

4. Describe Jack's view of the family. What does this tell you about the Mundy family?

5. To what extent do you think the general societal attitude to unmarried mothers is reflected in the play?

6. Look again at the key moment entitled 'Rose's Disappearance.' To what extent is this a family crisis?

7. What contributes to the breaking up of the Mundy family?

THEME: family relationships 32A

In this film about a journey to maturity, both Maeve's and Ruth's families are in crisis. In common with many texts, there is a breakdown of communication as each family is embroiled in its own conflicts.

Re-read the key moment entitled 'A Quiet Dinner Table' outlined in Chapter 2, where the drama revolves around Maeve, whose general friendliness seems lost in the silent atmosphere. Dessie is at the heart of the family conflict since he has been found in possession of drugs. Their displeased mother is unsettled by the giggles of the other siblings. Their father is overly aggressive towards Dessie, whose non-compliant attitude is at the root of the conflict. A further row ensues between Dessie and his mother when he leaves without permission. Maeve's parents are struggling to cope with his open rebellion and seek solace in each other.

Ruth's family is portrayed differently. Her single-parent family contrasts with Maeve's much larger one. On the surface it appears quieter. Ruth's mother goes out a lot, leaving her daughter on her own. While Maeve's family is strict, Ruth's has none of these prohibitions. But this is a deceptive calm. Ruth's father left home after a history of marital conflict. In fact, neither girl has a stable family environment.

Maeve's relationship with an older boy, Brian Power, leaves her open to greater isolation and manipulation. Her parents are unaware of their planned meeting at the local chip shop. In the key moment 'Maeve's Deception,' Maeve's mother is perplexed when her friends arrive looking for her daughter. They cover over a delicate situation, explaining that there must have been some confusion over meeting arrangements. Maeve is secretive here, using her friends as a pretext for secretly meeting Brian Power. Outside her protective family circle, Maeve is venturing into unfamiliar territory where she is emotionally and socially out of her depth.

Ruth is equally secretive in her dealings, not disclosing the details of her father's phone call. She has not been in contact with her father for years and brings her friends along to support her. Her father is unable to meet his daughter directly. Instead, he picks up the girls in his taxi. His general unease is well conveyed. Years have passed him by. His failure to disclose his identity is his own doing. The film highlights the difficulties of estranged family relationships. Re-read the key moment entitled 'Ruth Comes Face to Face with Her Father.' This moment of recognition is a shock for Ruth. She behaves childishly and hysterically. Her father tries to ameliorate the situation, but to no avail. She is horrified by her father's deception. Her hurt spills over and she shouts at him. Equally, he is unable to reach out to his daughter effectively.

Maeve's deception has caused a rift in her relationship with her father. In the key moment 'Maeve's Punishment,' the atmosphere is cordial until Maeve's father arrives. He has created a punishment for her. There is very little communication; both are distant. His earlier troubles with his eldest son, Dessie, may have coloured his response now.

However, this is not the only deception that is uncovered. Ruth's mother intercepts her ex-husband's letter. She is hurt by her daughter's deception and unnerved at the prospect of the girl's father being in contact. Hurt spills over on both sides, but it ends amicably enough.

Maeve does not give in to her feelings until her mother returns, as we see in the key moment entitled 'Maeve's Mother Arrives Home.' Maeve's father is desperate to protect his wife from his unhappy children who circle around her with their complaints. Even Dessie behaves in a childish fashion. Maeve sits there observing the commotion while her father snaps impatiently. The mother is the focal point of the family. Eventually, Maeve's mother asks about her friends. Finally, Maeve opens up, bursting into tears. Her mother expresses a willingness to put the past behind them.

The film *32A* explores different aspects of family life but the final scene resolves the family conflict. In the key moment 'Maeve's Birthday,' we see a happy family scene. It contrasts with the passive aggression demonstrated in the key moment entitled 'A Quiet Dinner Table.' Maeve expresses delight when she sees her four friends there. Her family stays at the doorway, demonstrating their togetherness. It is a happy resolution to the film as past conflicts are forgotten.

CLASSROOM **activities**

1. 'Troubled relationships are central to this film.' Discuss.

2. Comment on the different family relationships in the film. Refer to the key moment 'A Quiet Dinner Table.'

3. Describe the conflict in the key moment 'Ruth Comes Face to Face with Her Father.' Comment on Maeve's father's general response to her.

4. How important is the mother figure in the family as demonstrated in the key moment 'Maeve's Mother Arrives Home'?

5. In your opinion, how satisfactory is the ending of *32A*?

6

Answering the theme or issue question

Answering the theme or issue question

Once you have identified the core themes that run through each of your texts, your next task is to compare each text with the others. Daunting as the task may appear, take heart. This chapter breaks down the task into workable steps that can be used to answer the theme or issue question.

This chapter will:

- Outline ten steps that will help you tackle the theme or issue question
- Compare the treatment of the theme of exploitation in *Never Let Me Go*, *Sive* and *The Constant Gardener*, focusing on the 2002 question.

THEME OR ISSUE question — 2002 Leaving Certificate

'A theme or issue explored in a group of narrative texts can offer us valuable insights into life.'

Compare the texts you have studied in your comparative course in the light of the above statement. Your discussion must focus on one theme or issue. Support the comparisons you make by reference to the texts. *(70 marks)*

STEP 1 Understand the question

You must be sure what the question demands of you:

- What are the key words in this question?
- What is the question asking you to do?
- How can you connect the question with your knowledge of the subject?

The key phrases in this question are 'theme or issue,' and 'valuable insights into life.' The question is asking you to compare the texts under your chosen theme and then demonstrate the insights into life's experiences that these texts provide.

Planning your answer   STEP **2**

You should first plan the main points that you intend to highlight in your essay and then link your plan to the question, as outlined below. It is important to plan for the following reasons:

- Planning helps you trace the development of a theme in your texts
- A plan will help guide your essay
- A plan reveals possible comparisons between the texts
- It enables you to keep your answer relevant to the question asked.

Here is an example of how to plan your answer:

Never Let Me Go	*Sive*	*The Constant Gardener*
Insight: Life is unfair. Exploited to serve medical science.	*Insight:* Life is negative and mercenary. Exploited at home.	*Insight:* Life is a struggle and unfair. Poor Africans become pawns in the scientific testing of a new drug.
Key moment: 'Denied the Chance to Be a Mother.' Powerful vested interests: the medical profession, the guardians, the human population.	*Key moment:* 'Careful Plotting.' Powerful vested interests: Seán Dóta, the rich.	*Key moment:* 'The Treatment of Wanza.' Powerful vested interests: KDH, the medical profession, the high commission, the Kenyan police.
Type of exploitation: against the 'clones' as a group. Their lives are taken from them. They are medical pawns.	*Type of exploitation:* against the person, Sive. Sive is forced to marry Seán Dóta.	*Type of exploitation:* Lives are at risk. Africans are just medical pawns.
Key moment: 'Miss Lucy's Outburst.' Kathy's life is controlled. She has no control over her future. She is denied the right to life.	*Key moment:* 'Sive's Growing Isolation within Her Family.' Sive's life is controlled. She has no control over her future. She is denied the right to choose a husband.	*Key moment:* 'The Lack of Choice for the Sick.' Wanza's life is controlled. She has no control over her medical needs. She is denied the right to choose her healthcare and the right to life.
Key moment: 'Miss Emily's Chilling Truths.' Full exploitation. Tommy's tragic end and Kathy's tragic life.	*Key moment:* 'A Dispirited Sive.' Arranged marriage and exploitation of the youth. Sive's tragic end.	*Key moment:* 'One Little Girl and the Dangers of Africa.' Full exploitation. The little girl's tragic and uncertain life.

STEP 3 First impressions: writing the essential opening paragraph

The first paragraph is very important in an essay. It should assist in introducing the remaining paragraphs. You need to show in your opening paragraph that you have understood the question and what it is you are required to answer.

An opening paragraph should:
- Target the question you are asked
- Refer to the texts and their overall importance
- Highlight some of the key issues to be explored in your essay.

STEP 4 Writing the middle section of your answer

Refer to the question at all times. Refer to your plan as often as is required. Use this book to help plan answers to past exam questions, specifically chapters 3, 4 and 5. It is also essential to refer to a series of key moments which highlight the manner in which your chosen theme is treated in your texts. Use Chapter 2 to refresh your memory of the key moments in each text. In the exam, you should:
- Expand upon one point per paragraph
- Make clear comparative points in each of your paragraphs.

STEP 5 Lasting impression: writing the conclusion

The conclusion is essential as it brings all the main points in your essay together. It is important to write a conclusion as it:
- Helps draw the points in your essay together
- Reconstructs the points in your answer in a different way.

STEP 6 Re-read the question

Make sure you re-examine the question.
- Have you answered all aspects of the question?
- Is there any aspect that has not been examined?

STEP 7 Look at the plan

Ask yourself whether there is any aspect of the plan you have not included in your answer. Make sure all aspects of the plan relate to the question.

Re-read the middle section of your essay

STEP 8

This is the section in your answer that should provide the most detail.
- Make sure you have made as many comparative points as you can in each of the paragraphs.
- Did you refer to the question statement in each of your paragraphs?

Re-read the opening and concluding paragraphs

STEP 9

The opening and concluding paragraphs are important in your essay. They are essential in making a general and lasting impression.

Is there anything else?

STEP 10

Check if there is anything that has not been included in your essay which could be important. If you are happy with your answer, move on to the next question.

2002 Leaving Certificate

THEME OR ISSUE question

'A theme or issue explored in a group of narrative texts can offer us valuable insights into life.'

Compare the texts you have studied in your comparative course in the light of the above statement. Your discussion must focus on one theme or issue. Support the comparisons you make by reference to the texts. *(70 marks)*

The Theme of Exploitation in *Never Let Me Go*, *Sive* and *The Constant Gardener*

SAMPLE answer

Exploitation is a dominant theme that emerges in Kazuo Ishiguro's *Never Let Me Go*, John B. Keane's *Sive* and Fernando Meirelles' *The Constant Gardener*. As the theme unfolds in these texts, insights into life and its experiences can be gained. While the plot of *Never Let Me Go* appears to enter the realm of science fiction, *Sive* and *The Constant Gardener* have a realistic resonance. All texts ask provocative questions about the nature of what it means to be human and the callous means by which the eroding of the rights of others is justified.

In *Never Let Me Go*, Kathy, Tommy and Ruth's only reason for existence is to serve the requirements of medical science to provide a pool of organ donors for the human population. They are excluded from humanity at a stroke. Similarly, *The Constant Gardener* concerns the millions in the third world who unwittingly become pawns in the scientific testing of a new drug. In both texts, the excluded are denied access to information about their own predicaments. One of life's lessons to emerge from these texts is the importance of worldwide education to combat exclusion and exploitation. *Sive* makes a different point. Sive is exploited in her home environment. The play highlights how the evil machinations of one person, like Mena, can have a profoundly negative effect. The central characters in all three texts have striking disadvantages, either personal or social, which leave them open to being exploited by others in a mercenary fashion. Many insights can be gleaned by studying the presentation of the theme of exploitation in these texts.

In all three texts, exploitation is presented, but in different ways. The texts suggest that in life, exploitation can have different guises. In *Never Let Me Go*, the chilling exploitation of three young people is graphically presented. Like the starving millions in *The Constant Gardener*, the 'clones' are not afforded a voice. In *The Constant Gardener*, Wanza and her younger brother Kioko's vulnerability is more obvious than that of the characters in *Never Let Me Go*. On the surface, Hailsham appears very different from poverty-stricken Africa. It seems like a privileged boarding school, but as the story unfolds it becomes evident that this impression is deceptive. Hailsham is running a medical experiment like KDH, the Swiss–Canadian firm in *The Constant Gardener*. Likewise, Sive appears to be supported in her family environment when she is offered a better quality of education than the norm. However, the dominance of Mena and Thomasheen effectively means that Sive will be exploited for financial gain. Wanza is exploited when offered a drug which will have unknown side-effects. Like Kathy, Tommy and Ruth, she is being exploited by stronger forces in society which are beyond her control. All texts represent the effect of exploitation on the most socially excluded groups in society, though for different reasons. This offers an insight into life in that it demonstrates how easily certain groups are excluded from access to proper resources and highlights the fragility of human life.

Three key moments illustrate the theme of exploitation at the beginning of each text. Kathy has to grapple with Madame's bizarre reaction to her in the dormitory. In *The Constant Gardener*, Wanza is left dying in an underfunded African hospital because she is an unwitting participant in the experimental use of a new drug, Dypraxa. In *Sive*, Mena and Thomasheen conspire to encourage the young Sive into a loveless marriage to Seán Dóta for their own personal gain. Kathy's exploitation is more persistent, in that she is denied the right to be a mother, while Wanza will be denied the right to see her child, Blessing, grow up. In all three key moments, all these vulnerable characters are seen as pawns. In *Sive*, Thomasheen sees Sive as a pony that Seán Dóta is willing to buy at the highest price. Sive's 'bye-child' status and Wanza's poor African background leave them vulnerable to exploitation from vested interests. In *Never Let Me Go* and in *The Constant Gardener* these vested interests are powerful social forces, while in *Sive* it is individuals – Mena and Thomasheen mainly – who threaten to cause the most damage. Life in these texts is portrayed as very diverse; they explore the characters' helplessness in a variety of situations.

The theme of exploitation is well developed in all three texts. In *Never Let Me Go*, Madame and the guardians are overseers in a diabolical and inhumane project which involves the exploitation of Kathy, Tommy and Ruth to serve the interests of wider humanity. Their distance is unnerving. Equally, the actions of KDH and Sir Bernard are just as menacing and clinical in their precision. In *Never Let Me Go*, Miss Lucy's words show little sympathy for the plight of the young people: 'Your lives are set out for you. You'll become adults, then before you're old, before you're even middle-aged, you'll start to donate your vital organs.' In a similar fashion, this exploitation is shown in *The Constant Gardener* when Justin goes in search of Wanza's younger brother, Kioko. The doctors in the medical centre behave like the guardians in *Never Let Me Go*. Their willingness to be involved in a project which may result in the deaths of millions of people is unnerving. Both texts show how unfair life can be, how the most defenceless are so easily disregarded. *Sive* demonstrates exploitation on a minor level in comparison to the other two texts. Unlike the doctor in the medical centre and the guardians, Mena acts on her own initiative. She is instrumental in forcing Sive to marry Seán Dóta and labels her negatively when she calls her a 'bye-child, a common bye-child – a bastard.' Mena's action is personal whereas the guardians and KDH are more remote. Life can be very dark and depressing.

The theme of exploitation reaches certain pivotal moments in all three texts from which life's lessons can be discerned. The most explicit moment in *Never Let Me Go* is when Kathy and Tommy speak to Miss Emily. Her use of the word 'shadows' is reiterated, emphasising the students' sense of otherness and human ambiguity, thus justifying their exploitation. More openly, the little girl in southern Sudan is in grave danger, but Justin's pleas for her life are in vain. His concern is in contrast to the indifferent but factual responses that Miss Emily offers Kathy and Tommy. The African child's identity as the 'other,' rather than an aid worker, means that different rules apply. In both texts, the clones and the little girl are isolated and disregarded in society. Miss Emily claims that the most powerful in society want the students to return to the 'shadows.' This is exactly what happens to the vulnerable Sudanese child when she runs off; she becomes almost a dot on the landscape. Sive is just as helpless as Kathy or the little Sudanese child. Unlike Kathy, Tommy and the little girl, Sive is being forced to adopt a new identity as Seán Dóta's wife. She is denied even the right to choose her own clothes. She takes off her coat and hat at a slow pace, giving voice to her troubles: 'I think I'll go to bed instead. My head is on fire.'

All the characters under discussion here, however, respond passively to their plight. All are powerless. All three texts examine how the most dependent in society are afforded little voice and are ill-equipped to find a way out of their difficulties. In all the texts, the characters are exposed to constant danger, suggesting that life offers many challenges, and for some it is all too much. All texts examine how easily people can attempt to justify heinous crimes or simple crimes of neglect for their own purposes. *The Constant Gardener* emphasises the precariousness of life for many of the earth's population while *Sive* more powerfully conveys the effect of ill-treatment on one lonely individual. Both are realistic in that the events surrounding them are credible. John B. Keane's play, *Sive*, offers a commentary on arranged marriage, still happening in some parts of the world today. *Never Let Me Go* is a more surreal portrayal than *The Constant Gardener* or *Sive*. It demonstrates how easily people can become identified as the 'other,' thereby leaving them open to exploitation.

A sorry and tragic end awaits many of the characters in these texts. In *Never Let Me Go*, Tommy dies and Kathy is left alone. It is implied that her end will follow Tommy's relentlessly tragic path. A similar inevitability follows for many of Africa's poor in *The Constant Gardener*. Tess's cousin makes fitting observations. He claims that it is easy for KDH to test a new drug in Africa as there are 'no murders in Africa, only regrettable deaths.' Unlike the main characters in *Never Let Me Go* and *The Constant Gardener*, Sive chooses her own tragic end. While Justin's investigation ameliorates the suffering of some, Kathy's suffering is set to continue. Sive's suffering is at an end, but at least it has the positive effect of isolating Thomasheen, Mena and Seán Dóta in the final moments of the play. In contrast to *Sive* and *The Constant Gardener*, evil is not so resolutely vanquished in *Never Let Me Go*. All texts highlight the different ways in which suffering can destroy the lives of the vulnerable. All texts highlight human fragility, which is a life lesson in itself.

To conclude, the theme of exploitation is effectively conveyed in all three texts. Its depiction is chilling. The most memorable moments include Kathy looking out onto a deserted field, Nanna crying over Sive's body and the scramble to survive in a Sudanese village. The effect of exploitation on the most vulnerable characters in each text is well captured. All these moments highlight the ever-present reality of the unequal nature of society where those least able are often required to offer the most. This makes the reading and viewing of these texts unforgettable.

7

General Vision
and viewpoint

General Vision and viewpoint

In our everyday lives, sometimes the weather captures the overall mood of the day. Dark clouds signal depression while bright blue, sunny skies provide us with a sense of joy and exhilaration. These simple effects, as well as many more complicated images and strategies, can be used by authors to signify an optimistic or pessimistic outlook in a book, play or film.

General vision and viewpoint is one of the core modes of comparison. You need to discern the clues in each of the texts to uncover the level of optimism or pessimism that is reflected in each one.

This chapter will outline an approach to studying general vision and viewpoint in:

- Jennifer Johnston's *How Many Miles to Babylon?*
- Martin McDonagh's *The Lonesome West*
- Brian Friel's *Dancing at Lughnasa*
- Henrik Ibsen's *A Doll's House*
- Kazuo Ishiguro's *Never Let Me Go*
- Fernando Meirelles' *The Constant Gardener*
- Kenneth Branagh's *As You Like It*
- Damien O'Donnell's *Inside I'm Dancing*.

In assessing the mode of comparison, general vision and viewpoint, you should:

- Determine the importance of the opening and closing key moments
- Ascertain what view of life and relationships is emphasised
- Assess the level of hope conveyed in the texts
- Determine the characters' freedom to choose.

How Many Miles to Babylon?

GENERAL VISION AND VIEWPOINT

How Many Miles to Babylon? offers the reader a social commentary on class at the beginning of the twentieth century as well as portraying the agony and futility of war. The opening scene could not be more pessimistic. Flanders has become the centre of the world for 'tens of thousands of men' (p. 2). Sadly, Alec predicts that it will be the 'end of the world for many, the heroes and cowards, the masters and the slaves.' It is raining heavily. The ugliness of the scene is well captured by the phrase, 'a thick and evil February rain.' Even the choice of words, 'a hundred yards of mournful earth' (p. 2), suggests decay and destruction. The whole atmosphere of the book is almost one of perpetual mourning, where Alec's personal tragedy is allied to that of the countless others who have died in the conflict.

> It is raining heavily. The ugliness of the scene is well captured by the phrase, 'a thick and evil February rain'

The way the story is told underscores the prevailing doom and gloom. Alec is the narrator. His view of the world is pessimistic, especially because of the loss of Jerry. Time is meaningless for him. He writes that he has 'no future' (p. 1). From the beginning, the reader is aware that time is running out for Alec as he records the events of his life in his notebook, compounding the text's overall pessimism. The whole narrative of the novel is foreshadowed by the fact that Alec is awaiting execution. Time offers the reader a depressing finality.

Not only is there a pessimistic view of life in general in the novel, but relationships are also viewed negatively. The novel conveys the impression that important relationships do not last and the impediment of class affects people's freedom of choice. Re-read the text referred to in the key moment entitled 'Alec's Parents' Disapproval of His Friendship with Jerry,' detailed in Chapter 2. It is a dispiriting scene that shows relationships to be negative on almost every level. Alec's view of the world is coloured by the loneliness of his childhood. He describes being kept apart from the children of his own age 'by the traditional barriers of class and education' (p. 3). Alec's description of the loneliness of his childhood gives the text a dismal overview. Alicia is presented as a cold-hearted woman who is too self-absorbed to reach out meaningfully to her son. There are moments of tenderness conveyed between Alec and Frederick, but these are spasmodic and ineffectual. Alec's friendship with Jerry is the only relationship that has meaning.

The oppressive social world of the text becomes an evil force. The humanity of Alec and Jerry is contrasted with the coldness of Alicia and Major Glendinning. Major Glendinning is portrayed more as an institution than as a person. The authority figures in the text compound the overall pessimism of the novel as Alec is trapped on every level, both in Wicklow and in Flanders.

Another characteristic of this text is its hopelessness. The outcome for Alec and Jerry is somewhat predictable given the time and place in which the text is set. Giving Alec a lonely childhood increases the debilitating pessimism of the book, further supported by Alec's lack of freedom to manoeuvre when Jerry is sentenced to death. The key moment entitled 'Alec's Hopeless Pleas on Jerry's Behalf' should be re-read. This key moment conveys how hopeless the situation is for Jerry. All Alec's protestations are in vain.

> The major offers the reader a very pessimistic view of the world, arguing that it taught him to be evil

The major offers the reader a very pessimistic view of the world, arguing that it taught him to be evil. This is linked to his 'cold disapproval' of Alec and his general indifference to 'almost everyone.' Alec is deeply unsettled. His body shudders when Glendinning touches his shoulder while speaking about the firing squad (pp. 150–53). The situation is hopeless.

Alec is not free to make his own decisions. This is clearly expressed in the key moment 'A Simple Lack of Choice' outlined in Chapter 2. As an officer in the army, he is expected to obey his superiors without question. Alec strikes a fatalistic note at the end of this scene. He refers to the 'eternal recurrences' throughout life. This implies that life is a vicious cycle from which there is no escape.

Alec's last scene with Jerry is chilling. The novel ends pessimistically. Jerry's line 'I bear no hate against living thing' is contrasted with the opening page of the novel where Alec claims that he loves 'no living person' (p. 1, p. 155). This shows powerfully how the theme has been brought full circle. Within the confines of this story, nothing changes.

Throughout the novel, life offers little more than perpetual predictability and constant entrapment, with true happiness merely an illusion. This sombre view of life is well suited to this historical novel, with its deep, tragic undertones. Pessimism could not be better expressed than in *How Many Miles to Babylon?*

CLASSROOM activities

1. What does the opening scene convey to you?

2. What is your overall impression of the strength of the relationships in this novel?

3. 'The social world of the novel makes the novel pessimistic.' To what extent is this statement true? Give reasons for your answer.

4. 'In this novel there are examples of hopelessness and defeat.' Do you agree with this statement?

5. Are there any hopeful moments?

6. To what extent is Alec afforded the freedom to choose?

7. Is Jerry more restricted than Alec? Explain your point of view.

8. 'By the end of the novel, Alec is defeated.' To what extent do you agree with this statement?

9. What does the closing scene tell us about life?

10. What is your opinion of the ending of this text?

11. Examine the view of life presented in *How Many Miles to Babylon?*

The Lonesome West

GENERAL VISION AND VIEWPOINT

On one level, *The Lonesome West* highlights the futility of modern life in a country where inhabitants of certain areas are starved of the opportunity for social interaction. The opening scene provides a negative impression of life. Re-read the key moment entitled 'Fr Welsh's Conversation with Coleman' summarised in Chapter 2. Relationships have no meaning. After all, Coleman expresses very little distress over the death of his father, a point that is picked up later in the text.

Despite the pessimism in the opening scene, the text as a whole offers a very mixed view of life. Fr Welsh is dismayed on hearing the news of Tom Hanlon's suicide: 'A lonesome oul lake that is for a fella to go killing himself in.' He reflects on how it must have been for poor Tom, 'sitting alone there, alone with his thoughts' beside the 'cold lake.' He considers that life has positive aspects, which he lists as appreciating rivers, the prospect of travelling and football. Valene concurs with what he says about football. Fr Welsh considers that the hope of being loved is essential in life. He acknowledges that others are much worse off than Tom Hanlon. Valene interjects that the Norwegian girl born with no lips is surely one of them. Fr Welsh bemoans that Tom had no friends in 'this decent world' to support him in his hour of need. He repeats his question: 'Where were his friends then?' (Scene 3).

> *'A lonesome oul lake that is for a fella to go killing himself in'*

Fr Welsh's view suggests that life is full of need. Coleman agrees with the priest's view of life. Valene comments on Coleman's poverty: 'Never unbare are your cupboards.' Coleman is aware of this. 'I suppose they're not now, but isn't that life?' This suggests that life is a constant struggle.

Girleen sees life differently. She tells Fr Welsh that she spends some time in the graveyard. She reasons that even in her moments of sadness, this offers her the consolation that she is 'still better off than them lost in the ground or in the lake' (Scene 4). She thinks the dead are happy for her to have the chance of enjoying some of life's happiness, however fleeting.

The relationships portrayed convey a mixed impression of life. Coleman is implicated in the murder of his father. Valene makes his wayward, hot-tempered brother sign everything over to him. At one point in the play, Valene is more concerned about the melting of his figurines than about his father's murder. Still, despite the brothers' constant arguments and aggression, both demonstrate a concern for Fr Welsh. Re-read the key moment entitled 'Coleman and Valene's Reaction to Fr Welsh's Suicide' highlighted in Chapter 2. Coleman and Valene both show concern for Girleen, who was secretly in love with the priest. Despite the tragedy, there is a small flicker of hope amidst the gloom. Touching words are used throughout to emphasise this point.

Moments of hope persist, but conflicting forces are at work. The props used illustrate this: the knife, the double-barrelled shotgun, Girleen's chain, the crucifix and Fr Welsh's letter. The knife and the shotgun represent Coleman and Valene's dysfunctional form of communication, while Girleen's chain and Fr Welsh's letter symbolise the possibility of love and redemption. Coleman apologises for the murder of Valene's dog and their father while Valene apologises for making Coleman sign the deeds of the family home over to him. Valene promises that everything will be shared with Coleman again (Scene 7). This is positive and uplifting.

While violence appears to have been given a force of its own in the play, the characters still have the power to decide what course of action they want to take. The brothers reach a dangerous point in the closing scene. In the key moment 'A Tenuous Reconciliation?', Valene approaches his brother with a knife. Coleman has loaded the gun with live ammunition. Here, Fr Welsh's fears could easily have been realised. Valene puts the knife away and expresses his concern for the priest's soul. Valene acts constructively and Coleman, despite his protestations to the contrary, follows suit. The brothers can determine their own futures. The priest's letter acts as a catalyst for change. Do the brothers want to continue the vicious cycle of violence or can they break away from old patterns of behaviour? The play does not answer this question directly, but it implies that Coleman and Valene have a choice, highlighting the opportunity for individuals to have an impact on their worlds.

> Valene acts constructively and Coleman, despite his protestations to the contrary, follows suit

While there is undue focus on the brutalities of life in this play, both domestic and against the self, the playwright highlights the dread of loneliness and the genuine human need for the company of others. This text offers a mixed view of life.

CLASSROOM **activities**

1. What does the opening scene convey about life?

2. What is important to Coleman and to Fr Welsh?

3. Which character's view of life do you think is the most optimistic? Give reasons for your choice.

4. How would you describe the relationship between the central characters in *The Lonesome West*?

5. What picture does Fr Welsh paint of his parish? Is there anything positive to be found in its depiction?

6. In what way would you describe the social world of the text as unsupportive?

7. What do you think is the reason for Fr Welsh's crisis of faith?

8. How important is Fr Welsh's letter in the context of the brothers' partial reconciliation?

9. How much freedom to choose do the central characters have?

10. How satisfactory is the closing scene, in your opinion? Justify your view.

11. Have the brothers learned anything throughout the play?

12. There are moments of light and darkness in this play. Examine these moments. Re-read Chapter 2 in order to assist you in your answer.

13. Do you feel there is a point in conveying Valene and Coleman's constant disputes and arguments?

14. Do you think that Valene and Coleman's partial reconciliation in the closing scene ameliorates the pessimistic view of life which seems to be conveyed throughout?

15. Do you think that Coleman and Valene have learned anything about life throughout the course of this play?

GENERAL VISION AND VIEWPOINT: Dancing at Lughnasa

Dancing at Lughnasa presents a mixed view of life. There are positive relationships. However, a debilitating sense of fatalism runs through the play and darkens the text considerably. Fr Jack is a tragic figure, lost in Ireland after spending years as a missionary priest in Africa. There is a deep sense of foreboding throughout the play, but there is also a positive, optimistic sense of family life and togetherness. Re-read the key moment entitled 'Family Togetherness' detailed in Chapter 2. The sisters love to dance and are content in one another's company, but darker forces surround them. Rose's song makes reference to Mussolini's invasion of Abyssinia. Even though the wireless only hums out a few notes and the music soon stops, it does not hinder a playful Rose and Maggie from dancing around the room. From the opening, it is not quite clear what tragedy is to unfold.

The overall vision of the text is also evident through the view of life expressed by the characters. Kate has a deep sense of foreboding about life. She is deeply troubled and confides in Maggie that she fears 'control is slipping away; that the whole thing is so fragile it can't be held together much longer. It's all about to collapse' (Act 1). This suggests that Kate feels unable to support the family, life is a burden and that too many difficulties have threatened to overwhelm the family. Kate's view of life strikes a fatalistic note; she is swamped by the difficulties of life and she seeks outside reassurance. She tries in vain to hold on to a fragile faith.

Kate is not alone in viewing life in a negative vein. Many of the characters are escapist. Agnes and Rose appear to want to escape from Ballybeg. Michael narrates that perhaps the 'two of them just wanted away.' Equally, Maggie escapes internally by pretending to 'believe that nothing had changed.' Michael also records that 'in the selfish way of young men I was happy to escape' (Act 2). This presents a negative view of life in Ballybeg.

> Michael also records that 'in the selfish way of young men I was happy to escape'

Despite the injection of negativity, provided chiefly by Michael's narration, relationships are viewed more positively. Argumentative moments are depicted between Kate and some of her sisters, but the Mundy family is presented as a loving, supportive one. The sisters' concern is highlighted when Rose disappears. Re-read the key moment entitled 'Rose's Disappearance.' Chris, Agnes and Maggie are deeply concerned for Rose's safety. Her disability is more obvious in this scene. All the sisters are relieved when she arrives home. The sisters rally around to support one another in a time of difficulty, making this moment positive and uplifting.

Within this family context, the sisters are encouraged to realise their good fortune. Michael emphasises the power of dance to transform the ordinary, mundane domestic setting: 'Dancing as if the very heart of life and all its hopes might be found in those assuaging notes and those hushed rhythms and in those silent and hypnotic movements' (Act 2). Momentarily, the sisters feel the joys of life.

Despite this uplifting message, life's outer turmoil affects the Mundy family circle. The social world of this text is painted rather darkly. The parish priest sacks Kate from her position as schoolteacher because of her brother's wayward views. A new knitting factory sets up near by, diminishing their financial resources further. Ballybeg is portrayed as a difficult place to live as employment is scarce. Life in England is depicted as harsh for new emigrants in the insecure world of the 1930s. The sisters are driven apart by these malignant forces. The dark shades in the play enable the audience to analyse the nature of society in the 1930s.

While the situation becomes hopeless, the enduring values of love and togetherness are long remembered. Dancing strikes a positive note. Together, the sisters dance as if 'language no longer existed because words were no longer necessary.' Coupled with this, Fr Jack values Michael as a human being, rather than seeing him as a social disgrace. Even Kate appreciates the importance of Fr Jack's 'own distinctive search' (Act 2). This, in itself, sends a positive signal about life.

> *'I must put my trust in God, Maggie, mustn't I? He'll look after her, won't he?'*

The most eloquent of the sisters, Kate, is unable to control the external, negative forces that finally separate the family. In the key moment 'It's All about to Collapse …' we notice Kate's use of language in her conversation with Maggie. Words such as 'cracks,' 'slipping,' 'fragile' stress that a lack of control over events is a hallmark of human experience. Kate's chief concern is for Rose but her own faith in God is weakened by life's experiences: 'I must put my trust in God, Maggie, mustn't I? He'll look after her, won't he?' Notice the repetition of the line, 'I believe that.' This suggests she is trying to convince herself. Agnes's determination to emigrate may have been a chance for her to explore other options, but even she is ill-equipped for the challenges that she faces in a new environment. Both Agnes and Rose are left broken by poverty and hardship in England.

The closing scene provides the audience with the overall mood of the text.

This scene is marked by a sense of foreboding. There is the contrast between the happy family scene and the change which is soon to affect every member. It is a nostalgic memory. No positive change has occurred in the course of the play. This is graphically conveyed in the characterisation of Fr Jack. At the opening of the play, Jack is described as a 'shrunken,' rather tragic figure. Now in the last scene, his old army suit no longer fits him. Happiness is short-lived.

Overall, *Dancing at Lughnasa* presents a mixed view of life. The mood is nostalgic. There is a sense of the fleeting happiness of life, where the central characters are unable to control their destiny. It is this which adds to the debilitating pessimism of the play.

CLASSROOM activities

1. What does the opening scene convey about life? Re-read the key moment entitled 'Family Togetherness' detailed in Chapter 2.

2. What effect does Michael's narration have on the play as a whole?

3. What aspects of life are considered important in this opening scene?

4. Re-read the key moment entitled 'It's All about to Collapse …' How do you think Kate sees life?

5. What are Kate's values?

6. How important is Kate's conversation with Maggie in light of the eventual outcome for the central characters?

7. How do the other sisters deal with life?

8. What is positive about the relationship between the Mundy sisters?

9. In what way does the depiction of life in Ballybeg and further afield in England make the text's general vision and viewpoint a pessimistic one?

10. Why do you think Brian Friel chose to represent the 1930s in this way?

11. In what way is dancing important in the play *Dancing at Lughnasa*? What does the freedom to dance represent in the context of the play?

12. What do you see as the most uplifting moment depicted in the play *Dancing at Lughnasa*?

13. 'The characters in *Dancing at Lughnasa* are offered little freedom

to make choices affecting their own lives.' To what extent is this statement true? How does this add to the overwhelming sense of fatalism in the play?

14. **Compare the opening and closing scenes.** Re-read the key moments entitled 'Foreboding,' 'Family Togetherness' and 'The Last Scene of the Mundy Family Together and Michael's Narration,' outlined in Chapter 2, before you answer this question.

15. **'There are many happy moments in this play but such happiness came to an end due to unfavourable circumstances elsewhere.'** What does this tell us about life and its experiences?

GENERAL VISION AND VIEWPOINT — A Doll's House

A Doll's House paints a mixed view of life. Immediately we are struck by the title; it captures a sense of Nora's imprisonment in the suffocating confines of the Helmers' apartment. *A Doll's House* asserts the power of the individual. Relationships are not viewed positively. Helmer's relationship with Nora – confining, narrow and unequal – is pivotal. Nora's attitude undergoes change in the course of the play.

Initially, Nora's childlike excitability is underlined by her verbal and non-verbal responses. She listens at Helmer's study door and furtively eats some macaroons (Act 1). Re-read the key moment entitled 'Nora's Relationship with Her Husband, Helmer' detailed in Chapter 2. They delight in each other's company but Helmer puts constraints on his wife. Helmer and Nora adopt different attitudes to life. Nora is more open and optimistic while Helmer is anxious to avoid calamity.

> *'Yes, it's a wonderful thing to know that one's position is assured and that one has an ample income'*

Helmer warns Nora that a 'home that is founded on debts and borrowing can never be a place of freedom and beauty.' He is proud of his achievements and his social position. 'Yes, it's a wonderful thing to know that one's position is assured and that one has an ample income.' He is content that Nora does not have to make flowers over Christmas. He claims that the previous Christmas was boring. Nora insists that she 'didn't find it boring' (Act 1). This exchange illustrates the difference between Helmer and Nora.

Dr Rank adopts a fatalistic and negative approach to life. He is suffering from tuberculosis of the spine, the result of his father having lived a life of debauchery. Dr Rank confides in Nora about his illness: 'And all this to atone for someone else's sin? Is there justice in that? And in every single family, in one way or another, the same merciless law of retribution is at work' (Act 2). This offers the audience a very bleak view of the world.

Dr Rank's negative view of life is not supported by other characters. Mrs Linde finds fulfilment in work: 'I must work if I'm to find life worth living.' She calls it her 'only joy.' She also finds happiness with Krogstad. Her delight is barely concealed when she exclaims, 'What a change. Oh, what a change! Someone to work for – to live for! A home to bring joy into! I won't let this chance of happiness slip through my fingers' (Act 3).

Sophisticated Norwegian society has a veneer of respectability. Krogstad represents the corrupt underworld. He realises that Nora has committed a transgression and blackmails her. He delights in the prospect of Helmer being subject to him. He further tries to distress Nora by painting a frightening and graphic image of those who have drowned in the 'cold, black water' (Act 2). These images of death and destruction convey to the audience a pessimistic view of life.

Constant references are made to miracles throughout. Nora anticipates a miracle on many occasions. The word 'miracle' is the very last word of the play. A miracle has religious overtones. It is an amazing, unexpected event. Nora anticipates that Helmer will sacrifice himself for her even though she would refuse to accept. This outcome fails to materialise and Nora is forced to re-examine her relationship with Helmer. Re-read the key moment entitled 'Time Is Running Out.' Notice the way Nora is anxious and tense in this scene. She is trapped, unable to move or exert any influence over her future.

By the end of the play, this has changed. Nora has found her own voice and engages in her first adult-to-adult conversation with her husband. Re-read the key moment entitled 'A New Nora?' summarised in Chapter 2. The moment she takes off her fancy dress is symbolic of the shedding of her past imprisonment, where old societal roles are accepted. Helmer's inability to cope becomes

A Doll's House

Henrik Ibsen

FIRST PERFORMED:
1879, Royal Theatre, Copenhagen. The play – a scathing criticism of the roles men and women played in the marriages of the day – was reviled by some critics on moral grounds. *A Doll's House* was very popular with audiences, though, and played to full theatres night after night.

ABOUT THE AUTHOR:
Henrik Ibsen (1828–1906) was a major 19th-century Norwegian playwright, theatre director and poet. He is often referred to as 'the father of modern theatre,' largely because of his realism, which examined the uncomfortable truths that lie behind the 'respectable' façade of people's lives. His plays are still highly topical and widely staged, and include *Peer Gynt, Hedda Gabbler* and *An Enemy of the People.*

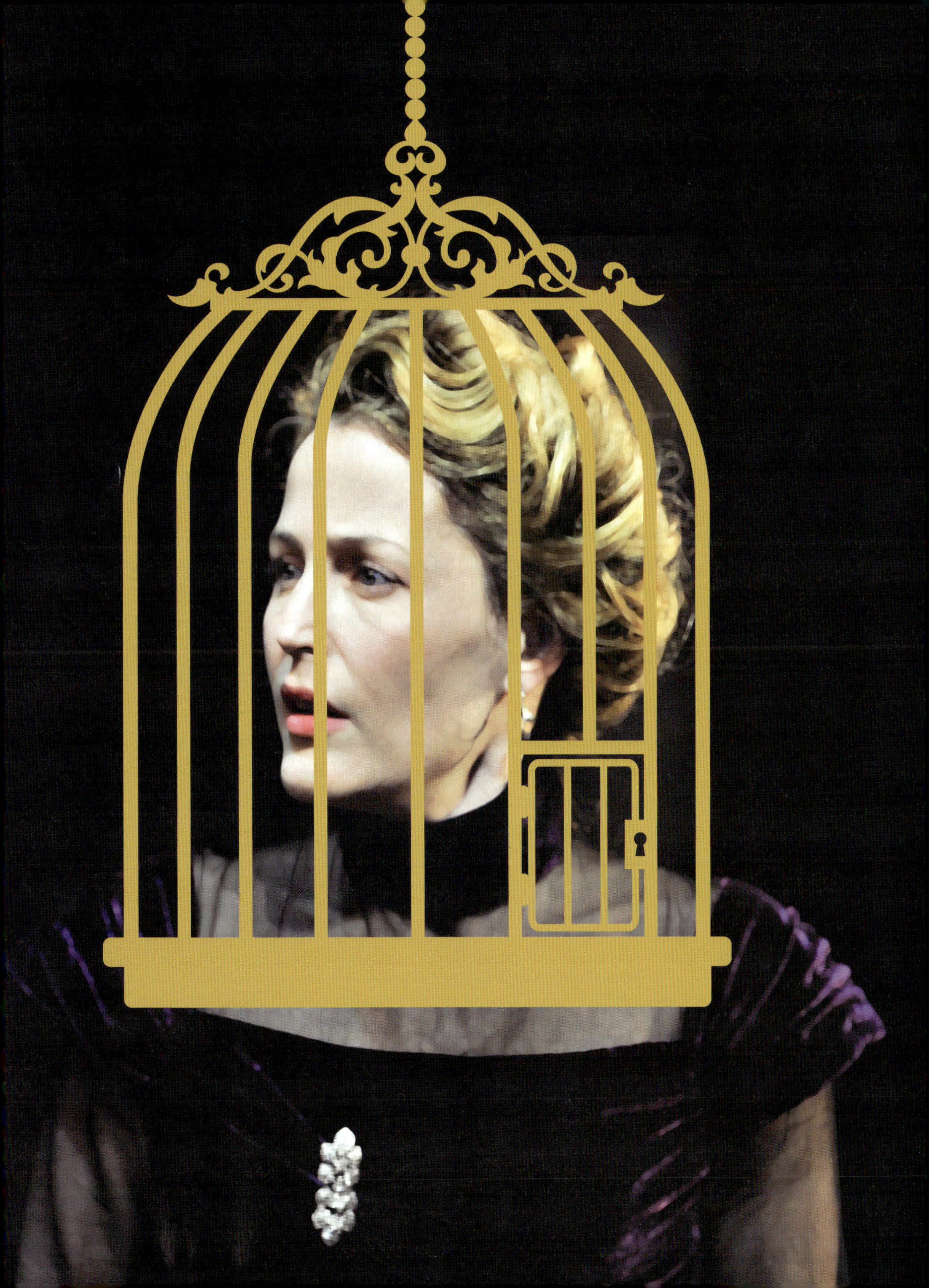

more obvious. He says he will protect her 'like a hunter dove' from the 'claws of a falcon' (Act 3). The claws of the falcon represent the horrors of life, but Nora is reluctant to be protected in this way again and, symbolically as well as literally, slams the door on their relationship. Notice that Nora is no longer 'prepared to accept what people say.' She is no longer going to be passively guided by others or conditioned by society. While Helmer comes across as a tragic character who loses what he loves most, Nora emerges as a stronger woman who is committed to making firm choices about her future. This suggests that people have the freedom to choose and the freedom to create the type of life they desire.

> Nora is reluctant to be protected in this way again and, symbolically as well as literally, slams the door on their relationship

The closing scene can be viewed positively or negatively. In a pessimistic vein, Nora's relationship with Helmer is in tatters. Helmer is forced to acknowledge the need for change but his change comes too late. He is left disconsolate, repeating Nora's words, 'miracle of miracles,' to himself. The fleeting hope that she might return is dashed when he hears her slam the door behind her. This closing scene presents a negative view of marriage and of relationships.

However, Nora is determined to create a new life for herself, to become more familiar with the ways of the world and no longer to be cocooned in the fairytale world of playthings. While her survival is not certain, the text re-asserts the qualities of courage and individuality. *A Doll's House* presents a mixed view of life.

CLASSROOM activities

1. What is the importance of the opening scene in determining the general vision and viewpoint? Re-read the key moment entitled 'Nora's Relationship with Her Husband, Helmer,' detailed in Chapter 2.

2. How does Nora grow and develop as a person throughout this text?

3. What does Nora's character development tell the audience about life and its experiences?

4. Which character adopts an optimistic approach to life? Explain your choice.

5. 'Dr Rank's view of life needs to be put into context.' Is this statement true? Explain your answer.

6. What is your first impression of Nora's relationship with Helmer? Explain your answer.

7. What does the text have to say about relationships?

8. Are the relationships positive or negative?

9. How does the social world of the text present an optimistic or pessimistic view of life? Explain your answer.

10. Re-read the key moment entitled 'Time Is Running Out' detailed in Chapter 2. Explain how the word 'miracle' is important in the context of the play as a whole.

11. In the key moment 'A New Nora?', how free is Nora to choose?

12. Do you think the ending of *A Doll's House* is optimistic? Justify your answer.

13. 'Overall, this play captures the view that life is a mixture of light and dark, optimism and pessimism.' To what extent is this statement true? Refer to the whole play in formulating your answer.

14. Is the presentation of life depicted in this play realistic? Explain your answer.

Never Let Me Go — GENERAL VISION AND VIEWPOINT

Pessimism prevails in this novel, but this is not apparent in the opening pages. Kathy, the narrator, describes her life as a carer. As she narrates, a degree of unreality is established. She is happy to be offered the opportunity to choose her donors but it soon appears that the freedom to choose is meaningless, as there are 'fewer and fewer donors left who I remember' (p. 4). Hailsham figures large in her memories and Kathy describes herself as 'lucky' to have grown up in such beautiful surroundings.

The view of life that predominates in this text is very fatalistic. Kathy, Tommy and Ruth are clones. Life is already mapped out for them. Miss Emily explains to Ruth and Tommy that 'all clones, or students, as we preferred to call you –

existed only to supply medical science' (p. 256). This view of life is deeply dark and pessimistic.

In such unusual circumstances, relationships have a new meaning. Kathy, Ruth and Tommy have no parents, and are denied the right to have long-term relationships. Despite this, all have the human desire to be loved. Re-read the key moment entitled 'Ruth's Deception and a Craving for Love' detailed in Chapter 2. When Kathy uncovers Ruth's deception she realises that all the students crave 'a spontaneous hug, a secret letter, a gift.' All are starved of the opportunity to develop proper long-term relationships with one another. Kathy attempts to hold back her emotions when she says a final goodbye to Tommy. They have been preparing all their lives for the moment of death. It is unavoidable and relentlessly deterministic.

In *Never Let Me Go*, one must be aware that appearances are deceptive. Hailsham is described as a 'beautiful place' (p. 4). It is painted as a boarding school for the privileged and looms large in Kathy's imagination. In contrast to Hailsham, there is the sinister depiction of the woods. Kathy describes two rumours about the woods. One concerns a boy who ventured outside Hailsham's boundaries and whose body was found two days later. The other rumour concerns a girl who travelled beyond the fence and who, when she returned, was denied access to the school. She subsequently died. There is a contrast between the confined world of Hailsham and the uncertainty of the world outside. Hailsham offers a veneer of respectability, but the guardians are overseers in a ghastly, inhumane project to serve the requirements of medical science.

> *'More scientific, efficient, yes. More cures for the old sicknesses. Very good. But a harsh, cruel world*

The guardians voice a view of the future which makes the situation hopeless, but *Never Let Me Go* is also pessimistic on other levels. Life is shown to be harsh, callous and cruel. Miss Emily asserts that life is superficial and valueless. Her words are chilling and devoid of feeling: 'You have to accept that sometimes that's how things happen in the world. People's opinions, their feelings, they go one way, and then the other' (p. 261). Madame's negativity is futuristic: 'More scientific, efficient, yes. More cures for the old sicknesses.

Very good. But a harsh, cruel world' (p. 267). Miss Emily's analysis supports this when she claims that the most powerful in society want 'the students' to return to 'the shadows' (p. 259). The phrase 'the shadows' is repeated, emphasising the students' sense of otherness and human ambiguity. The future will expose them to even greater threats.

Even Kathy's present life is devoid of hope. In the key moment 'Denied the Chance to Be a Mother,' we see how hopeless Kathy's situation is; her life is predetermined. She has no control over her future and is denied the right to have a family of her own, as she is not considered fully human. This key moment evokes pathos on many levels. Kathy is denied the right to have a child and the fictional woman's life mirrors Kathy's story, but Kathy's life is more tragic than any fiction ever fabricated. Madame's bleak predictions compound the prevailing pessimism in the novel. She thought Kathy was holding the 'old kind world' to her heart rather than a baby. She also sees the situation deteriorating for future clones, who will be forced to return to the shadows. This key moment highlights the sheer hopelessness of Kathy and Tommy's situation due to societal prejudices and determines the overall pessimism of the text.

> She also sees the situation deteriorating for future clones, who will be forced to return to the shadows

What makes this text particularly pessimistic is the lack of freedom afforded to the main characters to choose their own futures. In the key moment 'Miss Lucy's Outburst and the Truth,' her words are clinical and chilling: 'You'll become adults, then before you're old, before you're even middle aged, you'll start to donate your vital organs' (p. 79). The weather depicted fits in well with the overall mood. It is gloomy and raining outside. Their dreams are quashed; they are denied access to the human population. Throughout the speech, Miss Lucy highlights their separateness from the human population. Even after Miss Lucy's speech, her optimism about the sun reappearing does not serve to dispel the overall gloom.

Pessimism is well conveyed in Miss Emily's conversation with Kathy and Tommy. In the key moment, 'Miss Emily's Chilling Truths,' Miss Emily explains that she would look condescendingly upon them from her study window and feel 'such revulsion' (p. 264). The word 'revulsion' encapsulates Miss Emily's view of Kathy and Tommy. They are less than human; their very existence provokes horror, disgust and abhorrence. Her words are echoed by Madame's reaction to them, thus adding to the general pessimism of the novel. Such a view serves to justify their exploitation.

By the end of the novel, the reader is aware that Kathy and Tommy's lives are devoid of hope. Re-read the key moment entitled 'Kathy's Memories,' when Kathy is left looking at the field in Norfolk where rubbish of all kinds has become stuck on the trees. She imagines seeing Tommy and Ruth waving to her in the distance. Norfolk symbolises finding all that is lost, but the reader is aware that such a search is fruitless. Kathy soldiers on, but her future is already decided.

The novel's pessimistic, negative approach to life is well captured on many levels, both literal and symbolic.

CLASSROOM activities

1. What impression do you get of Hailsham from the opening pages of the novel?

2. What view of life is offered in this text?

3. What are the main difficulties facing Kathy?

4. 'Hailsham is actually a very negative environment.' Discuss.

5. 'Kathy's conversation with Madame emphasises how hopeless her situation is destined to be.' Comment on this view.

6. To what extent is it accepted that Kathy and Tommy will never be free?

7. What does the closing scene tell us about Kathy's future?

8. What is unreal about Kathy, Ruth and Tommy's lives?

9. What is your opinion of their treatment at the hands of civilised society?

10. Are there limits to medical progress?

11. Does the novel suggest that this progress is taken a step too far?

12. What is the point of the pessimism that prevails in this novel?

13. What does this novel have to say about humanity?

The Constant Gardener — GENERAL VISION AND VIEWPOINT

The Constant Gardener emphasises the fragility and precariousness of human life. This film depicts a brutal world where the poor are mercilessly exploited to serve the needs of the first-world economy. The pessimism is relentless, especially when aid workers such as Arnold and Tessa are savagely murdered, in an overall context of poverty and desperation. The opening scene advances the notion that relationships are very fragile.

Sandy conveys the hopelessness of the situation for ordinary Africans. He justifies his actions on the grounds that the testing of the drug is not 'killing people that wouldn't be dead otherwise. Look at the death rate. Not that anybody's counting.' This narrow and heartless view of life in Africa is the predominant view among the ruling classes. Tessa's cousin, Ham (also playfully referred to as 'Muffin'), argues that the lives of the starving millions are not considered. He claims that people think 'there are no murders in Africa.' He suggests that their lives are 'bought so cheaply.' The events of the film support this opinion.

Relationships are depicted very differently in this film. Justin develops a whirlwind romance with Tessa. Re-read the key moment entitled 'Justin's first Meeting with Tessa' detailed in Chapter 2. Despite the political discussion, Justin and Tessa become attracted to one another. Later that day, they kiss passionately. Justin's romantic attachment to Tessa is the driving force of the film and propels him to search for the truth surrounding her death. Most other relationships are depicted in a negative vein. Sir Bernard, Justin's boss, is untrustworthy. Sandy, Justin's friend, is implicated by being used as a stooge for his employer, Sir Bernard. Betrayal is everywhere and appearances are deceptive on almost every level. This portrays an undesirable view of life.

The social world of the text is depicted as corrupt. There are glaring inequalities between the rich and the poor in Africa. The pharmaceutical company is saving millions of dollars by using sick Africans to test its drug.

> He justifies his actions on the grounds that the testing of the drug is not 'killing people that wouldn't be dead otherwise'

Many people are complicit in this deception, including Sandy and Sir Bernard. Sandy spells out the advantages for the British government: KDH is providing jobs for people in Wales. The African landscape is bleak and barren. The villagers' vulnerability is highlighted when raiders invade their village and kidnap children for a harrowing life of slavery.

The situation is presented as hopeless for the sick millions, especially young children, in Africa. The key moment 'The Treatment of Wanza,' which looks at the death of a fifteen-year-old girl, is a pivotal moment in the film. She is a victim of KDH's drug, the side effects of which are deadly. An atmosphere of secrecy surrounds her death and her files are erased to make it seem she never existed. Wanza's short life story is a fitting portrayal of the diabolical treatment of the poorest in society, whose day-to-day lives are a constant struggle, one from which there is no escape. For most, the outcome is premature death. It is in this context that KDH's exploitation of the poor goes unnoticed. This demonstrates the hopelessness and futility of life in Africa. It is further compounded when Curtiss shows Justin where Wanza and some sixty others are buried in unmarked graves in the middle of a swamp.

One small flicker of hope remains. Justin's investigation is a success, as he uncovers the deception and highlights it for a wider audience at the end of the film. This, at least, could potentially have the effect of ending the trials and exposing the plight of the sick and dying in Africa. Sir Bernard's corrupt career is now over.

> A contrast between busy, bustling London and the windswept, barren landscape of Sudan is effectively conveyed

This positive development ameliorates the doom and gloom of the film.

People in the first world are free to make choices to improve their futures. A contrast between busy, bustling London and the windswept, barren landscape of Sudan is effectively conveyed. The poor have no choice at all over their futures. Re-read the key moment entitled 'The Lack of Choice for the Sick.' This key moment highlights the unjust exploitation of the sick in African society, who have become unwitting participants in serving the interests of the Swiss–Canadian pharmaceutical firm KDH. The poor woman's pleas go unheard. She won't consent to the use of the drug, Dypraxa, so she is prevented from accessing wider medical care. A fatalistic note is struck when

Curtiss describes both himself and Justin as 'marked men.' This creates a sense of foreboding as powerful forces have destroyed Curtiss's career and now threaten Justin's life.

A lack of freedom to manoeuvre is highlighted in the key moment entitled 'One Little Girl and the Dangers of Africa.' The raiders mercilessly ransack the village, targeting small children for further exploitation. The villagers are helpless to prevent such an attack and just scramble for safety. Attention turns to the plight of one small child. Mercilessly, she is exposed to the dangers ever present in Africa without any means of defending herself. As the plane lifts off, she becomes a dot on the landscape, prefiguring her helplessness and powerlessness in a cruel and vicious world.

Despite the prevailing negativity that colours the portrayal of life in this text, it vindicates Tessa's and, ultimately, Justin's search for the truth. The darker forces represented by Sir Bernard are vanquished at the end. He has to face the ensuing scandal. Justin is instrumental in highlighting the issue, but in searching for the truth, Justin pays with his life.

The Constant Gardener is a love story between Tessa and Justin interwoven with a tale of corruption involving high-ranking diplomatic officials, the Kenyan government and a pharmaceutical company. It highlights the glaring inequalities of life in Africa and the treatment of Africans as second-class citizens. The pessimism which colours this text acts as a commentary on the wide differentials that exist between the first and third worlds.

CLASSROOM activities

1. What does the opening scene suggest about what is important in life?
2. How is life in Africa depicted in this film?
3. Compare and contrast the positive and negative relationships in this text.
4. How negative an environment is the social world of the text shown to be?
5. Are there any hopeful moments in this film?
6. 'In the end, Justin's decision to investigate is crucial.' Discuss.
7. Is the closing scene inevitable?

8. '*The Constant Gardener* asks us searching questions about the nature of the world and how unequal and unfair life is in the third world.' Discuss this statement in the context of general vision and viewpoint.

GENERAL VISION AND VIEWPOINT
As You Like It

As You Like It depicts an optimistic view of life, but the opening scene conveys a more pessimistic and negative outlook. There is a sense of the good in life coming to an abrupt halt due to the villainy of Duke Frederick's forces. Re-read the key moment entitled 'A Siege in Progress' outlined in Chapter 2. The light-hearted atmosphere engendered by the duke's guests turns nightmarish when Frederick's soldiers storm the building. A sharp contrast is portrayed by the colourful display of the little gathering in the palace and the black attire of the invading soldiers. Frederick, armed and dressed in black, sternly faces his defeated brother; his victory darkens the text considerably.

Many of the characters adopt different attitudes to life throughout the film. At first, Rosalind is grief-stricken and overwhelmed by the prospect of life without her loving father; she finds it difficult to 'forget a banished father.' Celia boldly asserts that if Rosalind is to be banished, she will also be exiled from the palace. In this context, she lightens the burden of an uncertain future by proclaiming that she is going 'to liberty and not to banishment.' This demonstrates a positive approach to life despite its difficulties.

Relationships are represented in a variety of ways throughout *As You Like It*. On one level, there are the positive romantic relationships between Orlando and Rosalind, Jaques and Celia. On the other, there are the negative sibling relationships such as Frederick's antipathy for his older brother and Jaques' unfair and dismissive treatment of Orlando. A Machiavellian Jaques damages his younger brother's reputation so as to encourage the champion wrestler, Charles, to fight Orlando in the ring. This represents the darker force of the play. However, throughout *As You Like It*, relationships undergo change, suggesting that redemption is always possible.

> Throughout *As You Like It*, relationships undergo change, suggesting that redemption is always possible

The social world of the text provides a contrast between two opposing worlds. We have the playful gaiety represented by the abundant Forest of Arden, as well as the dark, enclosed world of Frederick's castle. The Forest of Arden represents romance; it is where a lovestruck Orlando writes odes to Rosalind and pins them on the bark of trees. It is likened to the golden age of Robin Hood and represents a paradise on earth, where they live in a state of timelessness. Frederick's castle is the opposite: a dark and deserted fortress. Everyone flees to the peace and serenity that the Forest of Arden represents.

Hope is a redeeming virtue throughout this film. Jaques' and Frederick's characterisation follow a similar path. A poisonous jealousy provokes them to treat their respective brothers unfairly, but both have a change of heart. Frederick, bitter and heartless, is determined to venture out with his army to kill his brother in the Forest of Arden. However, he has a surprising change of heart on his travels; he encounters a holy man who encourages him to re-examine his behaviour. Notice the way Jaques abruptly changes course once he realises that Orlando had been instrumental in saving his life. This film demonstrates that hope for a positive outcome is always within reach.

Villainy, represented by the paranoid Frederick and the cunning Jaques, appears to triumph. Re-read the key moment entitled 'Rosalind's Banishment.' Despite Frederick's autocratic presence, Frederick loses his daughter. Unashamedly, Celia declares her love for Rosalind and urges her father to banish her too. While Frederick's authority effectively banishes Rosalind from court, she is not silenced.

> Celia's defiance of her father's wishes illustrates that the powerful lord is not the only one with the power to choose

Cleverly, she argues that his mistrust of her cannot make her 'a traitor.' Celia's defiance of her father's wishes illustrates that the powerful lord is not the only one with the power to choose. This suggests that even the victims of villainy have the power to decide their future. It demonstrates an optimistic and uplifting view of life, where a character's destiny is within their own grasp and not dependent upon another's whim.

The last scene conveys a positive view of life. Villainy has been thwarted as its power has been negated from within. Look again at the closing scene, 'The Wedding Day,' which brings the film full circle. Many of the characters

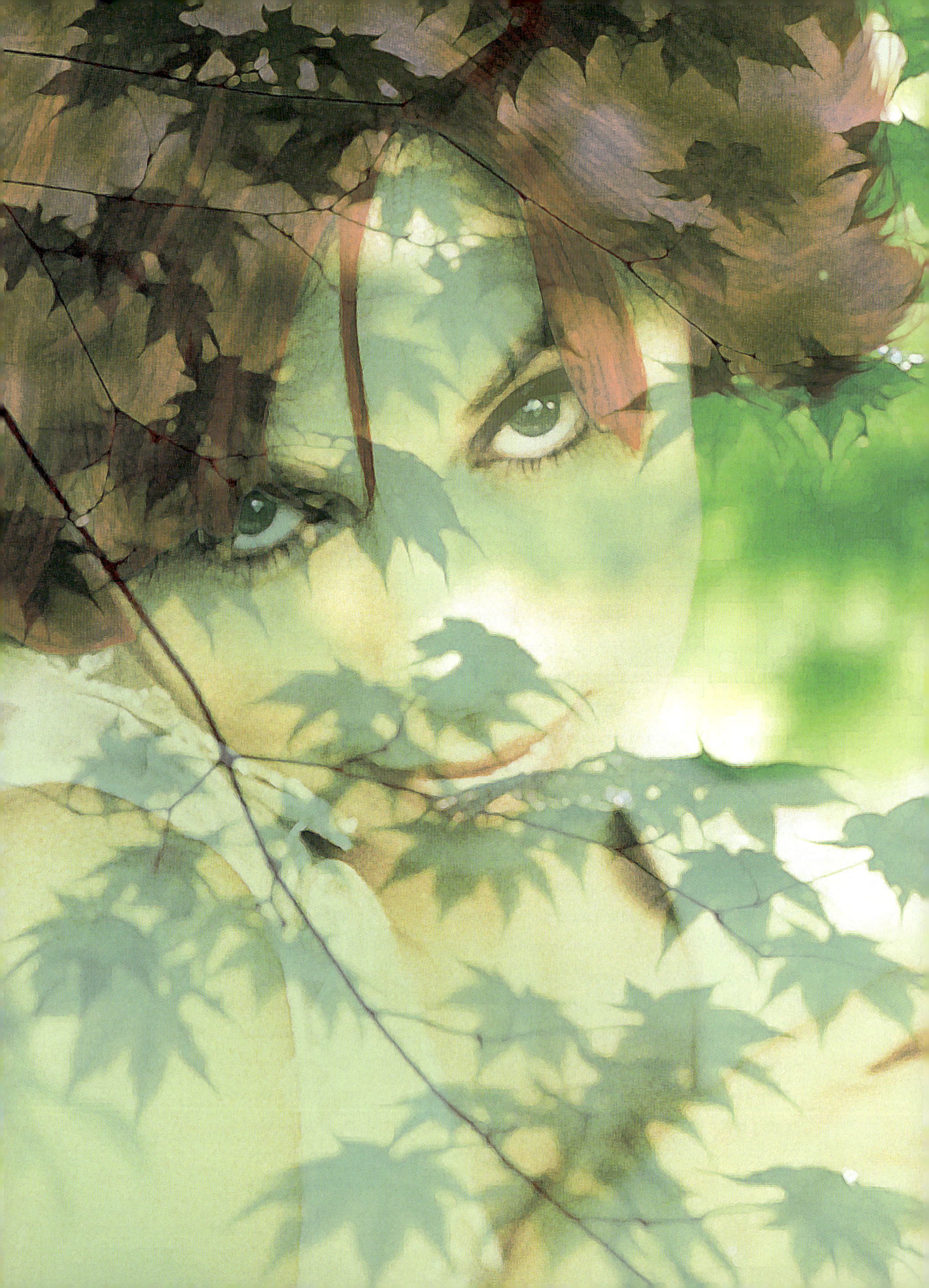

As You Like It

William Shakespeare

FIRST PERFORMED:
The year is uncertain but 1603 is a strong possibility.

ABOUT THE AUTHOR:
William Shakespeare (1564–1616) was born in Stratford-upon-Avon, the son of a successful merchant. Little is known of his early life but as a young man he moved to London to pursue a career in the theatre and as a writer. His immense body of work, which includes 38 plays, has led many people to regard him as the greatest writer that ever lived.

ABOUT THE CHOSEN ADAPTATION:
Released in 2006, Kenneth Branagh's film version was well received by some critics. *The Guardian* called it 'attractive, intelligent and elegant.' It stars Bryce Dallas Howard as Rosalind, David Oyelowo as Orlando, and Kevin Kline, who gave an award-winning performance as Jaques.

have been enabled to overcome their difficulties and develop a positive approach to life. It signifies that life offers infinite possibilities and that even in adversity there is a need to search for companionship. In the view of *As You Like It,* love rules the world.

CLASSROOM activities

1. Look again at the key moment 'A Siege in Progress.' What impression of life does the opening scene convey?

2. Evaluate the different approaches to life adopted by Celia, Orlando, the Duke and Frederick.

3. Assess the strength of relationships in *As You Like It.*

4. To what extent do characters have the freedom to choose?

5. 'The biggest conflict between good and evil is played out in the character of Jaques.' Discuss.

6. '*As You Like It* conveys that life is full of infinite possibility.' To what extent is this statement true?

7. What does the closing scene, 'The Wedding Day,' convey?

GENERAL VISION AND VIEWPOINT

Inside I'm Dancing

Inside I'm Dancing paints a mixed view of life in its portrayal of Rory and Michael's search for independence. At its heart, the film exudes a positive and uplifting message about life. However, this message is not obvious in the opening moments of the film. The opening scene, 'The Isolation of Michael Connolly in Carrigmore,' is a pessimistic key moment. Michael struggles to communicate, but he is misunderstood by the carers and fails to alert them to the oncoming danger. He is willing to participate in the world around him, but he is hindered by the fact that no one can see beyond his disability. The scene demonstrates Michael's isolation within his environment, as he is unable to communicate his needs or realise his potential.

Both Michael and Rory extol the virtues of freedom. Rory is prepared to break the rules on many occasions; he is even prepared to steal from the collection box. Michael protests but Rory justifies his decision, arguing that 'life is dishonest, Michael.' Later, Michael is looking out of the window waiting for Siobhán to arrive. Rory is unsettled by this as he wants them both to go out. He claims that Michael is letting life pass him by and that by being confined to his flat he is 'building a little Carrigmore.' For Rory, each day is a bonus. On the bridge the previous night, Rory urged Michael to grasp hold of the future. He claimed that Michael, unlike him, has a future. To Rory, this is a precious gift.

The text offers a mixed view of relationships. Rory and Michael's relationship dominates the film. Rory's innate rebelliousness contrasts with Michael's more even-tempered nature. Through their friendship, they learn from each other. An institutionalised Michael is encouraged to engage with the broader world beyond the narrow confines of Carrigmore. Rory offers Michael hope. In the key moment 'Siobhán's Rejection of Michael's Love,' the competing forces of light and dark are well captured on the bridge at night. The pouring rain mirrors Michael's distressed state of mind after Siobhán's rejection. However, the moment brightens at the end as the pair whirl around in the rain. This highlights the general importance of friendship in combating difficulties, such as isolation and depression.

> He claimed that Michael, unlike him, has a future. To Rory, this is a precious gift

Later, Michael has to face the prospect of losing his best friend, Rory. Characteristically, Rory tells his shaken friend that he is independent and self-supporting. Michael vindicates his friend's trust; his determination to demonstrate that Rory had the right to achieve independent living is testament to his friend's faith in him. In the key moment 'The Loss of a Friend,' despite this being a tragic and sorrowful scene, a note of optimism is struck. Michael is empowered to live life independently. However, it also suggests that in life, relationships are transient.

Hope is conveyed throughout *Inside I'm Dancing*. Rory paints Carrigmore as a prison from which he is happy to escape. His words convey this very forcefully. By gaining the right to live independently, Rory and Michael are empowered to live life to the full and face up to its challenges. While Carrigmore is portrayed as drab, their new accommodation is fitted with modern appliances, brighter colours, and creates an atmosphere of joy and energy. It suggests that change is possible and that disabled people can claim their rightful place in society. This offers hope to the viewer.

However, a sense of foreboding is created through the lyrics of 'Hurt' as sung by Johnny Cash, which highlights the negative aspects of life. The words of the song convey betrayal, loss and rejection. Life is a mixture of light and dark, of optimism and pessimism. Michael suffers the emotional loss of Siobhán and grief when he loses his best friend and companion, Rory.

At its heart, the text conveys the triumph of the human spirit in overcoming life's prejudices and difficulties. Uncharacteristically, it is Rory who loses heart when his application for independent living is rejected. An undaunted Michael reapplies and Rory nominates himself as his in-house translator. An optimistic note is struck. Michael and Rory are not portrayed simply as passive pawns in a hostile environment, nor as victims of societal prejudice. Rather, they are characterised as actively engaged in the world, attempting to bring about their desired ambitions. This presents a positive and uplifting view of life.

> Michael and Rory are not portrayed simply as passive pawns in a hostile environment, nor as victims of societal prejudice

The closing moment offers a mixed view of life. The key moment 'Michael on His Own' provides a contrast with the opening scene. Michael has moved away from the confining, passive existence that characterised his life in Carrigmore. Now, in this key moment, Michael is shown moving out on his own amid the hustle and bustle of everyday life. However, it appears that he has a lonely future ahead of him, which darkens the text slightly.

Inside I'm Dancing conveys a balanced view of life, highlighting the triumph of the human spirit in its exploration of life's potential.

CLASSROOM activities

1. What does the opening scene say about life and the general treatment of disabled people in society?

2. What does the text say about relationships?

3. 'Life's lessons are cruel.' Discuss this statement in the light of how the text views the importance of relationships in life.

4. Overall, do you see the social world of the text as positive or negative for Michael? Give reasons for your answer.

5. To what extent does *Inside I'm Dancing* convey a hopeful vision of life?

6. How satisfactory is the closing scene?

7. What message do you think this scene conveys about life?

8. How has Michael progressed from the beginning of the film? What does this progression say about life?

9. To what extent does this film offer you a positive and optimistic view of life?

10. Does the title encapsulate a view of life? What does it mean to you?

8

Answering the general vision and viewpoint question

Answering the general vision and viewpoint question

All texts demonstrate different views of life and its purpose. Through the study of this mode of comparison, you are encouraged to explore the world view presented in the text and how it is defined in the overall development of the plot. Make sure you are clear about your definition of the mode of comparison. You should also refer to the statement in the question in every paragraph of your answer. Be sure you understand what is required before planning and formulating your answer.

This chapter will:
- Outline ten steps that will help you tackle the general vision and viewpoint question
- Examine the 2010 Leaving Certificate question in relation to *How Many Miles to Babylon?*, *Sive* and *Inside I'm Dancing*.

Recent Trends

Over the years this mode of comparison has become more demanding. The 2010 question is the most analytical and challenging to date. Care needs to be taken when tackling the general vision and viewpoint question. It is not sufficient to simply learn off a pre-planned answer. While preparation is always essential, you are also required to think carefully in the examination hall. You must be able to:

- Determine how the central characters' freedom contributes to the overall optimism of any novel, play or film
- Establish how a character's lack of freedom contributes to the overall pessimism of the text

- Show how characters shape the texts on many levels, and are pivotal to the plot and the overall impact of the story.

2010 Leaving Certificate — VISION & VIEWPOINT question

'The general vision and viewpoint of a text can be determined by the success or failure of the central character in his/her efforts to achieve fulfilment.'

In the light of the above statement, compare the general vision and viewpoint of at least two texts you have studied in your comparative course. *(70 marks)*

Understand the question — STEP 1

You must be sure what the question demands of you:
- What are the key words in the question?
- What is the question asking you to do?
- How can you connect the question with your knowledge of the subject?

The key phrases in this question are 'general vision and viewpoint,' 'success or failure' and 'efforts to achieve fulfilment.' The question is asking you to compare the texts and evaluate whether the texts offer optimistic or pessimistic views of life depending on the extent to which their characters achieve fulfilment or not.

Planning your answer — STEP 2

You should first plan the main points that you intend to highlight in your essay and then link your plan to the question, as outlined below. It is important to plan for the following reasons:
- Planning helps you trace the general vision and viewpoint of the texts
- A plan will help guide your essay
- A plan reveals possible comparisons between the texts
- It enables you to keep your answer relevant to the question asked.

How Many Miles to Babylon?	*Sive*	*Inside I'm Dancing*
Opening scene: negative and gloomy. Alec is in prison – no future, unfulfilled. Similar situation to Michael in *Inside I'm Dancing*. Negativity in life.	*Opening scene:* Sive is the most fulfilled; opportunity for education. She is part of the social community; supported. Positive aspects of life.	Michael is unhappy, shut away in Carrigmore; likened to Alec's prison. Hopeless situation in both instances. Negative aspects of life.
Alec wants to be a breeder and trainer of horses. 'It's good to have the future fixed.' Joined army instead, dream unfulfilled; darkens the text. Alec's lack of success is linked to the negative overall vision of the text.	Sive had dream to finish her education; her mother's dream for her as well. This is cruelly denied her by Thomasheen's and Mena's menace. Unfulfilled dream; darkens the text; lack of success is linked to the negative overall vision of the text.	Michael had a dream of living independently; a new world opened up to him by Rory; application successful but in order to live out the dream he has to ask his father for money; consequences of Fergus's neglect. One dream fulfilled, another denied. This text has the most optimistic vision.
The situation becomes hopeless for Alec. Relentless cycle of negativity. Sadness is conveyed.	Evil is vanquished, but at a cost; tragic end of life; cruelty of life. Sadness is conveyed.	Hope is conveyed; change possible. Michael discovers the true meaning of independent living.
Life is an impossibility.	Cruelties of life.	Triumph of the human spirit.

STEP 3 First impressions: writing the essential opening paragraph

The first paragraph is very important in an essay. It should assist in introducing the remaining paragraphs. You need to show in your opening paragraph that you have understood the question and what it is you are required to answer.

An opening paragraph should:
- Target the question you are asked
- Refer to the texts and their overall importance
- Highlight some of the key issues to be explored in your essay.

STEP 4 Writing the middle section of your answer

Refer to the question at all times. Refer to your plan as often as is required. Use this book to help plan answers to past exam questions, specifically Chapter 7. It is also essential to refer to a series of key moments which highlight the manner in which the general vision and viewpoint is treated in your texts. Use Chapter 2

to refresh your memory of key moments in each text. You should also:
- Expand upon one point per paragraph
- Make clear comparative points in each of your paragraphs.

Points for reflection include:
- How is life presented?
- What options are available to the characters?
- How do the characters respond to their situations?

You could also reflect on the portrayal of relationships in each of the texts:
- Are the relationships in the text supporting and loving or dysfunctional?
- Do the dynamics between different characters change throughout the texts?
- Are there positive and/or negative aspects in all texts? Identify these and their overall effect on the narrative or drama.

Focus on opening and closing key moments. The last page of the novel might be the most momentous, or the last scene the most dramatic as matters reach a climax. Ask yourself:
- What are the closing moments in each of the texts?
- How do these moments compare in each text?

Lasting impression: writing the conclusion STEP 5

The conclusion is essential as it brings all the main points in your essay together. It is important to write a conclusion as it:
- Helps draw the points in your essay together
- Reconstructs the points in your answer in a different way.

Re-read the question STEP 6

Make sure you re-examine the question.
- Have you answered all aspects of the question?
- Is there any aspect that has not been examined?

Look at the plan STEP 7

Ask yourself whether there is any aspect of the plan you have not included in your answer. Make sure all aspects of the plan relate to the question.

STEP 8 Re-read the middle section of the essay

This is the section in your answer that should provide the most detail.
- Make sure you have made as many comparative points as you can in each of the paragraphs.
- Did you refer to the question statement in each of your paragraphs?

STEP 9 Re-read the opening and concluding paragraphs

The opening and concluding paragraphs are important in your essay. They are essential in making a general and lasting impression.

STEP 10 Is there anything else?

Check if there is anything that has not been included in your essay which could be important. If you are happy with your answer, move on to the next question.

VISION & VIEWPOINT question: 2010 Leaving Certificate

'The general vision and viewpoint of a text can be determined by the success or failure of the central character in his/her efforts to achieve fulfilment.'

In the light of the above statement, compare the general vision and viewpoint of at least two texts you have studied in your comparative course. *(70 marks)*

SAMPLE answer

The General Vision and Viewpoint conveyed in *How Many Miles to Babylon?*, *Sive* and *Inside I'm Dancing*

The general vision and viewpoint conveys a view of life. As each character strives to achieve a certain goal, he/she can be thwarted in a variety of ways. This is true in Jennifer Johnston's novel *How Many Miles to Babylon?*, John B. Keane's play *Sive* and Damien O'Donnell's film *Inside I'm Dancing*. These texts examine the issue of fulfilment in different ways. Both Alec's and Sive's struggles end in disaster for different reasons. In *Inside I'm Dancing*, Michael hopes to be understood by the wider community and eventually values Rory's goal of independent living. Only Michael emerges successfully; Sive resorts to desperate measures to avoid her fate of being forced to marry Seán Dóta. Neither Alec nor Sive achieves their objectives in life, thus darkening these texts considerably. Overall, the vision of life conveyed in the texts is linked to the characters' struggle for fulfilment in attempting to attain their goals.

Alec in *How Many Miles to Babylon?* and Michael in *Inside I'm Dancing* are both restricted from the outset. Alec is trapped in prison while Michael is confined as a patient in Carrigmore Nursing Home. Both are unfulfilled and alone. For Alec, life is described as meaningless, while Michael's facial expression communicates his frustration at being misunderstood. In *How Many Miles to Babylon?* Alec's overall mood is gloomy: 'The fact that I have no future except what you can count in hours doesn't seem to disturb me unduly.' He awaits execution.

Of the three characters, Sive appears to be the most fulfilled initially. She has been offered the opportunity of education, which has been denied to previous generations, and is widely supported by the community. Her hopeful expectation is in contrast to Alec's gloom. She enquires about her mother: 'Go on, Gran! Tell me more!' while Alec is bitter towards his mother: 'My heart doesn't bleed for her.' Sive is part of the community while Alec is shut out: 'How alarmed were they by the lurking demons of my mind.' Alec is an isolated, unfulfilled character without a future. Like Alec, Michael is isolated but he is also demeaned. He is shown the alphabet when he tries to alert the manager in Carrigmore to oncoming danger. Both Alec and Michael are dejected figures, whose failures serve to darken the texts and add to a prevailing pessimism created in the opening key moments.

Alec and Sive become unfulfilled while Michael achieves independent living. This serves to darken the general vision of *How Many Miles to Babylon?* and *Sive*, but the view of life expressed in *Inside I'm Dancing* brightens. All three characters have dreams, but only one is realised. Alec wants to become a breeder and trainer of horses. He plans to work with Jerry, who is an accomplished horseman: 'It's good to have the future fixed.' However, Jerry is aware of the difficulties involved: 'He grinned. He was undoubtedly wiser than I.' Like Alec, Sive has her dream of being provided with a good education while Michael espouses Rory's ambition of independent living away from the confining life in Carrigmore.

Both Alec's and Sive's dreams are cruelly repressed by the meddling of others. Alicia and Mena play similar roles. Instead of pursuing his dream, Alicia's demands and revelations spur Alec into the war effort and he becomes an officer. The thought of war does not appeal to Alec: 'I really don't feel I have any right to go and shoot people. I mean, for a cause I neither understand nor care about.' He does not share his mother's sense of patriotic duty and refers to the dangers on the battlefield. Like Alec, Sive does not share societal values; she resists the thought of marrying a rich elderly farmer: 'I could never live with that old man.' If Alicia stresses the importance of family position, of love of country, Mena emphasises the value of money and social advancement and displays a mercenary view of life: 'You will have no enemy when you have the name of money.' Mena denies Sive the right to schooling, which was her mother's ambition for her beloved daughter: 'It must be an ease for you to get away from the nuns and the books, but sure we won't have much more of the schooling now.' At this, Sive is despondent under such pressure, looking 'bewilderedly at Mena.' The word 'bewilderedly' suggests Sive's deep-seated unease at her young life changing before her very eyes. It shows that her mother's dream for a better future for her daughter is Sive's also.

Like Alec and Sive, Michael has to cope with obstacles. When Rory's application for independent living is rejected, Michael takes up his friend's ambition and applies instead. His application is successful, but he is despondent when he discovers that neither of them has enough money to provide for their accommodation. Like Alec and Sive, it seems that Michael's dream has come to an end, especially when it involves the unpleasant task of seeking money from his estranged father, Fergus Connolly. In Michael's case, his disappointment is momentary, while Sive's and Alec's unhappiness is persistent. Their dreams remain unfulfilled, while Michael's dream is realised. This is linked to a general understanding of general vision and viewpoint. The central characters' fate – their success or failure – determines the overall optimism or pessimism of any text. Michael's success conveys an optimistic view of life while Alec and Sive's failures emphasise the negative and pessimistic aspects of life.

Alec and Sive are forced to live lives that others require of them, rather than ones they aspire to themselves. Unlike Alec and Sive, Michael is free to live his life, even if he is labelled unfairly due to his disability. He can still map out a life for himself, a personal freedom denied to Alec and Sive. Alec joins the war effort, despite his protests, when his mother tells him that Frederick is not his father. At that moment, his resistance to her weakens and he is aware of his mother's triumph. Equally, Mena is triumphant when it appears that Sive has no choice but to acquiesce. Both Alec and Sive are despondent, unsuited to and unfulfilled in their new roles; Alec as army officer and Sive as a potential partner to Seán Dóta. Alec and Sive are aware of this. Alec notes his inadequacies as an officer: 'I am useless as far as the men are concerned. I could neither control them nor give them comfort in any way.' Both resist the pressures of others, only outwardly acquiescing. Sive stares into a future life with Seán Dóta, reflected in her wearing adult clothes: 'Sive enters and stands self-consciously in her new clothes.' She exchanges her high-heeled shoes for low ones, indicating her refusal to fit this role. Like Alec and Sive, Michael has to meet obstacles and social prejudice. He meets the father who rejected him at birth. He has kept clippings of his father's successful legal career, but the pain of rejection leaves him speechless approaching him. Fergus stands rigidly at the table, speaking in a calculated way. Michael's dream of a reunion with his father is effectively dashed on that day. However, Michael is given a freedom to manoeuvre denied to Alec and Sive; he has the money to achieve his dream.

Both Alec and Sive meet tragic ends, making the chance of fulfilling their dreams impossible, while Michael realises his. Alec shoots Jerry to prevent him being sent to the firing squad and is arrested and sentenced to death; Sive meets her tragic end by committing suicide. Alec dies as a failed officer while Sive's suicide ends her life as a 'tormented child.' Alec is aware of being misunderstood in a cruel world: 'They will never understand. So I say nothing.' Sive's last moments are captured in Liam's description: 'I saw her running across the bog with only the little frock against the cold of the night.' Like Alec, Michael loses his friend when time runs out for Rory. Unlike Alec or Sive, he has a future on his own.

Sadness is conveyed in all three texts but only in *Inside I'm Dancing* is there a fulfilment. Sive and Alec's lack of freedom to manoeuvre is linked to their lack of fulfilment in life. Both act defiantly. Sive's suicide is an act of defiance and desperation in her refusal to marry someone she does not love. Equally, Alec's shooting of Jerry strikes a fatalistic note. For Alec and Sive, true happiness is merely an illusion. For Michael, some happiness is possible, once he no longer builds a 'little Carrigmore' for himself. Through his friendship with Rory, he discovers the true meaning of independent living.

To conclude, the success or failure of a central character in his or her quest for fulfilment lightens or darkens a storyline and is linked to the view of life projected in each text. Alec's and Sive's failures evoke pathos and dismay, darkening the view of life, while Michael's success in achieving his goal serves to brighten the text. All characters attempt to resist the pressures of others and all are thwarted in some way, but only Michael is ultimately successful. The intricate tangle of plot and subplot makes each story riveting and interesting on different levels.

9

Literary Genre:
novels

Literary Genre: novels

A novel is one means of telling a story. All novelists draw the reader into a voyage of discovery; a voyage into an unfamiliar world through the power of the printed word on the page. A novel is also a work of the imagination. Through the study of the novel, the reader is drawn into the inner psychology of the central character. With the central character's development, the story unfolds.

This chapter will outline an approach to studying literary genre in:
- Thomas Hardy's *Tess of the d'Urbervilles*
- Jennifer Johnston's *How Many Miles to Babylon?*
- Kazuo Ishiguro's *Never Let Me Go.*

The novel, a relatively young art form, rose to prominence in the nineteenth century. By this time the Reformation and the division of Europe along sectarian lines had concluded. The century, a time of tumultuous change with an increasing role for science and a diminishing role for religion as the age of revolution swept Europe, moved civilisation towards the creation of a modern society.

Some aspects of the novel are similar to films and plays. All involve characters, suspense and conflict. What makes the novel unique is its reliance on the printed word to convey the thoughts, the hopes, the emotions and the dreams of the central characters and their relationships and conflicts (internal or external). Like other art forms, the novel is a two-way process. The novelist creates a work of art while the reader reacts to that creation.

The aspects of literary genre which will be examined in this chapter are as follows:

- The importance of the title
- The narrator (implied and actual) and the type of narration
- Character development
- The importance of the plot and the order of narration
- The character's choice or lack of it and the subsequent design of the novel
- The use of suspense and tension
- The use of description.

Tess of the d'Urbervilles
LITERARY GENRE: novels

This novel is dominated by the story of a young girl whose life and dreams are destroyed through a series of calamities that lead her to murder Alec, the man who took advantage of her. The reader is actively encouraged to follow her life story as she journeys from innocent young girl to adulthood. *Tess of the d'Urbervilles* is one of Thomas Hardy's darkest Wessex novels. Other novels by Hardy include such well-known titles as *Far from the Madding Crowd* (1874) and *The Mayor of Casterbridge* (1886).

In its day, *Tess of the d'Urbervilles* was plagued by controversy, centring on the author's tacit criticism of Victorian morality. The title emphasises the central character's overall importance and the subservience of other characters, such as Alec and Angel, who wrestle for Tess's affections.

The novel is told through omniscient (all-seeing) narration. The author provides a panoramic view of the story. However, subtle changes occur at certain points. During Alec's assault of Tess another voice appears to intrude. Later, certain events are viewed from different points of view. Tess's love for her child, Sorrow, is conveyed as Tess narrates it. To Sorrow 'the cottage interior was the universe, the week's weather climate, new-born babyhood human existence, and the instinct to suck human knowledge' (Maiden No More, Ch. 14). At once this emphasises the tragic brevity of the child's life as seen from the point of view of his anguished mother. On other occasions, Tess is seen through Angel's charmed eyes, and

> In its day, *Tess of the d'Urbervilles* was plagued by controversy, centring on the author's tacit criticism of Victorian morality

later minor characters view events as they unfold. Re-read the key moment entitled 'Tess's Murder of Alec,' detailed in Chapter 2. This moment is seen through the eyes of Mrs Brooks, the landlady, who eavesdrops on Tess and Alec's final argument. Her view is a partial one, distancing the reader from the horror of the violence: 'The dead silence within was broken only by a regular beat' (Fulfilment, Ch. 56). Later, Alec and Angel are seen through the caretaker's eyes and he is struck by their 'innocent appearance.' The novel is given a more rounded existence through these occasional narrative veins.

Tess's characterisation is well developed. She is associated with the plight of the wounded pheasant and the bleeding calf. From the outset, this locks her characterisation in combat with the forces of the past. Tess comes across as a spirited character who defies definition and who attempts to exert some control over her own life. Her characterisation passes through certain phases, linked to the overall structure of the novel. She is seen through the eyes of two characters, those of the lustful Alec and the idealising Angel. Angel compares her to Artemis and Demeter, both goddesses at one with nature (The Rally, Ch. 20). They do not provide a definition with which she can relate, emphasising that it is a depiction seen only through Angel's eyes. He changes his mind later. It is more accurate to argue that Tess's character defies definition, partly because she undergoes such momentous change.

After Sorrow's death, Tess becomes a changed, more reflective person, noticeable in her body and in her tone of voice: 'Symbols of reflectiveness passed into her face, and a note of tragedy at times into her voice (Maiden No More, Ch. 15). However, the line 'quite failed to demoralize' is interesting as it highlights her inner strength and transforms her into a heroic character. However, she is defeated by the negative forces at work in society, but not before she gives vent to her anger by murdering Alec. Tess is a complex character who defies simple definition. The past and her ancestors have a powerful effect on her tragic demise. This is emphasised in the final page: '"Justice" was done, and the President of the Immortals (in Aeschylean phrase) had ended his sport with Tess' (Fulfilment, Ch. 59). Hardy gives the heroine an unparalleled significance. His acute character analysis, in-depth exploration of issues and graphic portrayal of social alienation makes his novel a precursor to modern works of literature. The novel is structured around the phases of Tess's life, starting with her as a young woman and finishing with her death. The structure emphasises the overall importance of Tess's characterisation.

The unfolding tragedy is foreshadowed by the author. The overall significance of colour is highlighted with Tess's red ribbon. Red symbolises danger as well as love. The colour red follows Tess, memorably after the description of Alec's murder: 'The oblong white ceiling, with this scarlet blot in the midst, had the appearance of a gigantic ace of hearts' (Fulfilment, Ch. 56). Tess is executed in a building made of red brick on a sunny day. Another colour takes over, a black flag signifying the end. We have been forewarned, however. In the key moment entitled 'The Tragic Death of Prince and Tess's Isolation,' Tess is deeply distressed by the death of the horse. Even Abraham, her young brother, appears visibly older. All the talk about a 'blighted star' has become a reality: 'Her face was dry and pale, as though she regarded herself in the light of a murderess' (The Maiden, Ch. 4). At this point, this is a judgement that Tess makes of herself, but it has a predictive significance. It recurs in Tess's conversation with Alec after her trauma. In the key moment 'Tess's Distress,' Alec pours cold water on her torment but he is robustly rebuked by an angry Tess. The description of her latent anger is significant in the context of the novel as a whole. She is described as 'turning impetuously upon him, her eyes flashing as the latent spirit (of which he was to see more some day) awoke in her' (Maiden No More, Ch. 12). The death knell is struck with this line. Passivity is not Tess's natural state of being. The implication is that her anger can reach boiling point, when it will ultimately explode.

> *Her face was dry and pale, as though she regarded herself in the light of a murderess*

Hardy's language is very varied throughout. He changes from the past to present tense and uses complex language: architectural, pagan and religious allusions are splashed with the colour of local dialect. The language used varies and is suited to the moment. This is reflected in the person of Tess, who speaks two languages (her parents' dialect and Sixth Standard English), thus conveying the impression that she inhabits two worlds.

Natural order imagery recurs throughout the novel and reflects Tess's increasing vulnerability and pain. In the key moment 'The Tragic Death of Prince and Tess's Isolation,' the natural world reacts to Prince's death: 'The atmosphere turned pale, the birds shook themselves in the hedges, arose and twittered; the lane showed all its white features, and Tess showed hers still whiter' (The Maiden, Ch. 4). Tess's shock is reflected in nature. Later, Tess is compared to a 'sunned cat' (The Consequence, Ch. 27). Tess epitomises nature: 'She went stealthily as a cat;' and nature is personified: 'The trees have inquisitive eyes' (The Rally, Ch. 19). In one conversation with Angel she speaks of her attachment to the natural world. The condition of the natural order, whether it is peaceful or disrupted, adds to the overall mood of the text.

Hardy effectively explores the downfall of Tess, a tragic heroine, whose characterisation is so lifelike she almost becomes a real person. *Tess of the d'Urbervilles* is a direct antecedent of many works of modern literature.

CLASSROOM activities

1. What is the significance of the title?

2. How well developed is Tess's character? Identify a moment that makes Tess an almost lifelike figure. Give reasons for your choice.

3. Comment on Hardy's narration and the order in which it is told.

4. 'Tess is a solitary figure.' How well drawn is Tess's alienation throughout the novel?

5. 'Alec and Angel wrestle for the soul of Tess.' Outline the importance of the men in Tess's life. Are they both flawed?

6. In what way is the tragedy foreshadowed? Explain how this might add to the pathos of the moment.

7. Provide examples of good description in *Tess of the d'Urbervilles*. Comment on their overall effectiveness.

8. In what way could this novel be regarded as a classic?

9. What is striking about Hardy's allusions to the natural world?

10. What do you regard as Hardy's greatest skill as a novelist?

How Many Miles to Babylon?

LITERARY GENRE: novels

The tragedy at the centre of *How Many Miles to Babylon?* is set against the backdrop of a broken landscape. Hope seems eternally beyond reach: 'How many miles to Babylon? Four score and ten, sir.' This is part of a childhood rhyme that recurs throughout the book, emphasising the patterns that 'weave and unweave' throughout history. Alec is trapped socially, emotionally and literally.

How Many Miles to Babylon? is written as social realism. The novel provides a commentary on life during World War I and how prejudices persist from Wicklow to Flanders. It reads like an eye-witness account of the horrors of war. Jennifer Johnston weaves the political and social landscape into her novel. It is a desolate and harsh environment where, as Bennett remarks, soldiers' lives are prematurely cut short: 'After all there's a man killed every minute' (p. 82). Alec's unfolding tragedy is linked to the ongoing catastrophe of countless lives lost on the battlefield in Flanders.

'After all there's a man killed every minute'

The narrator of this text is Alec. Jennifer Johnston has chosen to write in the first person. This has the effect of enabling the reader to empathise with the central character and see the world from Alec's point of view. This view is only partial as it is heavily dependent on Alec's memory, which is sometimes fragmented: 'I can juggle with a series of possibly inaccurate memories, my own interpretation' (p. 1). The type of narration chosen creates an immediate effect. Alec is viewed in different situations, as a soldier awaiting execution, as a lonely child shut out by his parents' perpetual squabbles, as a failed officer who struggles to save Jerry's life, as a friend to Jerry and as a prisoner in the midst of conflict.

It is through Alec's narration that readers are afforded an insight into his state of mind. In one conversation with Major Glendinning, he remarks that not sending Alec to school was a 'grave error of judgement on your parents' part' (p. 120). Secretly, Alec agrees with Glendinning. The reader alone shares this with Alec. Major Glendinning, the stern villain of the piece, is seen through

Alec's eyes. Alec captures aspects of his person while leaving his life story incomplete. One line sums up Glendinning's dismissal of Alec as a soldier and as an officer: 'Cold disapproval, a nod, the papers, the pens, the neatly folded hands' (p. 150). Only the stationery put in front of Glendinning is emphasised. It highlights his unyielding authority as seen through the eyes of a younger officer. By emphasising specific aspects of the major's persona, Alec's growing isolation on the battlefield is underlined.

The reader is distanced from certain characters, largely due to Alec's unfavourable narration. Alicia is triumphant at the thought of him joining the war effort. Her powerful presence is captured in Alec's perception: 'I was conscious of a radiance coming from her, a feeling of triumph' (p. 66). The reader is drawn to her triumph rather than to her general characterisation. Through Alec's narration, a window into an unfamiliar world is opened for the reader. Alec emphasises Frederick's vulnerability on a number of levels, which creates mood and atmosphere. He shares Frederick's vulnerability and mirrors Frederick's actions and responses. Re-read the key moment entitled 'Frederick's Misery in His Marriage to Alicia,' outlined in Chapter 2. In this significant moment Alec is just about to join the army. He sees his parents locked in vicious combat amid the superficiality of their life together: 'They would be there, immaculate themselves, their heads elegantly bent towards the morning papers and the cream-drenched porridge, starched damask napkins folded neatly across their knees' (p. 63). Alec is the onlooker, the observer, yet what he shares colours the reader's response to those he describes. He captures his father's unease and his mother's triumph. His own joke highlights his fear: 'The condemned man did not eat a hearty breakfast.' A sense of foreboding is created and established by Alec's narration of these events from jail. A sense of finality is created. His life with his parents is over and a new role as a soldier has begun.

> *'The condemned man did not eat a hearty breakfast'*

The consequence of Alec's narration is that the story is incomplete. Alec records the events only from his vantage point. The truth about Alec's parentage is shrouded in mystery, as is Bennett's reaction to Alec's choice. Equally, Alicia and Frederick's reaction to their son's impending execution is ignored. The leading player in the unfolding tragedy is Alec, rendering other characters obsolete once their prominence fades. Only Alec's friendship with Jerry supersedes everything.

Another consequence of Alec's narration is its order. *How Many Miles to Babylon?* is told in flashback. It starts with Alec's impending execution and then relates in retrospective mode the depiction of Alec's lonely childhood in Wicklow, his befriending of Jerry, his adulthood and his life as an officer in Flanders during World War I. It follows a circular pattern, ending as it began with Alec listening to the shelling. The same phrase is repeated: 'Because I am an officer and a gentleman, they have given me my notebooks, pen, ink and paper' (p. 1). This circular pattern has consequences for the plot and the overall telling of the tale. The order of narration emphasises the ebb and flow of history, from which there is no escape.

> The order of narration emphasises the ebb and flow of history, from which there is no escape

The narrator is not just observing the events as they unfold, he is also the subject. Alec's friendship with Jerry is a flashpoint. Alicia, Frederick and Major Glendinning belittle its importance. Alec reads Jerry's mother's letter slowly. 'The words stood nervously upright on pale-blue lines' (p. 129). A sense of foreboding is well captured as Alec pores over its contents: 'I read it twice, mainly because I didn't know what to say to Jerry, then I folded it into its folds again.' A staccato conversation follows: '"Would?"... "Glendinning. Leave. You wondered"' (p. 130). Alec anticipates that Glendinning will refuse Jerry's request for leave: 'I hated the thought of the cold and the dark and the Major, colder and darker than the night itself' (p. 130).

Major Glendinning's refusal sets in train a series of events that lead to the deaths of both Jerry and Alec. Jerry has reached a point where he can either ignore his mother's request or go in search of his father. He chooses the latter, leaving Alec in an impossible situation. Jerry's decision to leave his duty as a soldier and find his father is pivotal. He justifies his decision: 'I did what she wanted me to do. I'd do it again. I've harmed no one. The British Expeditionary Force is no worse off' (p. 141). It speeds up the subsequent plot and places their friendship centre stage. Alec has to grapple with the implications of this. The atmosphere is dark and eerie as he imagines Jerry trawling over the lost soldiers on the battlefield. The events leave Alec even more isolated and alone, in keeping with the prevailing darkness and conflict-ridden environment. Jerry's choice means that Alec is forced to act in ways that would have seemed unimaginable before. After pleading with Major Glendinning to reconsider Jerry's case, he takes the most drastic action of all: he shoots Jerry. This moment is unexpected, and not related until the final pages of the novel.

In the key moment 'Alec's Shooting of Jerry and His Wait for Execution,' we see the horrific implications of this event. A sense of trepidation is conveyed: 'I took the damn gun out from under my coat and looked at it' (p. 155). He notes that it is in 'good working order.' Alec shoves the gun away on hearing footsteps, but these fade away. The footsteps and the gun add to the suspense and tension. They are alone once more and the reader is invited to concentrate on Alec's action: 'No steps, no voices. I got up and moved over to where he was sitting.' Their friendship is conveyed through a touch. 'I put my left hand on his. His fingers clenched around mine.' Jerry smiles at Alec and Alec is struck by the blueness of his eyes. Both shut their eyes and Alec pulls the trigger. Then the reader is drawn to the sounds of a shout, of the echo of the shot and of the door opening. The sequence evokes great pathos. We are at the heart-rending consequence of Alec's choice. Then there is the repetition of the first phrase of the novel: 'Because I am an officer and a gentleman ...' (p. 156). The reader is invited to feel the impact of Alec's choice.

Swans symbolise Alec and Jerry's friendship. Alec's mother feeds the swans in Wicklow. Swans are associated with air and water, not the earth. They take on powerful significance: 'The beating of our hearts was like the cracking wings of swans lifting slowly from the lake, leaving disturbed water below' (p. 141). Jerry's fate is linked to Alec's. One of Alec's men kills a swan: 'An ugly mass of flesh and feathers fell to the ground' (p. 149). Alec's horror is emphasised by his inability to take command of the situation: 'My voice was blown back at my own face by the wind.' His fear is emphasised: 'All the muscles in my face were trembling' (p. 150). Alec highlights the soldier's reaction: 'He shrugged, dismissing me and the dead swan simultaneously' (p. 150). Alec's fate is now linked to the dead swan, heightening the tension for the reader.

In keeping with the story, time is frequently referred to throughout the novel. Time suggests that life is transient. From the outset, time is described as meaningless: 'I have no future except what you can count in hours' (p. 1). Frederick gave Alec his gold watch before he left: 'I don't need a watch these days. The whole house full of damned clocks. Ticking everywhere. Put it away' (p. 68). The reader is aware of the idea of time passing, the narrative time of the novel when Alec's life will meet an untimely end. The sense of a premature end is also highlighted in Bennett's chilling words: 'After all there's a man killed every minute' (p. 82). Time becomes meaningless as Jerry faces the agony of waiting in his cell: 'It's the waiting. Hours. Minutes. Each hour seems so long. I can't think of anything to think about, if you get me' (p. 154). Jerry's agony becomes Alec's, who passes the time by relating his story up to now: '… so I sit and wait and write.' Even the word 'wait' is laden with tragedy; Alec is waiting for his end.

Throughout *How Many Miles to Babylon?* Jennifer Johnston recreates a world of privilege in the midst of the turmoil of war, as seen through the eyes of a son of the landowning classes. Alec's depiction is modern in outlook, providing the reader with an effective bridge between the unfamiliar world of the text and the modern reader.

CLASSROOM activities

1. Comment on the novel's effectiveness as an historical novel. To what extent does the historical backdrop to this text restrict the novelist?

2. Comment on the advantages and disadvantages of the use of first person narration.

3. What impression does the circular pattern of this novel convey to you, a modern reader of the text?

4. Identify pivotal moments in the text and illustrate their importance for the overall story, the development of the plot and the creation of character.

5. Comment on the use of the symbol of the swans in *How Many Miles to Babylon?*

6. Identify passages of good description. Justify your choice.

7. How important are references to time in the overall narrative of the novel?

8. What do you regard as Jennifer Johnston's greatest skill as a novelist?

LITERARY GENRE: novels — Never Let Me Go

Never Let Me Go highlights the exploitation of three 'clones' to serve the medical needs of the human population. The title has profound significance for the unfolding of the plot. The imagination of the narrator, Kathy H, is caught by the Judy Bridgewater track, 'Never Let Me Go.' Re-read the key moment entitled 'Denied the Chance to Be a Mother' outlined in Chapter 2. She imagines that in the song a woman is told that she cannot have children. She then has a child, but she fears that the child will die or could be taken away from her. This is merged into Kathy's own story as Tommy relates the ghastly truth: 'So when she saw you dancing like that, holding your baby, she thought it really tragic, how you couldn't have babies' (p. 72). Another story is built around the song, centring on Madame's bizarre reaction. Figuratively, Madame sees Kathy holding the 'kind old world' that is passing away. The cost of scientific advancement will result in diminished rights for the 'students.' Madame describes this as a 'harsh, cruel world' (p. 267). The title of the book could imply Kathy's yearning for the lost companionship of friends, Tommy and Ruth.

Kathy is the narrator in this text. As a narrator, she has only a partial grasp of the issues. The full extent of her exploitation becomes apparent gradually. Much is left unsaid. Kathy's limited vocabulary serves to heighten this overall effect. Initially, only a glimpse of the ghastly future is presented. 'So you're waiting, even if you don't quite know it, waiting for the moment when you realise that you really are different to them; that there are people out there, like Madame, who don't hate you or wish you any harm, but who nevertheless shudder at the very thought of you – of how you were – and brought into this world and why – and who dread the idea of your hand brushing against theirs' (p. 36). The narrative presents a disturbing view of humanity. The use of 'you' allows the reader to identify with Kathy's plight. Life has lost its familiarity: 'It's like walking past a mirror you've walked past every

> As a narrator, she has only a partial grasp of the issues. The full extent of her exploitation becomes apparent gradually

day of your life, and suddenly it shows you something else, something troubling and strange' (p. 36).

Kathy and the other characters are humanely drawn before the reader is aware of their identity as 'clones.' In contrast, the human guardians seem like callous agents in the medical project. Even the rebellious Miss Lucy, who interrupted their gathering, is devoid of any humanity. The reader sees the world through the eyes of the exploited. This is graphically illustrated by the 'look' of the guardians. Readers see Madame's eyes from the perspective of the narrator, Kathy H. The importance of Madame's fearful stare is highlighted throughout the novel. At first, it is Ruth who is most conscious of it. Kathy notices that Madame responds strangely towards them. Madame 'froze' as the 'students' passed her by. Kathy explores her underlying feelings about this moment: 'And though we just kept on walking, we all felt it; it was like we'd walked from the sun right into the chilly shade'

> *'And though we just kept on walking, we all felt it; it was like we'd walked from the sun right into the chilly shade'*

(p. 35). Madame's coldness is emphasised in the comparison drawn between the students and spiders: 'But she was afraid of us in the same way someone might be afraid of spiders' (p. 35). Spiders provoke fearful reactions from some people. Madame's 'look' is one process in the students' dehumanisation. This idea recurs throughout the novel and the comparison is appropriate. The students are powerless over their lives and exist like spiders in the shadows. Madame's fear is phobic, irrational and ingrained, like the human fear of spiders. As before, the reader is encouraged to see it from Kathy's point of view.

Re-read the key moment entitled 'Denied the Chance to Be a Mother' outlined in Chapter 2. Kathy is captivated by Madame's gaze. Readers are positioned nearer to Kathy than to Madame: 'Except this time there was something else, something extra in that look I couldn't fathom' (p. 71). The guardians' terror is best expressed by the clinical Miss Emily: 'We're *all* afraid of you. There were times I'd look down at you all from my study window and I'd feel such revulsion' (p. 264). Miss Emily's fear of looking at the clones is stressed in her reactions. Her eyes 'flashed' (p. 264). The fearful eyes of the

Kazuo Ishiguro
never let

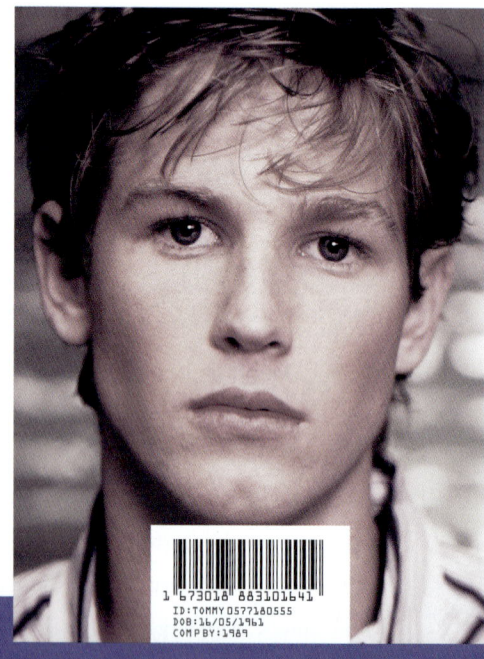

FIRST PUBLISHED:
2005, Faber & Faber. *Time* magazine named it the best novel of the year and included it in their 100 best English language novels from 1927–2005.

ABOUT THE AUTHOR:
Kazuo Ishiguro was born in 1954 in Nagasaki, Japan, but grew up in Surrey after his family moved to England in 1960. He is one of the most celebrated contemporary fiction authors in the English language and has received four Man Booker Prize nominations. He won the prize outright in 1989 for his novel *The Remains of the Day*.

ADAPTATION:
Never Let Me Go was adapted for the screen in 2010 by Mark Romanek and starred Carey Mulligan as Kathy, Andrew Garfield as Tommy and Keira Knightley as Ruth.

me go

guardians look at the students as if they were like Frankenstein's monster rather than people.

Each meeting with Madame is momentous as it draws the plot forward. Here a guardian combats her fear of touching a 'clone,' the object of her terror. In an instant, Kathy realises that Madame's terror re-emerges, but this moment is different: 'I could feel a trembling go all through her body, but she kept her hand where it was, and I could see again tears appearing in her eyes.' She whispers, 'Poor creatures' (p. 267). Madame is not released from her fear but she is drawn closer to Kathy than anyone could have predicted at the outset of the book. Kathy, as narrator, draws this reaction out of Madame. Throughout, it is the students rather than the guardians who behave in a humane fashion, the direct opposite of how they are conceived by society.

> Throughout, it is the students rather than the guardians who behave in a humane fashion, the direct opposite of how they are conceived by society

Never Let Me Go is told in flashback. Now in her thirties, Kathy narrates her life in Hailsham and then returns to her present life as a carer. At the end, the tension surrounds the prospect of seeking a reprieve for at least a few years. In a circular pattern, Kathy and Tommy return to Hailsham, only to find that it is a changed place and the guardians are powerless. Life there is depicted as a vicious circle from which there is no escape.

The forces of light and dark compete in this novel. Certain imagery is strongly evocative. One image is of the students being imprisoned in Hailsham. The world outside is unknown territory, where students are not permitted to travel. An eerie atmosphere surrounds Hailsham, not openly apparent at the beginning of the novel. Hailsham is not a boarding school for the privileged but a prison for the students. At first, it appears that the dangers lurk outside. The woods are unexplored territory. There is a story of a boy who ventured into the woods only to come to a ghastly end and another of a girl who strayed from Hailsham's walls only to find herself perpetually locked out. Hailsham is portrayed as separate from the wider world. This prefigures the students' separateness from the human population: 'This might all sound daft, but you have to remember that to us, at that stage in our lives, any place beyond Hailsham was like fantasy land' (p. 66). This illustrates their separateness from the human population.

Kathy and Tommy embark on a search to uncover the truth, which is packed with moments of tension and suspense. The reader is led to appreciate the importance of their search. They fall in love and hope that this might give them three years' reprieve. They decide to test out the deferral theory by returning to Hailsham. Finally, they meet Madame and, as before, Madame's coldness is highlighted. The image of spiders re-emerges, emphasising Madame's fearful reaction towards the students in the past. 'I don't know if she recognised us at that point; but without doubt, she saw and decided in a second *what we were,* because you could see her stiffen – as if a pair of large spiders was set to crawl towards her' (p. 243). This moment heightens the tension further as Kathy struggles to find the words: 'I'd gone over it during the long car journeys, and while sitting at quiet tables in service-station cafes' (p. 246). Kathy meets Madame and then Miss Emily emerges from the shadows. In the key moment 'Miss Emily's Chilling Truths,' all the threads of the novel are drawn together. It becomes clear that there is no hope of deferring, though Kathy is calm about the revelation: 'I felt surprisingly calm, even though Miss Emily's words should have crushed us.' The implication of Kathy and Tommy's search for the truth is that their lives have been determined. Miss Emily accepts that they are 'pawns.' She reiterates the chilling words of Miss Lucy and explains that their lives form part of a process: 'It just so happens you grew up in a certain point in the process' (p. 261). Kathy is close to rebellion here when she robustly emphasises the unfairness of the whole design: 'But for us, it's our life' (p. 261). The consequence of Kathy and Tommy's choice to return to Hailsham is to discover that their lives are predetermined.

> *'But for us, it's our life'*

Kathy and Tommy's lives are shown to be shrouded in darkness, highlighting the obscurity of their existence. This is graphically illustrated by the novelist as Kathy and Tommy journey home from their conversation with Miss Emily: 'I kept us on the most obscure back road I knew where only our headlights disturbed the darkness' (p. 267). Kathy compares her own life to this back road, suggesting that the students are excluded from full access to the joys and wonder of life. The 'glittering motorways' are only for the human population. Motorways have better access routes and greater options. The back roads are masked in darkness and cars travel slowly on them. Back roads become an appropriate metaphor for Kathy and Tommy's lives, given their restrictions and separateness from the human population, highlighting what the students once were: 'shadowy objects in test-tubes' (p. 263). It also stresses that real choice in life is denied them. The darkness fits in well with the overall mood of the novel at this point.

Norfolk has significance in this novel. The students' idea of Norfolk emerges from Miss Emily's Geography class when she describes it as a 'hump jutting into the sea.' Norfolk is the 'lost corner' of England (p. 65). In the students' minds, this reminds them of the 'lost corner,' where lost property is found. Norfolk becomes a 'lost corner,' where all that is lost can be found, in Kathy's fevered imagination. She finds a copy of her lost single 'Never Let Me Go' in Norfolk and at the end of the novel she surveys a field in Norfolk where she sees faint images of Tommy and Ruth waving to her. The key moment 'Kathy's Memories' evokes pathos as Kathy surrenders to her fate in life. Norfolk is figuratively explored as the place where the lost can be found.

The language used in the novel is unnerving. Words take on new meanings. Some words have clinical connotations, such as 'donor' and 'machine.' The ghastly idea of Tommy being switched off encapsulates the horror of the students' situation. The word 'guardians' is a euphemism, as patently these people do not guard or care for the young people in their control.

Kazuo Ishiguro creates a surreal world of horror where Hailsham is a prison for the students before they embark on their final journeys.

CLASSROOM activities

1. Describe how the title of the song has significance in the overall story.

2. Outline the advantages and disadvantages of first person narration.

3. How well developed is Kathy's character? Justify your answer.

4. The image of the spider is well explored in *Never Let Me Go*. Comment on the appropriateness of this image.

5. 'The forces of light and dark compete in this novel.' How important is this in the context of the telling of the tale as a whole?

6. Identify pivotal moments that explore an eerie atmosphere. Justify your choice.

7. 'Norfolk is more than a place.' Comment on the importance of Norfolk in Kathy's narration, in the central characters' childhood fantasies and in the final moments of the novel. Re-read the key moment entitled 'Kathy's Memories.'

8. Explore the impact of suppressed emotion in Kathy's narration.

9. Comment on the use of language in the novel.

10. What do you regard as Kazuo Ishiguro's most adept skill as a novelist?

10

Literary Genre:
plays

Literary Genre: plays

a dramatic production does not stand still; it is shaped and re-shaped in each dramatic performance. Many plays centre on the external conflicts of the leading characters, which propel the drama and heighten the dramatic tension and suspense for the audience. Conflict can be demonstrated through gripping dialogue interlinked with the visual depiction of the characters' actions, gestures, the overall stage design and performance.

This chapter will examine various aspects of literary genre in:
- Sophocles' *Oedipus the King*
- Henrik Ibsen's *A Doll's House*
- Brian Friel's *Dancing at Lughnasa*
- Martin McDonagh's *The Lonesome West*.

Literary genre means the manner in which the story is told. There are many aspects of a play that make it different from a novel or a film. The use of a narrator echoes the Greek theatrical heritage. In a play, the actor holds the attention of the audience for up to three hours and his or her identity is immersed in the character for all that time. Characters are pivotal in any dramatic performance, and to ensure excellent performances, actors need to be well cast. The sequence in which the narrative is told is essential to the story. The plot and subplot and the manner in which they are connected or disconnected are part of the overall structure of the play. The plot has an impact on the audience, who interpret the play as the story unfolds. As in all texts, the title can be significant and emphasise a certain point of view.

Plays revolve around the external conflicts between the characters. The term *mise en scène* means 'that which has been placed in the picture.' Every element that appears on stage is placed there deliberately, to help provide the essential building blocks in the dramatic performance. Aspects of a dramatic performance include:

- The lines a character says
- The tone of voice
- Facial expression
- Gesture
- Body movement
- Costumes
- The overall design
- The appropriate use of lighting, music and background noise to create an effect.

The text does not exist outside the performance nor does the performance fully exist outside the text.

Oedipus the King
LITERARY GENRE: **plays**

Sophocles (496–406 BC) was one of the great Greek innovators of his day and is regarded as providing the genesis of modern theatre. He wrote 120 plays, of which only seven survive, among these *Oedipus the King, Antigone* and *Oedipus at Colonus*. Sophocles' values are traditionalist; he is proud of the Athenian democratic model and Athens' powerful position in the Adriatic. Sophocles' work expanded upon the theatrical model inherited from the older Aeschylus, but he experimented with a new design of his own choosing. He diminished the chorus's early prominence in the drama, preferring to concentrate instead on the inclusion of different actors and consigning the chorus to the role of commentator, in which it becomes an intermediary between the actors and the audience.

Sophocles' play *Oedipus the King* was performed in a semi-circular, open-air theatre in fifth-century BC Athens. Many plays are cathartic; they serve to purge the audience of negative emotions as they lose themselves in the unfolding drama. *Oedipus the King* achieves this effect because the audience identifies with the central character's suffering, which evokes pity and fear.

In this play, the title is intricately linked to the plot itself. Oedipus means 'swell foot,' which highlights how his feet were bound as an infant when he was sent away so as to avoid the tragic prophesy. The tragedy projected is deep and personal, emphasising the fragility of the human condition in contrast to the omnipotent power of the gods. The plot centres on the moment of Oedipus's self-realisation. It is a moment that is laden with dramatic irony. Re-read the key moment entitled 'The Unspeakable Truth' detailed in Chapter 2. The detective who unwittingly set out to solve the murder of the former King of Thebes is revealed as the culprit. Ironically, Oedipus pledges to search for the murderer with the same resolve as he would if he were looking for his own father's killer.

Much emphasis is placed on Oedipus's characterisation. Oedipus is a man on a journey to find his own identity but unwittingly brings about his doom. His identity is to be the origin of his shame and self-mutilation. Oedipus, the man who saved Thebes from the Sphinx, is unable to solve the riddle of the self.

The way the story is told impacts on the dramatic narrative itself. Events are told retrospectively as Oedipus slowly begins a journey of self-revelation. The story is told by involving the same characters in two important events each. The Theban shepherd who saved Oedipus from being killed as a baby is also the survivor who witnessed Laius's death. The Corinthian shepherd who gave the child to the childless King and Queen of Corinth is also the messenger who informs Jocasta and Oedipus of the death of Polybus. This use of coincidence gives the drama a relentless predictability; there is no escape from divine providence.

External conflict is the driving force of good drama. Centre stage in *Oedipus the King* is the conflict that emerges between Oedipus and the blind prophet Tiresias. In the key moment entitled 'Seeing the Truth,' notice the contrast between Oedipus's pride and the prophet's humility and how these are shown in word and action. The imagery of blindness highlights Oedipus's groping in the dark in search of his identity. Ironically, Tiresias's blindness will also be Oedipus's future fate.

Given the immense size of the vast auditorium in ancient Greece, a greater emphasis is placed on dialogue than on gesture to convey emotion. Naturalistic masks were used to highlight a character's gender or social position. Words have a powerful effect in evoking emotion and exposing Oedipus's self-loathing: 'Born of outrage, outrage to the core' (1530). Oedipus speaks of being imprisoned in a 'loathsome body' (1520) and highlights the corruption of the self: 'O Polybus, Corinth, the old house of my fathers, so I believed – what a handsome prince you raised – under the skin, what sickness to the core' (1527–1530). Recurring sight–blindness imagery is highlighted throughout, so much so that Oedipus greets the truth with the line 'O god – all come true, all burst to light!' (1231–1310). Emotive language combines with the imagery of light to convey Oedipus's plight. The paradoxical truth at the heart of this human tragedy is well expressed in the language used by the blind prophet, Tiresias. He notes that the day of recognition for Oedipus will bring him 'birth and your destruction' (490) and emphasises that Oedipus's 'great fortune' in solving the riddle and becoming the King of Thebes is also his 'ruin' (503).

'O god – all come true, all burst to light!'

The unfolding tragedy is captured well by Jocasta's actions and gestures, however limited their treatment. She rushes through the palace doors, leaving the chorus to ponder 'Where's she gone?' They then foreshadow doom by predicting that 'something monstrous may come bursting forth,' so adding to the dramatic tension of the moment (1182).

The most violent scenes occur off-stage and are conveyed to the audience through the use of a messenger, which could have an anaesthetising effect on the audience. This approach differs from most modern treatments where violence is enacted centre stage. Sophocles, incidentally, is credited with the introduction of a scenic backdrop in his plays.

Oedipus the King highlights the frailties of the human condition. Sophocles prefigures much of later drama where the external dynamics between characters are more strongly emphasised.

CLASSROOM **activities**

1. How important is the title in the context of the plot?

2. How does the manner in which the story is told affect the audience's attitude to the plot?

3. How do the characters contribute to the drama as a whole?

4. How does the external conflict between Oedipus and Tiresias add to the suspense and tension of the play?

5. In what way is language effectively used to support the theatrical experience?

LITERARY GENRE: plays — A Doll's House

Henrik Ibsen (1828–1906) transformed the European theatrical experience through his diversity of approach, which included the satirical *Love's Comedy*, verse dramas like *Peer Gynt* and realist domestic dramas such as *A Doll's House*. Religious images are intricately blended into many modern texts in an art form which began as a dedication to the wine god, Dionysus. While the god Apollo's distant and underlying influence is felt in early Greek drama, Nora, in *A Doll's House*, openly criticises narrow religious values in an effort to assert her individuality.

The title *A Doll's House* is significant. It suggests that Nora is in need of protection and that she lives a sheltered life. Her existence is likened to that of a doll. In the Helmers' apartment, Nora does feel at home, but an apartment is a very confined space in which to operate. Tension is created between individual freedoms and societal pressures. In calling his play *A Doll's House*, Ibsen is emphasising how marriage can stifle individuals.

The title is also linked to the plot itself, which focuses on the importance of Nora's character and development. Nora's deception is quickly uncovered and Krogstad's blackmail adds great impetus to the drama. The subplot of Mrs Linde's and Krogstad's relationship is carefully interwoven into the main plot, which examines Nora's relationship with Helmer. Mrs Linde reflects Nora's position, but by the end of the play the roles are reversed and it is Nora, not Mrs Linde, who embarks upon an uncertain future. Dr Rank's slow death is another subplot. All the characters are trapped, living unfulfilled lives. This sense of claustrophobia persists until Nora releases herself from her caged existence.

> All the characters are trapped, living unfulfilled lives

The Graeco–Roman heritage influenced Ibsen in his choice of a limited number of characters (Nora, Helmer, Mrs Linde, Krogstad and Dr Rank). Initially, Nora is depicted as the dutiful wife. She appears childlike, as highlighted in Helmer's question, 'Has my little squander-bird been overspending again?' (Act 1). Another side to her character is yet to emerge. Re-read 'Nora's Monologue' outlined in Chapter 2. Her frailties come to the surface and her fears are exposed. By the end of the play, Nora's character has changed dramatically. Gone is her excitable nature. She asserts herself. The roles in the marriage have been reversed.

> 'Has my little squander-bird been overspending again?'

Ibsen is a master of characterisation. Notice the way Helmer's and Krogstad's characterisations mirror each other. At the beginning of the play, Helmer is careful to draw comparisons between his character and that of Krogstad; his sense of superiority towards Krogstad is effectively drawn. Yet, as the final acts emphasise, Helmer is little different from his arch-rival, and Krogstad had predicted Helmer's reactions perfectly. Helmer ends the play in a similar position to Krogstad; he becomes a single man with children. Krogstad and Mrs Linde's characters are not as well drawn as their counterparts Helmer and Nora, but their introduction serves to heighten the tragedy unfolding in Helmer and Nora's marriage.

The play is told in linear sequence but the influence of past events work their way effectively into the drama. Nora took out a loan without Helmer's knowledge by forging her father's signature as guarantor for the loan. As she comes to the realisation that her deception will be revealed, Nora desperately tries to stall the inevitable. The key moment 'Time Is Running Out' shows how past events impact on the present storyline. Nora waits for her deception to be discovered. In presenting the sequence of the play in this way, Ibsen cleverly creates an air of expectation that Helmer and Nora's relationship will survive. Krogstad's return of the IOU could have led to a happy ending. However, there is a twist in the tale as Ibsen concentrates on the gripping internal and external dynamics between Helmer and Nora.

External conflict is at the heart of drama and is reflected in the actors' use of gesture and action as well as delivery of dialogue. Tension is masterfully incorporated into the key moments 'Helmer's Horror at Nora's Deception' and 'A New Nora?' At first, the audience is encouraged to ponder the likely outcome. Will Helmer forgive his wife? What will happen after Helmer's outburst? Will their relationship change? Will Nora change her mind and stay with Helmer? However, deeper changes are under way. Nora has shed her former persona, both literally and symbolically. Helmer's power to exert any influence over the situation is seriously eroded.

Stage directions are another crucial aspect of a play. We notice how the apartment is depicted and how the porter brings in a Christmas tree for Nora to decorate. In Act 2, the Christmas tree 'stands, stripped and dishevelled, its candles burned to their sockets.' This stresses the destruction which develops over a period of time as well as reflecting Nora's fears for the future. It could be linked to the previous act when Nora is startled by Helmer's words: 'Corrupt my little children–! Poison my home!' (Act 1). Further stage directions cast more light on the play's inner meaning. The sound of the door slamming represents the termination of Nora and Helmer's marriage. Helmer's frustration and defeat is well captured by gesture and action: 'Helmer (sits down on a chair by the door and buries his face in his hands) "Nora! Nora!" (Looks around and gets up) "Empty! She's gone!" (A hope strikes him) "The miracle of miracles–?" (The street door is slammed shut downstairs)' (Act 3). This passage conveys Helmer's defeat and hopeful expectation through facial expression. A note of finality is struck in the sound of the slamming door, which effectively captures the significance of this final act.

The title *A Doll's House* provides the most striking image in the play: 'Our home has never been anything but a playroom' (Act 3). Nora extends this image further by contending that she has been 'a doll-wife, just as I used to be papa's doll-child. And the children have been my dolls' (Act 3).

Krogstad paints a frightening and graphic image of those who have drowned in the 'cold, black water' (Act 2). This dark and depressing imagery compounds the overall mood built into the scene.

Dialogue is, of course, the ultimate driving force of drama. It has symbolic power. At first, Nora's discourse is similar to that of an excitable child while Helmer's is melodramatic. Krogstad's language is notable for its rigidity.

There is also the fitting use of dance, which has a symbolic as well as literal meaning. Nora is frantic as she dances the tarantella for the last time. The dance has tragic undertones. It has a poetic power of its own – Helmer is transfixed by its rhythm – but Nora's distress abruptly breaks up the sequence, leading to the climax of the play.

A Doll's House is a powerful, intricately produced play.

CLASSROOM activities

1. How important is the title in the context of the plot and subplots?
2. How does the manner in which the story is told affect the audience's attitude to the plot?
3. Assess the importance of Nora's monologue.
4. How do the characters contribute to the drama as a whole?
5. The best example of external conflict between Nora and Helmer is kept until the end. Why do you think Ibsen chose to do this?
6. How important are the stage directions in the play?
7. Examine the effectiveness of the use of imagery in the drama.
8. Evaluate the importance of dance in the telling of the tale.

Dancing at Lughnasa

LITERARY GENRE: **plays**

Brian Friel's works act as a dynamic commentary on social pressures through different historical epochs. *Philadelphia Here I Come!* offers a novel approach to tackling the subject of emigration and *Translations* deals with the colonisation of language in the nineteenth century. By setting *Dancing at Lughnasa* around the Lughnasa weeks of 1936, Brian Friel focuses on the clash between the festival of Lughnasa and the Catholic religion. Michael's narration provides the background for the events as they unfold.

The title *Dancing at Lughnasa* is significant because it emphasises the power of dance to release the Mundy sisters from the restricted environment in which they live; dance is an act of self-expression. The competing forces of freedom and submission are powerfully worked into the drama; they are played out in the clash between the pagan festival of the god Lugh (which espouses a celebratory approach to life) and the stoical approach of the Roman Catholic Church.

Characters are hugely important in propelling the drama. Kate's unyielding and taciturn manner is well contrasted with the humorous Maggie. Rose's free, loving nature is highlighted in her love of dancing. Agnes is Rose's special protector and tends to take too much responsibility upon herself, a factor in her tragic demise. Chris is a spirited member of the family, easily infatuated with Gerry. Gerry's easygoing temperament strongly contrasts with Kate's rigid manner. Fr Jack is in the process of his own spiritual discovery, which is a source of conflict for his superiors.

Unusually, one character acts as narrator, evoking the traditional Greek chorus which commented on the drama. Michael also foretells the future, which provides a sense of foreboding. Initially, he links together three significant events. The first is the arrival of the wireless. Michael tells the audience that Kate insists that the wireless is called 'Marconi.' Maggie's whimsical name, 'Lugh,' is viewed as too pagan by the religious Kate. Second, Michael speaks about the earlier arrival of Fr Jack from the leper colony. Instead of being the hero that Michael imagined him to be, he is described as a 'forlorn figure' who is 'shuffling from room to room as if he were searching for something but couldn't remember what' (Act 1). Third, there is the arrival of Michael's father, Gerry. Change is seen as a negative force as Michael speaks of 'things changing too quickly before my eyes, of becoming what they ought not to be' (Act 1).

Michael's role goes beyond that of a mere commentator; he is also intricately enmeshed in the family. This play is presented in flashback as Michael casts his mind back to 'that summer of 1936' where 'different kinds of memories' are evoked (Act 1). The audience is heavily reliant on Michael's subjective memory to relate the events of that summer. The dialogue between the different characters is interrupted by the short intervals of Michael's narration at different points in the play.

Brian Friel uses many 'devices' in the play. The use of the tableau breaks the action deliberately and has the effect of giving the audience pause for thought. Re-read the key moment entitled 'The Last Scene of the Mundy Family Together and Michael's Narration' outlined in Chapter 2. Michael's narration is carefully linked into the overall drama and unites the stories of the Mundy sisters into a cohesive whole. All the characters are affected by one another. There is the sense of a family breaking apart due to forces outside its control. The moments of togetherness are lost for ever and the audience is forced to rely on Michael's memory.

External conflict is another driving force of good drama. Kate's overpowering presence is a flashpoint, especially when the other sisters begin to assert themselves. In the key moment 'Family Arguments and the Arrival of Gerry,' what is most characteristic about this moment is what is left unsaid. Agnes is secretly in love with Gerry but this secret is shared only with the audience. It highlights the individuality of the Mundy sisters, whose characterisation is very realistic. Agnes's gestures emphasise her frustration in this scene.

> There is the sense of a family breaking apart due to forces outside its control

This is not, however, the only conflict-laden scene. Kate's dominant character almost smothers the other sisters, but her authority does not go unchallenged. In the key moment 'Rose's Disappearance,' Kate's authority is questioned as Rose politely tells her that she has a life of her own. Notice how the scene gently moves to the moment when Kate interrogates Rose and is taken aback by the strength of her reply. Both these key moments highlight the central importance of external conflict in developing the drama.

Stage directions are vital for a well-worked performance. The play is set in the Mundy family home and details are provided of the characters' visual appearance, which add to the overall dramatic effect. Rose wears wellingtons in the summer. Her dress sense is inappropriate, suggesting she is 'simple.' Maggie and Agnes wear aprons, highlighting their constant domestic work. Fr Jack's chaplain's uniform visually represents his past. The exchange of hats between Gerry and Fr Jack symbolises empathy between these wayward characters. Sound effects create an effective background against which the drama unfolds.

Gesture is well used in Act 2 when a fearful Agnes sees Gerry up a tree. Her gestures – she covers her eyes – are easily understood by the audience and are supported by the line: 'You're going to fall! I'm not looking! I'm not watching!' (Act 2). These words are further supported by her action; she

FIRST PERFORMED:
1990, Abbey Theatre. *Dancing at Lughnasa* opened to great critical acclaim and after a very successful run transferred to London's National Theatre in 1991, when it won several Olivier Awards. The following year it opened on Broadway and garnered the Tony Award for Best Play. It went on to become one of the most successful and universally acclaimed plays of the decade.

ABOUT THE AUTHOR:
Brian Friel was born in Omagh, Co. Tyrone, in 1929, the son of a primary school teacher. He followed in his father's footsteps and taught in Derry for ten years, during which time many of his short stories were published in the *New Yorker*. Encouraged by this success, Friel quit teaching in 1960 to become a full-time writer, and never looked back. He is widely recognised as one of the greatest contemporary dramatists writing in the English language. Some of his other important works include *Philadelphia, Here I Come!, The Freedom of the City* and *Translations*. He lives in Donegal with his wife, Anne.

ADAPTATION:
Dancing at Lughnasa was adapted for the screen in 1998. Directed by Pat O'Connor, it starred Meryl Streep as Kate and Michael Gambon as Fr Jack.

Dancing at Lughnasa

BRIAN FRIEL

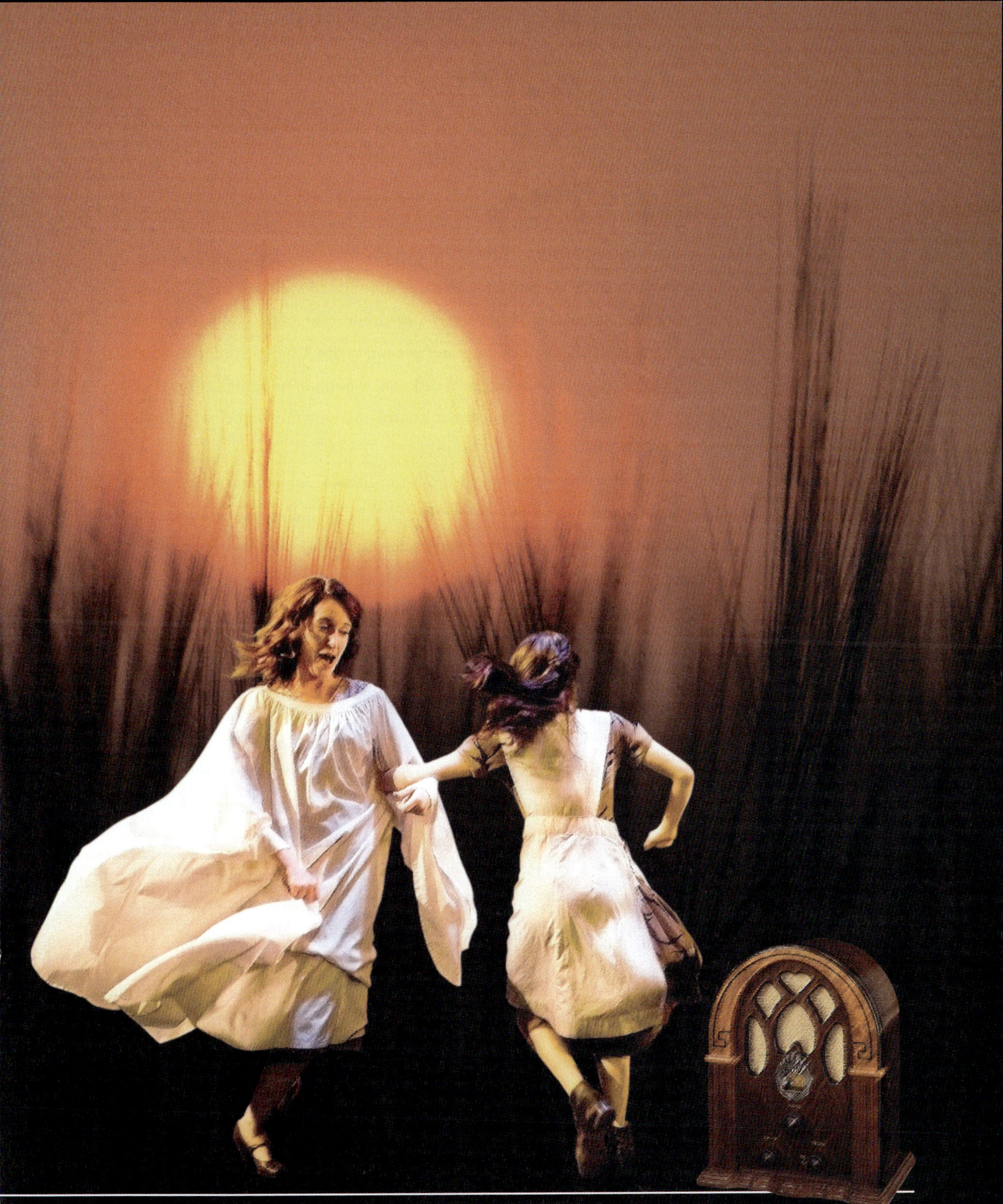

dashes into the house.

The imagery is very expressive. The sisters are forever inventing names for ordinary objects. The wireless almost becomes a character in the drama. Much of the imagery in the play evokes a sense of defeat. Michael's descriptions of Fr Jack – 'forlorn,' 'shuffling,' 'searching,' 'couldn't remember' – stress that Fr Jack has lost his youthful exuberance and is soon to die. Change, in the form of the passage of time and the ravages of old age, is seen in negative terms. The rigidity of traditional Catholic religion is contrasted with the Celtic pagan god of the harvest, Lugh.

Music is also incorporated throughout the drama. An ordinary domestic scene is transformed into a lively performance through the power of music and dance. Dance as a form of expression is strongly developed throughout the play: 'Dancing as if language had surrendered to movement – as if ritual, this wordless ceremony, was now the way to speak, to whisper private and sacred things, to be in touch with some otherness' (Act 2).

Cleverly, Brian Friel goes further by integrating dance into the overall design as a 'wordless ceremony'; it competes with language as a means of cultural expression. This emphasises the limitations of words to convey the totality of the human person and experience. Agnes's hurt spills over at one point in the play and while that alerts the audience to her unspoken romantic attachment to Gerry, Maggie and Kate are unaware of their sister's predicament. While the dialogue conveys movement and a quick turn of phrase, much is left unsaid, as in Agnes's resolute note. *Dancing at Lughnasa* is a powerful play on many levels.

CLASSROOM activities

1. How important is the title in the context of the plot and subplot?

2. How does the manner in which the story is told affect the reader's attitude to the plot?

3. Michael's narration is pivotal to the telling of the story. To what extent does this mean that the play revolves around memory?

4. How do the characters contribute to the drama as a whole?

5. How does the external conflict between the sisters add to the suspense and tension of the play?

6. Assess the importance of Kate's character in terms of conflict.

7. How important are the stage directions in the play?

8. Assess the importance of music in the play.

9. Assess the importance of the 'tableau' in the staging of *Dancing at Lughnasa*.

The Lonesome West
LITERARY GENRE: plays

The Lonesome West examines a family tragedy as it unfolds in a rural farmhouse through a diverse array of props and astute use of lighting, which are intricately drawn into the telling of the tale itself.

The title *The Lonesome West* highlights the loneliness at the heart of the play. It also contains a veiled reference to the 'wild west'. Other elements, such as the shotgun, 'Lassie' and *Alias Smith and Jones* evokes images associated with the American western.

Fr Welsh stresses the isolation of the bachelor brothers Valene and Coleman. Fr Welsh, however, is also depicted as a lonely, tragic figure. Even the lake is described as lonesome: 'A lonesome oul lake that is for a fella to go killing himself in' (Scene 3). This is further compounded by a reference to the tears shed by Tom Hanlon's family. The central plot involves the confrontational relationship between Valene and Coleman. Girleen's love for Fr Welsh is a subplot. The plot and the subplot highlight the heartbreak of loneliness on different levels. Girleen's unspoken love for Fr Welsh makes the priest's act of suicide evoke even greater pathos. In effect, the characters represent those lost, bereft and adrift in the modern tide of rapid social and economic change.

The play concentrates on only a select few characters (Valene, Coleman, Girleen and Fr Welsh) and all characters are well explored. The play does not have a narrator but we are provided with the point of view of each of the four characters. Fr Welsh's letter substitutes for a monologue.

Valene and Coleman are the two most developed characters. Re-read the key moment entitled 'Who Owns the House?' summarised in Chapter 2. This key moment highlights aspects of Valene's and Coleman's characters. The audience is introduced to the petty squabbles and violent contests which are the driving force of the play. Coleman is the more hot-tempered of the two brothers, while Valene's spiteful pettiness is clearly demonstrated. Fr Welsh vows to undertake the task of reconciling the warring brothers.

The manner of the telling has an impact on the overall structure of the play, which is told in linear fashion. The influence of the past has an impact on the present dramatic moment. The murder of Valene and Coleman's father is related retrospectively. The climax of the key moment 'The Murder of Coleman and Valene's Father' occurs when Fr Welsh discovers that Coleman murdered his father. This gives the event greater power and overshadows much of the drama. Many past issues are interwoven into the plot and demonstrate the impact of the past on the present moment.

External conflict is essential in propelling the drama forward. It is represented onstage by Valene and Coleman's mutual distrust and apparent antipathy for each other. The key moment 'A Tenuous Reconciliation?' is loaded with suspense and tension. The audience is invited to ask many questions: Did Coleman load the gun? Will he shoot Valene? Will Valene approach him with a knife? Gestures and actions complement the dialogue.

> The audience is invited to ask many questions: Did Coleman load the gun? Will he shoot Valene?

Stage directions are essential in any dramatic performance and in *The Lonesome West* a selection of props are well worked into the drama. Plastic Catholic figurines marked with a 'V' and the framed photograph of a black dog are associated with Valene. The double-barrelled shotgun has been used in the murder of the brothers' father. The bottle of poteen is associated with Girleen.

Lighting in the dramatic context of a performance can have an important input as it creates the mood and atmosphere. The audience is immediately drawn to the light. The emphasis is placed on Girleen's chain and the priest's letter. The priest's letter and the crucifix have symbolic importance in that they emphasise the possibility of redemption. However, Fr Welsh writes the letter and commits suicide at night; darkness has a symbolic significance in that it highlights the tragedy that is about to unfold.

Violent, brutal imagery is used to portray certain characters and to highlight the barbaric actions of some in the parish. Valene argues with Fr

Welsh that 'a great parish it is you run, one of them murdered his missus, an axe through her head, the other her mammy, a poker took her brains out' (Scene 1). Fr Welsh replies that God has 'no jurisdiction' in this parish.

Valene, Coleman and Fr Welsh use local dialect. This emphasises the realism of the play. Black humour is effectively used throughout. Valene claims that Fr Welsh's soul is burning in hell because of the brothers' arguments. Coleman replies: 'Well, did we ask him to go betting his soul on us? No. And, sure, it's pure against the rules for priests to go betting anyways, neverminding with them kinds of stakes. Sure a fiver would've been overdoing it on us' (Scene 7). At another point in the play, the sight of two men sitting down munching Tayto crisps and reading women's magazines creates its own sense of hilarity.

The Lonesome West acts out the drama of modernity in an ordinary farmhouse. The play represents the tensions and stresses of modern life that lead to a rise in violence and the breakdown of effective communication. The use of horrific violence within this familiar context makes it all the more thought-provoking for a modern audience. This is not a tragedy in the traditional sense. Unusually, the tragedy of Fr Welsh's suicide does not result in a further downward spiral, except for Girleen. Instead, the priest's letter acts as a catalyst for change in encouraging the brothers to re-examine their behaviour. While this play has many of the tragic elements associated with much of Greek drama, the protagonists' downfall is only partial, ameliorated by an abrupt change of mood and a surprising turn of events.

CLASSROOM **activities**

1. How important is the title in the context of the plot and subplot?
2. How does the manner in which the story is told affect the reader's attitude to the plot?
3. How do the characters contribute to the drama as a whole?
4. How are the plot and subplot linked?
5. How does the external conflict between Valene and Coleman add to the suspense and tension of the play?
6. How important are the stage directions in the play?
7. Assess the importance of lighting in the staging of *The Lonesome West*.

11

Literary Genre: film

Literary Genre: film

films are readily accessible. In an instant, they capture the meaning of a look, a expression or a gesture. Look at Michael Connolly's frustrated expression in Carrigmore nursing home when he finds it impossible to alert the carers to the approaching danger in the opening scene of the film. Notice the anguish on Justin's face when he has to identify his wife's body.

This chapter will outline aspects of literary genre in the world of the film in:
- Damien O'Donnell's *Inside I'm Dancing*
- Fernando Meirelles' *The Constant Gardener.*

As well as exploring the meaning of certain terms used in the study of film, this chapter will also examine aspects of literary genre, such as:
- The significance of the title and of social commentary
- The camera as narrator
- The development of characters and motivation
- The dramatisation of the moment by the actor, the acquired persona
- The story and the overall direction of the plot
- Unity or disunity in the overall design
- The power of the moving image: instant accessibility
- Special effects: lighting and sound
- The importance of the dialogue.

Inside I'm Dancing

LITERARY GENRE: film

The title *Inside I'm Dancing* is significant. Overall, the film highlights the interweaving lives of two disabled people as they journey to maturity and greater self-expression. The title emphasises the willingness to break free and overcome prejudicial attitudes to disabled people on a variety of different levels.

Michael is unsuccessful in winning the love of his life, Siobhán, and as the film draws to a close, he embarks on a lonely life. A positive approach to life is actively encouraged by Rory, whose time is running out due to his condition. The importance of enjoying life to the full is conveyed in the film. This is highlighted by the tagline for the film, 'Live life like you mean it.'

The camera is the omniscient narrator in this text. *Mise en scène* literally means 'what has been put in the picture.' The lighting, the angle and type of shot, the movement of the camera, figure behaviour (the actions and gestures of the characters), as well as props and setting, all form part of the overall design. In this case,

> *'Live life like you mean it'*

aspects of Rory's and Michael's demeanours are used as a form of artistic expression. Re-read the key moment entitled 'The Isolation of Michael Connolly in Carrigmore' outlined in Chapter 2. Michael is confined to his wheelchair. He is viewed at a different angle from the other patients in the home, symbolising his separateness. He lives in an isolated environment as no one can understand him. He is viewed from different angles, highlighting his importance in the overall story. All the faces in this scene are expressionless. Unlike the others, he has a name. Eileen calls out his name, which immediately draws the viewer's attention to his character. His actions are spontaneous as he tries to alert the cleaner to the oncoming danger, but to no avail. The cleaner responds like a robot, while those in authority come across as inept.

Rory's introduction is quite momentous. At first, the viewer is drawn to the prison bars as Rory emerges in his wheelchair. He questions Eileen about a key but she refuses to give him one. Almost immediately this paints Carrigmore as an unyielding prison and casts Rory in the role of a rebellious inmate. Rory and Michael's friendship is developed and Michael shares Rory's willingness to escape the confines of Carrigmore. Different angles and types of shot are used here. In films, central importance is given to the camera in the telling of the tale. The camera, as omniscient narrator, is able to manipulate the type and angle of the shot, as in all films.

The movement of the camera is crucial. In *Inside I'm Dancing* there are many emotive moments. In the key moment 'Siobhán's Rejection of Michael's Love,' Michael's visual distress is well captured. He is crushed after Siobhán's rejection of him and goes out in the pelting rain. The word 'home' is reiterated. Rory is unsettled by his friend's distress and charges after him. Many shots combine to give an overall impression.

- First there is a full shot of Michael in his wheelchair on the bridge. He looks a dejected figure. The rain emphasises Michael's emotional turmoil.

- The camera captures his movement along the bridge. Rory's voice is heard.

- Then there is a full shot which takes in the whole bridge from afar. Rory's voice seems closer but he and Michael appear like small dark figures on the bridge, prefiguring their helplessness in the situation. Immediately, the camera draws the viewer closer.

- A medium shot is shown of Michael and Rory together. Michael has his back to the camera while Rory's position is at a right angle to Michael.

- Viewers are made aware of Michael's distress as he moves his head. He speaks. This fits in well with Rory's line: 'I know it hurts. You're not the only one with a broken heart.' Close-up shots of Michael show him turning towards Rory.

- Soft music plays as Rory continues to speak: 'You have a future, Michael. That's what I call a gift. Don't give it up. You can't give it up. You have the whole world in your hands.' The camera alternates between Michael and Rory.

- A shot of Michael's back and Rory's sideways positioning is repeated.

- A close-up shot highlights Michael and Rory's pain. There is talk of suicide. Michael says it is too high to jump.

- High-angle shots show that the moment lightens as they swirl around in their wheelchairs, re-enacting the moment in the nightclub.

- A high-angle shot shows Rory and Michael going home.

The type and angle of shot gives the viewers a chance to see this emotive moment from different perspectives. The moment demonstrates the importance of Michael and Rory's friendship. The contrasting light and darkness of the shots highlight their emotional turmoil.

Character is developed not just through characters' actions, the use of space or the angle of the shot, but also through words. Rory's constant use of witticisms emphasises his difference, and sets him apart as a rebellious character. He uses biting sarcasm and often foul language. His opening speech to the patients in Carrigmore echoes the viewers' initial impression: 'Always so much fun, or is today someone's birthday?' When Michael tries to explain his annoyance at paint being splashed in his face, Rory comments that his 'Swahili is a little off the boil.' Tommy's dismissive attitude to Michael on account of his cerebral palsy is quickly countered by Rory: 'And you'd be Stephen Hawkins, would you?' Rory's ability to understand him brightens Michael's demeanour and overall attitude. Rory compares Michael to famous actors like Hugh Grant. Michael sees Rory as the 'embodiment of independence.' Their feelings are mutual.

> *'Always so much fun, or is today someone's birthday?'*

Michael's character is transformed. First, there is the institutionalised Michael who finds it difficult to cope with the loud music emanating from Rory's room. Then there is Michael the friend, who participates in Rory's activities. Later, there is the active Michael who takes up Rory's cause of independent living as his own. Later, Michael grows in maturity after facing the humiliation of Siobhán's rejection. At the end of the film, Michael is conscious that he had just a partial understanding of the term 'independence.'

Michael and Rory have one unifying goal: to achieve independence by living on their own. Their quest is a reaction against Carrigmore, the symbol of restriction and imprisonment in the film. Carrigmore (literally 'big rock'),

INSIDE I'M

RELEASED:
2004. Released in the USA as *Rory O'Shea Was Here*

STARRING:
Steven Robertson as Michael Connolly, James McAvoy as Rory O'Shea and Romola Garai as Siobhán

STORY BY:
Christian O'Reilly

AWARDS:
Edinburgh International Film Festival Audience Award 2004

REVIEWS:
'This is a lovely, moving tale of a powerful friendship'
– *USA Today*

'O'Donnell should be lauded for offering a sensitive portrayal of disabled people without ever being patronizing'
– *Empire Magazine*

ABOUT THE DIRECTOR:
Damien O'Donnell, born in 1967, is a native of Beaumont, Dublin. After graduating from Coláiste Dhúlaigh in 1987 with a degree in Communications and Media Production, he co-founded Clingfilms with three friends. In 1995 he wrote and directed what is probably the most successful Irish short film ever, *35-Aside*. Working with BBC Films and Film 4, his first feature, *East is East,* won the 2000 BAFTA award for Best British Film and a Best Debut award for O'Donnell at the Empire Awards. His other full-length film, *Heartlands,* was released in 2002.

DANCING

seems harsh and unyielding and symbolises all that is negative in Michael and Rory's life. Michael is institutionalised, knowing nothing of life 'out there.' Rory's friendship is instrumental in introducing Michael to a broader world beyond the confines of Carrigmore, with the film being shot in different locations around Dublin.

Rory's introduction helps build the tension of the film. When he wakes residents in Carrigmore by playing loud music, he is reprimanded by Eileen, the manager. His stereo is snatched from him. He roars at this and shouts out that he is 'alive.' He calls himself the 'Carrigmore 1,' implying that he is unjustly imprisoned like the 'Birmingham 6' or the 'Guildford 4.' Michael is shown to have lived in Carrigmore all his life. Rory asks him, 'What crime did you commit?' Michael matches Rory's witticisms: 'Unarmed robbery.'

Rory applies for independent living. As before, his request is denied. Noticing his despondency, Michael applies for independent living, with an interpreter. They are successful but financial concerns mean that Michael has to seek help from his negligent and estranged father, Fergus Connolly. Carrigmore is painted as a grey prison full of restrictions, but Michael and Rory's new home is bright and airy; Rory calls it 'cripple heaven.' However, the boys are actively encouraged throughout the film to grapple with the meaning of the term 'independence.'

> Carrigmore is painted as a grey prison full of restrictions, but Michael and Rory's new home is bright and airy; Rory calls it 'cripple heaven'

The film is narrated in a linear manner. Michael's meeting with Rory in Carrigmore sets in motion a chain of events which encourages them to live independent lives. Specific moments, such as Siobhán's rejection of Michael, and Rory's death, test Michael's commitment to his new-found independence.

Time has a different meaning. The film centres on a few years of Rory and Michael's lives. Michael's life up to now has been characterised by mindless tasks unsuited to his age and capabilities; his time has been wasted. Time is running out for Rory. His lifelong quest for independent living is his final wish before he dies. However, it is only in the closing minutes of the film that this becomes possible. Michael finds an unconscious Rory in a sea of red lights, symbolising danger. There is a tense moment as Rory is put into the ambulance. A distressed Michael watches his friend from a distance. Rory is well aware of his condition. A dying Rory tells a distraught Michael that he can achieve independence. This moment evokes great pathos. It emphasises the transience of time. The film conveys Michael's 'gift' of a future.

An actor's task is to bring a script to life. For the duration of the film, actors assume their respective roles by living out their characters' experiences, communicated by tone of voice, facial expression, a look, an action or movement. All reality is suspended for a time as the actor becomes 'the bridge' between the world of script and film. The completely different roles of Michael and Rory are played by Steven Robertson and James McAvoy. Michael's ability to communicate with the viewer rests on the actor's use of facial expression. Rory is trapped in his wheelchair and unable to move, but the wheelchair, a mechanical device, also becomes a form of bodily movement. Rory's choice of music also depicts aspects of his persona.

The use of costume has a particular significance in *Inside I'm Dancing*. Rory dresses as Dr Strangelove while Michael chooses Richard Gere's role from the film *An Officer and a Gentleman* (1982). Michael is trying to fill a heroic role to win the woman of his dreams. However, like the costume, it is mere role-play. It is an act within an act and doomed to failure. Siobhán falls for the man who plays the pirate, the antithesis of the heroic naval officer. After the party, Michael's costume is laid on the chair. At this moment, Siobhán rejects Michael. Later, she introduces their new carer, a qualified care assistant. It is a moment of truth: 'I can't help who I love. I can't help who I don't love.' Rory's criticism of her is biting, but she has her own version of the truth. Michael is visibly distressed while Rory is characteristically defiant. Notice the costumes are cast aside. All illusion is gone.

> *'I can't help who I love. I can't help who I don't love'*

Music is another component used to good effect in the film. Each character is associated with different songs. In the key moment 'The Isolation of Michael Connolly in Carrigmore,' the patients are watching *Bagpuss*, a BBC children's programme from the 1970s. At first sight, it seems inappropriate. The focus is on the little ballerina dancing 'all by herself,' which forms the introduction to the film. Unlike the patients in the home, Rory chooses his own music, which he plays at high volume. He plays music which immediately emphasises his different, less compliant attitude. All the patients are disturbed by Rory's music. Siobhán plays Johnny Cash's version of 'Hurt,' which contributes to a sense of foreboding: 'Everyone I know goes away in the end.' This foreshadows Michael's loss of Rory and Siobhán's rejection of him. All this music is diegetic, meaning the source of the music is visible in the film itself. The other form of music in film, non-diegetic (mood music or background music), is also present, for example in the key moment 'Fergus Connolly's History of Isolating His Son.'

'Everyone I know goes away in the end'

Soft music can be heard as an accompanying soundtrack. After Fergus says 'Okay,' Michael faces his father for the first time. Fittingly, the music reaches a crescendo at this point, accentuating Michael's inner turmoil after years of neglect by his father. In this way, songs and music form part of the expression of the tale itself.

The dialogue in *Inside I'm Dancing* sparkles, with witticisms effectively used throughout. For example, when Rory tells Fergus Connolly's secretary that they have an appointment, she requests the date of his appointment. Rory gives Michael's birthday: '1981. Traffic was murder.' He calls Michael's case a 'blatant case of criminal neglect.'

Certain words are reiterated throughout. One is the word 'home.' Rory tells a stone-faced Fergus that Michael needs a 'home.' When Michael is rejected by Siobhán, he tells Rory that he is going 'home.' The word 'home' tugs at the viewer's heartstrings, as we are aware that Rory and Michael have to create a home for themselves. Another word is 'gift.' Michael calls Rory's ability to translate for him a 'gift.' Rory scoffs at the suggestion. Later, Rory tells Michael, 'You have a future. That's what I call a gift. Don't give it up. You can't give it up.' The gift is his ability to grasp the future, with all its unknown possibility, underscoring the film's positive overview. A sad note is struck too, since Rory is denied a future on account of his condition.

The line 'whole world in your hands' recurs at different moments. The song 'He's Got the Whole World in His Hands' has religious connotations, but its meaning here is secular. It is played in Carrigmore and later the tune is played at the party just before Siobhán rejects Michael. However, on the bridge, it is given a new meaning by Rory. He tells a sorrowful Michael that he has the 'whole world' in his grasp, and pleads with him to become an independent person and explore the possibilities life has to offer.

Inside I'm Dancing conveys the light and dark shades of life with a strong emphasis on the primary importance of the power of the individual to decide the course of his or her life. Through dialogue, character, facial expression and cinematography, Michael and Rory's world is imaginatively enacted.

CLASSROOM activities

1. **Explain the central importance of the title *Inside I'm Dancing*.**

2. **Explore the manner in which the camera is instrumental in the telling of this tale. Refer to angle of shot, type of shot and movement of the camera.**

3. **Identify the differences between Rory's and Michael's characterisation.**

4. **Identify the importance of the unified goal of independence throughout *Inside I'm Dancing*.**

5. **What is the importance of the director's choice of location in the overall design?**

6. **Analyse the importance of time throughout the film.**

7. **Choose a key moment in the film which demonstrates how language can be conveyed verbally and non-verbally.**

8. **What do the costumes suggest about Rory and Michael's idealised sense of self?**

9. **Give examples of the effective use of music throughout *Inside I'm Dancing*.**

The Constant Gardener

LITERARY GENRE: **film**

The title ***The Constant Gardener*** is significant. Justin is a low-grade official in the high commission who loves gardening, but he is in conflict with powerful institutional forces, represented by Sir Bernard Pellegrin and Sandy Woodrow. He grows flowers in Kenya, keeping them controlled with insecticides. Sandy perceives this as a betrayal. The insecticides contain the same chemical properties as Dypraxa, the drug at the centre of the film. Justin is also engaged in discovering the truth. Sir Bernard speaks to Justin about the danger of 'poking around under rocks,' especially in foreign gardens. Justin's uncovering of the truth is a threat to these forces.

The camera narrates the story. It is an example of omniscient narration. The director's role is a form of artistic expression; he deliberately allows viewers a window on the third world.

The film is an adaptation of John Le Carré's thriller *The Constant Gardener*, but there is a different emphasis in the film. The director, Fernando Meirelles, changes the perspective to focus on the third world. This is especially pronounced in the treatment of powerless characters, such as Kioko and Wanza, and adds to the pathos of the film. At times, it seems like a documentary as Tessa and Dr Arnold Bluhm wander through poverty-stricken Africa.

> At times, it seems like a documentary as Tessa and Dr Arnold Bluhm wander through poverty-stricken Africa

A moving image is instantly accessible to the audience. *Mise en scène,* or 'what has been put in the picture,' encompasses many aspects of a film's composition. The lighting, the angle and type of shot, the movement of the camera, figure behaviour (the actions and gestures of the characters) all form part of the overall design.

Certain emotive moments heighten the tension and suspense. In the key moment 'One Little Girl and the Dangers of Africa,' the camera is adept at describing the movement of the frantic villagers as they scramble for survival in a harsh terrain. View this moment again.

- A full shot of children running shows the chaotic situation.

- The raiders are spotted from a distance. It is a low-angle shot. The viewer is invited to feel the villagers' vulnerability and powerlessness in the face of the raiders' armed superiority and dangerous intent. The raiders travel on horseback from over the hill, provoking panic among the villagers. The music fits in well with their warrior intent. Frantic villagers run to and fro. The camera captures their movements. There are random shouts and the doctor narrates the oncoming danger.

- There is a close-up of the back and side of the doctor's head. His line,

'Maybe we should leave,' suggests that time is running out. There follows a medium shot of the doctor turned towards the makeshift hospital.

- There are medium shots of Justin and the doctor. A man in a white coat is shown running towards the hut. A shot of the same man from the open door of the hut suggests tension. His line, 'They are leaving in five minutes,' emphasises the danger. The suspense and tension is heightened. The camera captures the movement of the doctor and Justin as they hastily collect their things.

- As the raiders come closer, the suspense and tension is increased.

- Full shots of aid workers speedily running away suggest that even they are a target.

- There is a shot of a boy running. Only his legs are shown. This is his only means of escape from the mercenary raiders. Then there is a medium shot of the same boy from the side and behind.

- Shots of the raiders on horseback illustrate the danger clearly.

- The doctor and Justin jostle. Close-up shots convey the doctor's fear and Justin's unbridled anger. There are full shots of villagers running away amidst screams.

- A full shot of the same boy with a red top who is now running with other children as the animals are pushed away. A shot rings out. The raiders are in close proximity.

- Shots of the horses' legs suggest their superior speed. Dust is blown up furiously.

- The legs of a child are shown. The camera appears to shake, giving the impression that this is amateurish documentary footage of a live raid.

- A low-angle shot of a raider on horseback identifies their military superiority over the civilian villagers. Movement is well captured.

- Frantic villagers drive away cattle and run for their lives.

- A close-up shot of children stealing away into a hut shrouded in darkness in an attempt at escape by a different means.

- Full shots of a raider coming towards the camera while defenceless villagers flee in the opposite direction.

- A shot is fired and a woman falls.

- The camera tracks the doctor and Justin's movements.

- A raider on horseback fires aimlessly.

- Fleeting shots of a dead child and a raider attacking a defenceless woman.

- A high-angle shot of children running away down a hill emphasises their panic and fear. Then the most harrowing moment of all is depicted.

- A slow mournful African tune provides background music as one of the raiders captures a child amidst the burning remains of the village.

- As people run to and fro almost aimlessly, one dazed villager is shown surveying the destruction of his home and livelihood.

- A shot of children running amidst a barren landscape is a recurring image. The white plane is shown and then a group of women are turned away. The plane is about to take off.

- Justin and the doctor run towards the plane. A raider is shown chasing them while firing into the crowd. Justin and the doctor run for cover. Another shot rings out. In the chaos it is hard to determine who has been shot. The doctor gets up. The shot of Justin staring at the lifeless body of a female villager is powerfully conveyed. His slow action is in contrast to the doctor's frantic movement.

- There is a shot of the plane moving off and a little girl sitting down patiently.

- The doctor and Justin reach out to her. A high-angle shot from the plane shows three small figures running towards it.

- As they all scramble on to the plane, a medium shot of Justin and the captain is shown. Justin's words, 'This is one we can help,' encapsulate his concern for the little girl's safety. It is an emotive moment as Justin produces money. The camera shows the captain, Justin and the little girl.

- There is a high-angle shot of the little girl running from the plane, as Justin calls her back. Momentarily, she turns around, but then continues onward. It is an emotive moment. The high-angle shot of the little girl from the window of the plane shows her running along a dusty roadway set against a barren landscape. This shot is cut by the wing of the plane. The angle of the shot and its brevity prefigure this little girl's helplessness in a mercenary world.

- African music plays. A shot of another child's legs and her little dog is shown. Then a medium shot of this same little girl appearing lost amidst the ruins of her deserted village.

This key moment is gripping and harrowing on different levels. It highlights the importance of the camera in the telling of the tale. The camera captures movement and chaos.

Characters and their motivation are essential to the working of the film. Tessa and Justin are different characters who meet and fall in love. Justin is a shy official who works in the high commission. Tessa is different. Her espousal of third-world causes makes her an activist. Her job as an aid worker in Africa gives her an opportunity to view at first hand the use of the trial testing procedure by a giant pharmaceutical company, KDH. Justin's love for Tessa is instrumental in his search to uncover the truth. Her untimely death sets in motion a chain of events which will result in uncovering corruption and collusion in British government circles. Justin's goal is singular and resolute. His search into Tessa's murder brings him into direct conflict with the forces of evil and corruption represented by Sir Bernard.

Through his search, Justin becomes a more courageous character, whose concern for the poor and sick in Africa supersedes his concern to further his own career or his personal safety. The actors, Ralph Fiennes and Rachel Weisz, inhabit their characters, igniting the script into seemingly spontaneous performance. Notice how their use of movement, tone of voice, gesture and facial expression are all intricately worked into the performance. A film production is a team effort that seeks to engage with a wider viewership. In this sense, all participants play a part, but the actors' ability to engage with the camera is paramount.

The correct order of narration is essential to how the story is told. Re-read the key moment entitled 'Justin's Final Farewell to Tessa.' The viewer hears the sound of footsteps. There is a medium shot of Justin and Tessa together. Justin waves her off from behind. The camera captures Justin's view of Tessa and Dr Arnold Bluhm walking to the plane. Tessa turns around briefly to say goodbye. Dr Arnold and Tessa fade out, emphasising the way they have been dramatically wiped out of Justin's life. Then there is a cut to a burnt-out car. Tessa's murder triggers Justin's search to uncover the truth, while his moments with Tessa are told in flashback. These flashbacks are an important device as they afford the viewer the chance to see Tessa the person. There is a circular effect to the overall order of narration as Justin's tragic end is on the same spot as Tessa's. He imagines Tessa is calling him home. A shot of soldiers' feet suggests that the end is nigh for Justin. He turns around and then looks towards the water. He closes his eyes.

> Justin's past with Tessa is a catalyst for his relentless search for the truth

The importance of the recurring images is linked to the narrative time. Justin's past with Tessa is a catalyst for his relentless search for the truth. The past and present are placed side by side. As Justin drives along in his car, Tessa appears in the car window. As he continues to drive, he sees her smiling at him with a camera in her hand. Tessa's image forms part of Justin's memory of her. He wonders why she did not share her secrets with him. Their declaration of love for each other ends the sequence and Justin is brought back to the present. The order of the film highlights the importance of Tessa's relationship with Justin as the film flashes backwards and forwards in time.

The film is set in Kenya, Southern Sudan, Germany, the UK and Manitoba, Canada. Much of the filming of *The Constant Gardener* took place in Kibera, Kenya. The film captures the poverty-stricken hovels of the Kenyan poor and their struggle for survival, set among the wider rugged landscape. The film inhabits many worlds. In positioning the film in this way, the first- and third-world experience is placed side by side.

Film is a visual medium. Images are cleverly juxtaposed. At the end of the film, there are camera shots of Sandy playing ball with his son, the KDH advertisement, smiling Africans amidst the squalor of their environment, Kioko scrawling Wanza's name on a wall in an effort to preserve her memory, and Tessa's graveside. These images are well matched and convey the essential aspects of the film.

Music is used effectively at the most dangerous moments. In the midst of the harsh and barren African landscape, there is a car chase. Justin is fearful as an unknown driver chases him. The tension and suspense is heightened by the music, which reaches a crescendo when this strange car catches up with Justin near the precipice. Music is used in film to help create mood and atmosphere and also as a form of cultural expression. The film aptly conveys the hustle and bustle of a lively town with African music being played off set.

Dialogue seems to take second place in the film's overall structure. If you turn the sound down, the actions and the facial expressions of the characters convey many essential aspects of the film. However, words have an emotive power. Every word, even seemingly random ones, can be significant. There is constant reference to the word 'home.' A dishevelled Justin is in constant battle with strong institutional forces. In his conversation with the 'resident spy,' Tim Donohue, the word 'home' is reiterated. Tim asks him to return home but Justin is resolute: 'I don't have a home, Tim. Tessa was my home.' Notice the power of dialogue in a confrontational moment between Justin and Sandy Woodrow in the key moment 'Sandy's Revelation to Justin':

Sandy: Not paid to be bleeding hearts. You know that, Justin. Not killing people who wouldn't be dead otherwise. Look at the death rate. Not that anybody's counting.

Justin: You were a bleeding heart, Sandy. Tessa was your salvation. Wasn't she, in all this? You loved her, remember.

Sandy: Pellegrin said that the report was too damaging. She had to be stopped.

Justin: Oh yes, she was stopped.

This is a powerful piece of dialogue on many levels. The words 'bleeding heart' take on two different meanings. To Sandy, a 'bleeding heart' is a reference to Justin's espousal of the cause of the dispossessed and sick in Africa. To Justin, a 'bleeding heart' is a reference to Sandy's unreciprocated love for Tessa. The line, 'Tessa was your salvation,' has religious overtones. The word 'stopped' is immediately taken up by Justin, implying that she was murdered in order to silence her permanently.

Words have dual meanings in *The Constant Gardener*. It is easy to misunderstand Tessa's line when she speaks to Arnold about a 'marriage of convenience, and the only thing it is going to produce is dead offspring.' At face value, that might seem to refer to Tessa's relationship with her husband and her miscarriage. On closer examination, it refers to the KDH partnership with Curtiss, an English businessman in Africa, and their involvement in test trials which lead to death.

The film *The Constant Gardener* is a powerful adaptation of John Le Carré's thriller for cinema viewers. Its third-world emphasis might unsettle viewers but it is a gripping film from beginning to end, with good cinematography and characterisation and atmospheric music.

CLASSROOM activities

1. What is the significance of the title of the film?

2. Outline a scene that shows the camera as the omniscient narrator in this film. Justify your choice.

3. Re-read the key moment entitled 'One Little Girl and the Dangers of Africa' outlined in Chapter 2. Look at this moment again.

    (a) Describe the elements that add to the suspense and tension for you, the viewer.

    (b) Which shot conveys this moment best? Justify your choice.

    (c) Look at the story from the point of view of the little girl in southern Sudan. Assess her importance in this scene.

    (d) Study the angles of shot (low, high, etc.) and types of shot (long, close, medium, etc.). What effect do these have on you, the viewer?

    (e) What does the seemingly amateur footage convey?

4. Choose an image from the film which best captures movement. Justify your choice.

5. Describe the central importance of Justin's relationship with Tessa in the context of the film as a whole.

6. Is the order of narration effective? Give reasons for your answer.

7. Assess the realism conveyed in *The Constant Gardener*.

8. In the key moment 'Sandy's Revelation to Justin' and the passage of dialogue above, what adds to the tension of this moment?

9. Choose your favourite passage of dialogue from the film. Assess its effectiveness.

10. Assess the role of music in *The Constant Gardener*.

12

Answering the literary genre question

Answering the literary genre question

Literary genre examines how the story is told. It is one of the most challenging modes of comparison, but with a clear understanding of the term, you will appreciate more deeply the texts you are studying and become more than capable of answering an exam question on literary genre.

This chapter will:
- Outline ten steps to help you tackle the literary genre question
- Examine the 2004 Leaving Certificate question in relation to Jennifer Johnston's *How Many Miles to Babylon?*, Henrik Ibsen's *A Doll's House* and Damien O'Donnell's *Inside I'm Dancing*.

LITERARY GENRE question — 2004 Leaving Certificate

'Texts tell their stories differently.'

(a) Compare two of the texts you have studied in your comparative course in the light of the above statement. *(40 marks)*

(b) Write a short comparative commentary on a third text from your comparative study in the light of your answer to question (a) above. *(30 marks)*

STEP 1 Understand the question

You need to be sure what this section demands of you:
- What are the key words in the question?
- What is the question asking you to do?

- How can you connect the question with your knowledge of the subject?

Planning your answer

STEP 2

You should first plan the main points that you intend to highlight in your essay and then link your plan to your answer. It is important to plan for the following reasons:

- Planning helps you trace the constituent elements of literary genre in the texts
- A plan will help guide your essay
- A plan helps reveal possible comparisons between the texts
- It enables you to keep your answer relevant to the question asked.

How Many Miles to Babylon?	*Inside I'm Dancing*
Alec is narrator: Alec's inner life, well explored through printed word. It is coloured by Alec's perspective. The printed word creates meaning.	*Camera is omniscient narrator:* Michael's and Rory's inner worlds not explored except externally. Angle, type of shot, camera movement pivotal in expressive content.
Dialogue: dialogue with mood and atmosphere is conveyed.	*Dialogue:* dialogue combined with visual content.
Character development: Alec as narrative object, i.e. the subject of the story. Jerry's character shown through dialogue/action.	*Character development:* Michael and Rory are camera's objects. Rory's character shown by the use of stereo, his costumes, use of wheelchair as body language and spoken word.
Sound effects: referred to indirectly, sound of gunfire etc.	*Sound effects:* referred to literally, part of performance, actual sound.
Location: Wicklow, Flanders communicated through descriptive language.	*Location:* Dublin communicated visually and literally, use of camera.
Order of narration: flashback, sense of foreboding.	*Order of narration:* linear sequence.
Symbolism: swans represent friendship between Alec and Jerry.	*Symbolism:* visual costumes, characters' idealised sense of themselves.

A Doll's House

Style of narration: omniscient; inner and outer worlds conveyed.

Dialogue: language use is different in each text. Dialogue is the driving force of plays like *A Doll's House*. Nora is the only character who alters her language style.

Characterisation: role of theatre actor different from *Inside I'm Dancing*'s actors. Less emphasis on slight differences in facial expression and more on tone to lift voice to the back of theatre. Real performance, not imagined sequence as in *How Many Miles to Babylon?*

Sound effects: the dance, tarantella, has tragic undertones, sourced on stage, no wide musical repertoire as found in *Inside I'm Dancing*.

Location: the Helmers' apartment, the most fixed location of all texts. Staging has meaning. The Christmas tree has symbolic significance in the context of the unfolding drama.

Order of narration: linear sequence but unlike *Inside I'm Dancing* the past has an influence on the present moment conveyed through Krogstad's menace. No flashback like *How Many Miles to Babylon?*

Symbolism: black shawl prefigures tragedy like different use of costume in *Inside I'm Dancing*.

STEP 3 ## First impressions: writing the essential opening paragraph

The first paragraph is very important in an essay. It should assist in introducing the remaining paragraphs. You need to show in your opening paragraph that you have understood the question and what it is you are required to answer.

An opening paragraph should:
- Target the question you are asked
- Refer to the texts and their overall importance
- Highlight some of the key issues to be explored in your essay.

STEP 4 ## Writing the middle section of your answer

Refer to the question at all times. Refer to your plan as often as is required. Use this book to help plan answers to past exam questions, specifically chapters 9, 10 and 11. It is also essential to refer to a series of key moments to highlight the manner in which the literary genre is treated in your texts. Use Chapter 2

to refresh your memory of the key moments in each text. You should also:
- Expand upon one point per paragraph
- Make clear comparative points in each of your paragraphs.

Lasting impression: writing the conclusion   STEP 5

The conclusion is essential as it brings all the main points in your essay together. It is important to write a conclusion as it:
- Helps draw the points in your essay together
- Reconstructs the points in your answer in a different way.

Re-read the question   STEP 6

Make sure you re-examine the question.
- Have you answered all aspects of the question?
- Is there any aspect that has not been examined?

Look at the plan   STEP 7

Ask yourself whether there is any aspect of the plan that you have not included in your answer. Make sure that all aspects of the plan relate to the question.

Re-read the middle section of your essay   STEP 8

This is the section in your answer that should provide the most detail.
- Make sure you have made as many comparative points as you can in each of the paragraphs
- Did you refer to the question statement in each of your paragraphs?

Re-read the opening and concluding paragraphs   STEP 9

The opening and concluding paragraphs are important in your essay. They are essential for creating a general and lasting impression.

Is there anything else?   STEP 10

Check if there is anything that has not been included in your essay which could be important. If you are happy with your answer, move on to the next question.

LITERARY GENRE question: 2004 Leaving Certificate

'Texts tell their stories differently.'

(a) Compare two of the texts you have studied in your comparative course in the light of the above statement. *(40 marks)*

(b) Write a short comparative commentary on a third text from your comparative study in the light of your answer to question (a) above. *(30 marks)*

SAMPLE answer (a)

Comparing the Story-telling Styles of *How Many Miles to Babylon?* and *Inside I'm Dancing*

How Many Miles to Babylon? and *Inside I'm Dancing* explore the pivotal role of friendship on life's journey towards maturity through the characterisations of Alec and Jerry, Michael and Rory. In *Inside I'm Dancing*, Michael and Rory's journey is readily accessible whereas Alec's torment is implied through the power of words. This crucial difference affects the response of the reader and viewer. Unlike *Inside I'm Dancing*, *How Many Miles to Babylon?* uses the printed word to convey Alec's thoughts, hopes, dreams and his conflicts (internal and external). This internal world of the character is not explored in the same way in *Inside I'm Dancing*.

Both texts explore friendship between two central characters (Alec and Jerry, Rory and Michael), but the style of narration changes the readers' and viewers' perspective. In *How Many Miles to Babylon?* Alec, the son of a privileged Irish landowning family during World War I, is the narrator of the book whereas in *Inside I'm Dancing* the camera is the omniscient narrator. Jennifer Johnston has chosen to write in the first person singular. Alec narrates his life as a soldier awaiting execution, as an only child shut out by his parents' squabbling, as a failed officer who struggles to save Jerry's life and as a prisoner in the midst of the conflict. In contrast to *How Many Miles to Babylon?*, viewers are not made aware of the secret thoughts of Michael or Rory. The camera is the narrator, not the characters.

There is no *mise en scène* in *How Many Miles to Babylon? Mise en scène* refers to the setting, props, lighting, make-up, etc. All these aspects are intricately woven into a production to convey a sense of plot, setting, era and atmosphere. In contrast to *Inside I'm Dancing*, *How Many Miles to Babylon?* conjures the world of the text solely through the power of the printed word. In *Inside I'm Dancing* the script is brought to life on screen, while in *How Many Miles to Babylon?* readers are encouraged to create the scene using their imagination. Alec's narration, however, leaves the story incomplete from certain angles. The truth about Alec's parentage is shrouded in mystery, as is Bennett's reaction to Alec's decision to disobey a military command.

The camera is able to alter the viewers' perspective. There are close-up shots of Rory, Michael and Siobhán. Facial expressions communicate feelings and heighten the differences in characterisation. *Inside I'm Dancing* does not convey the inner world of the central characters as clearly as does *How Many Miles to Babylon?* As readers, we are invited into Alec's inner world and inner pain. Just before Alec is about to leave for the war, he sees his parents together at the breakfast table: 'They would be there, immaculate themselves, their heads elegantly bent towards the morning papers and the cream-drenched porridge, starched damask napkins folded neatly across their knees.' Alec is the onlooker, the observer.

Film as a narrative form does not depend on the printed word but on visual depiction. In that momentous scene on the bridge, Michael's inner turmoil is echoed by the pouring rain. There is a contrast between light and dark, literally and figuratively. One shot takes in the whole bridge at a distance where Michael and Rory appear like small dark figures on the bridge, prefiguring their isolation. Unlike the film, in the novel Alec's isolation is captured unequivocally through the medium of words: 'As a child I was alone.' Michael's distress is implied through facial expression, through the weather and the prevailing darkness, whereas Alec's is shared directly through words. This affects the reader's or viewer's position in both texts; in *How Many Miles to Babylon?* the reader looks from the inside out, whereas in *Inside I'm Dancing* we look from the outside in.

While *Inside I'm Dancing* uses spoken words to convey mood and atmosphere, priority is given to the visual medium. During the film certain words are reiterated, such as 'home' and 'gift,' but greater use of words to create meaning is found in *How Many Miles to Babylon?* It is not just the words themselves, but also the manner of delivery (tempo, pitch and tone of voice) that communicates the message in *Inside I'm Dancing*, whereas this is not important in *How Many Miles to Babylon?* Dialogue creates immediacy in both *How Many Miles to Babylon?* and *Inside I'm Dancing*, but it is accomplished in different ways. In *How Many Miles to Babylon?* dialogue is linked to mood and atmosphere and is coloured by Alec's impressions. An example occurs when Alec reads Jerry's mother's letter. There is a description of the letter itself: 'The words stood nervously upright on pale-blue lines.' Then, there is Alec's impression: 'I read it twice, mainly because I didn't know what to say to Jerry, then I folded it into its folds again.' This conversation is coloured by Alec's sense of foreboding, which is depicted in the darkness of the atmosphere: 'I hated the thought of the cold and the dark and the Major, colder and darker than the night itself.' In *Inside I'm Dancing*, witness the tempestuous last conversation between Rory and Siobhán. Dialogue is supplemented by the positioning of characters (Siobhán is placed away from Rory and Michael), by bright lighting, by gesture and facial expression. In this way, dialogue is used in both texts but is presented differently.

Characters are central to books and films. However, *How Many Miles to Babylon?* and *Inside I'm Dancing* use different means to show the development of characters. Alec, the narrator of the novel, is not just observing the events as they unfold, he is also the subject of the narrative. He is involved in the plot as it unfolds. Unlike Alec, neither Michael nor Rory is a narrator. Instead they are the objects of the camera's attention. The camera tracks their movements, alters the angle and type of shot to convey their reactions to certain events in their lives.

Rory and Jerry are quite similar characters. Both rebel through music, but this is conveyed differently. Jerry sings to Alec, while Rory plays music on his stereo. Rory's rebellion is shown by his use of the stereo, his costumes, his use of his wheelchair as a form of body language and his biting sarcasm through the actor's interpretation of the part, while Jerry's rebellion is shown more indirectly through dialogue and in his actions (he leaves the regiment to find his father). Jerry is portrayed in words, and we have to imagine him as a figure, whereas an actor develops Rory's character. Jerry's description is hazy, leaving room for the reader to fill in the details, while Rory's character is part of a living performance. In *Inside I'm Dancing*, Steven Robertson and James McAvoy play the parts. For the duration of the film, the actors assume their respective roles by living out their characters' experiences, communicating them by tone of voice, facial expression, an action or movement. This is not the case in *How Many Miles to Babylon?* There are as many images of Alec or Jerry as there are readers.

Sound effects are implied in *How Many Miles to Babylon?* but they are directly conveyed in *Inside I'm Dancing*. Alec refers to the sounds of heavy bombardment, of crying soldiers on the battlefield, the gunshot that ends Jerry's life and which reverberates through Alec's entire being. Unlike the novel, a film uses actual sound. The pelting rain sounds realistic.

The use of music is intricately woven into the overall production of *Inside I'm Dancing*. Rory's music is loud. His choice of music emphasises his rebelliousness. In the novel, Jerry is also rebellious and in his final moments he sings an Irish rebel song: 'At the siege of Ross did my father fall.' Readers are invited to imagine this music but in the film viewers actually hear it. Siobhán plays Johnny Cash singing 'Hurt' and a sense of foreboding is effectively created: 'Everyone I know goes away in the end.' This foreshadows Michael's loss of Rory and Siobhán's rejection of him. Background music is also used effectively in the film, for example in the scene where Michael and Rory meet Fergus Connolly. There is a wider musical repertoire and it is used more effectively in *Inside I'm Dancing* than in *How Many Miles to Babylon?*

Location has a powerful effect in both texts. Carrigmore can be compared with Alec's prison both visually and through the spoken word, whereas place description is highly accomplished in *How Many Miles to Babylon?* Rory calls himself the 'Carrigmore 1' implying he is like a wrongly imprisoned man. By contrast, *How Many Miles to Babylon?* uses description to provide an image of the desolation of the battlefield. The phrase 'a hundred yards of mournful earth' seems to suggest that the soil is grieving for the countless souls lost on the battlefield. This personification is not needed in *Inside I'm Dancing* as the camera can show different locations in and around Dublin. However, Wicklow and Flanders can be imagined in our mind's eye because of the powerful descriptions in *How Many Miles to Babylon?*

The order of narration differs in both texts. Alec narrates his life through flashback. This creates a sense of foreboding as the reader is aware from the outset that Alec is languishing in his cell. By comparison, *Inside I'm Dancing* is narrated in a linear sequence. The order of narration is free from the circular pattern found in *How Many Miles to Babylon?* and has a clear beginning, middle and end, just as Michael and Rory's relationship also goes through these phases.

Symbolism is also used differently in the texts. Swans symbolise Alec and Jerry's friendship. The shooting of the swan prefigures Jerry's tragedy. By comparison, symbolism is conveyed through the use of costumes in *Inside I'm Dancing*. Michael's costume represents his idealised sense of self. Rory dresses as Dr Strangelove while Michael chooses to dress as the Richard Gere character in the film *An Officer and a Gentleman*. Michael is trying to assume a heroic role to win the woman of his dreams.

How Many Miles to Babylon? and *Inside I'm Dancing* explore similar storylines, but quite differently. *Inside I'm Dancing* brings the script to life visually whereas *How Many Miles to Babylon?* relies solely on the printed word to ignite the reader's imagination.

The Story-telling Style of *A Doll's House*

SAMPLE **answer**
(b)

A Doll's House is a theatrical production. Henrik Ibsen's drama does not stand still; it is shaped and re-shaped in each dramatic performance, which is markedly different from *Inside I'm Dancing* and *How Many Miles to Babylon?* The external conflict between Nora and Helmer reaches a climax and can be demonstrated through gripping dialogue interlinked with the visual depiction of the characters' actions, gestures, the overall stage design and performance.

As already outlined above, the narrator alters the reader's or viewer's perspective. In *A Doll's House*, the external world is best represented in the external dynamics between Helmer and Nora. Unlike *How Many Miles to Babylon?* as discussed in part (a), it uses *mise en scène,* where setting, props, lighting, make-up, costumes, etc. all form part of the overall performance.

In contrast to *Inside I'm Dancing*, *A Doll's House* alludes to the inner world of the central character by the use of monologue. The play allows room to explore a central character's private thoughts through the use of monologue, as Alec's narration does in *How Many Miles to Babylon?* In *A Doll's House*, however, the audience alternates its focus between the main characters, with Helmer's torment being laid bare at the end of the play when he cries out for Nora and echoes her words, 'The miracle of miracles–?'

Dialogue is more central to *A Doll's House* than to either *How Many Miles to Babylon?* or *Inside I'm Dancing*, as discussed in part (a). Dialogue reflects a difference in character which is not shown in *Inside I'm Dancing* or in *How Many Miles to Babylon?* Nora's language is infantile but changes to an adult tone to reflect her change of role. Krogstad uses courtroom-style language and Helmer's language reflects his pompous attitude. Dialogue passages are longer than in *Inside I'm Dancing* and spoken rather than printed as in *How Many Miles to Babylon?* Dialogue has a primary role, and gestures and tone of voice supplement the spoken word. This is in contrast to *Inside I'm Dancing*, as noted above, where dialogue competes with the moving image, which has its own expressive power.

As mentioned in part (a), character development is crucial. However, the actor's task in the theatre is different from that in the world of film. In *Inside I'm Dancing*, the living performance adds a different dimension to the narration of the tale, whereas there is no performance in *How Many Miles to Babylon?* However, the actor in *Inside I'm Dancing* plays to the camera, whereas the actor in *A Doll's House* plays to the audience. The stage actor uses a greater range of tone in an attempt to reach all the audience in a large auditorium, but the actor's words in *Inside I'm Dancing* are supplemented by the use of the motion picture: the angle and type of shot and the movement of the camera itself. An actor in *A Doll's House* is in a live performance, whereas in *Inside I'm Dancing* the performance is filmed. Both use gestures and bodily expression but an actor's movement needs to be more pronounced in a play than in a film, where close-up shots can be very effective. Also, facial expression is different; Michael's distress is related through his eyes, whereas in *A Doll's House* facial expression is harder to convey as the theatre does not have the advantage of the film screen to show every movement. Helmer's distress is not just shown by his tone of voice but through easily visible movements, for example sitting on a chair and burying his face in his hands.

Sound and music have different significance in *A Doll's House*. Nora is frantic as she dances the tarantella for the last time. The dance has tragic undertones. It has a poetic power of its own and Helmer is transfixed by its rhythm, but Nora's distress abruptly breaks up the sequence. This is deliberate as it warns the audience that events are leading to a climax. Unlike *A Doll's House*, *Inside I'm Dancing* uses a greater musical repertoire. In the film, music is sourced inside and outside the set; there is music and dance in the nightclub, music played on a stereo. In *A Doll's House*, music is played on the piano alone and in contrast does not come from outside the action, as is possible in *Inside I'm Dancing*. In contrast to

How Many Miles to Babylon?, the music in *A Doll's House* is live.

The location in *A Doll's House* is the Helmers' apartment. Location is not as diverse as in the texts discussed above, but props are given a symbolic significance. The Christmas tree 'stands, stripped, dishevelled, its candles burned to their sockets.' This alludes to Nora's fear of the corruption of her children and Helmer's words in the previous scene. Props are not given the same significance in *Inside I'm Dancing* or in *How Many Miles to Babylon?*

The order of narration is different in *A Doll's House* from the texts discussed above. The play is told in linear sequence but the influence of past events works its way effectively into the drama. It is largely through Krogstad's blackmail that the audience learns about Nora's deception and the IOU. Only then are props used; the letter is placed in the letter box, thus adding to the suspense and tension of the moment. By contrast, in *Inside I'm Dancing* the scrapbook charts Fergus Connolly's career before the character is introduced, so the props here are used in a different order from *A Doll's House*.

Symbolism, as discussed above, is utilised differently in *A Doll's House*. Instead of costumes representing an idealised sense of self as in *Inside I'm Dancing*, costumes reflect Nora's state of mind. Nora wears a black shawl which prefigures her inner turmoil and suicidal thoughts. She dresses in Italian costume while Helmer wears a black coat, representing the death of their relationship. Symbolism has a different meaning in *How Many Miles to Babylon?* where, as alluded to in part (a), swans represent Alec and Jerry's friendship.

To conclude, all texts tell their stories differently. *A Doll's House* emphasises dialogue and external conflict whereas *Inside I'm Dancing* relies more on the camera to tell the story and *How Many Miles to Babylon?* on the printed word. This crucial difference changes how the story is presented, as does the order of narration. Through these different means, the stories are brought to life in different ways.

13

Cultural context

Cultural context

every text is set against a colourful background. Characters have to breathe, live, work and survive in the environment depicted; thus the social world of a text has a huge impact on the main characters. Each text is also set at a particular time. A text could be set at a time of relative peace or at a time of conflict. Imagine what it would be like if the reader, audience or viewer had no idea of where and when a text was set; the experience would be a much poorer one.

This chapter will outline the cultural context in the following texts:

- Jennifer Johnston's *How Many Miles to Babylon?*
- Martin McDonagh's *The Lonesome West*
- Jane Austen's *Emma*
- Thomas Hardy's *Tess of the d'Urbervilles*
- Sophocles' *Oedipus the King*
- Marian Quinn's *32A*
- Fernando Meirelles' *The Constant Gardener*
- Michael Curtiz's *Casablanca*.

When beginning to study cultural context, you should ask yourself the following questions:

1. Do I have a good understanding of the term cultural context?
2. What do I need to examine?
3. How can I use this information to expand upon the definition of cultural context?

How Many Miles to Babylon? CULTURAL context

How Many Miles to Babylon? highlights the parochial nature of Anglo-Irish society before and during World War I. The old world order is very much in place. Frederick represents the landed gentry whose lack of interest in the international scene emphasises the narrowness of their world. Throughout the novel, this particular mindset is well described through the characterisation of Frederick and Alicia.

The modern reader is invited into the historical world of the text through Alec's narration. The novel is infused with a gripping psychological portrayal of Alec's constant torment. The rural environment of County Wicklow is graphically described. We are provided with detailed descriptions of Alec's house with its expansive garden, lake and stables, where Jerry works. The second social world of the text is the dangerous, vile and ghastly realm of war-torn Flanders. The fighting is so close that Alec hears the sound of gunfire from his prison cell: 'By now the attack must be on. A hundred yards of mournful earth, a hill topped with a circle of trees, that at home would have belonged exclusively to the fairies, a farm, some roofless cottages, quiet unimportant places, now the centre of the world for tens of thousands of men' (pp. 1–2). This passage describes the bleak, depressing landscape where the war is fought in an isolated location in foul February weather.

Family life for Alec is very isolating. His parents are unhappily married and, while growing up, Alec is kept from children of his own age 'by the traditional barriers of class and education' (p. 3). His mother is a formidable influence in the home and Alec is expected to set himself apart from the people of the locality. Re-read the key moment entitled 'Alicia's Shock Revelation' outlined in Chapter 2, where family is portrayed as a negative force in Alec's life and parentage is linked to status and class. Alicia's attitude towards Alec is dismissive and harsh. His emotional needs are undervalued and Alec feels alienated. However, Alicia's revelation that he

> His mother is a formidable influence in the home and Alec is expected to set himself apart from the people of the locality

is not Frederick's son appears to release him from family ties.

Throughout his life, Alec is provided with great opportunity because he is rich. He is privately tutored and has had the advantage of piano lessons. The piano teacher is soon dismissed, however, due to Alec's lack of progress. In contrast, Jerry is afforded fewer opportunities. He has to leave school early, highlighting the link between family income and access to educational advancement.

Class is unimportant to Alec, but in this world class dictates how friends are chosen. Alec's friendship with Jerry threatens the established order and Alicia tries to prevent its development. Both Alicia and Major Glendinning perceive class distinction to be part of the very fabric of society, without which life would descend into chaos. They also emphasise the importance of duty and obedience above social conscience.

Johnston depicts the Big House – where the Anglo-Irish upper class reside – as being associated with triviality. It is kept insulated against the winds of change from the international front: 'We paid very little attention to the war when it happened first. Belgium and Flanders seemed so far away from us. Our fields were gold and firm under our feet' (p. 35). The prestige of the Anglo-Irish gentry is still intact; power is assured by their substantial ownership of land.

> *'Our fields were gold and firm under our feet'*

Marriage is also part of the social fabric of society. In this text it is linked, like family, to class and religious affiliation. In the key moment 'Frederick's Misery in His Marriage to Alicia' we see how Alicia's marriage to Frederick is destructive on every level. Divorce is frowned upon, however. Frederick and Alicia represent a social elite who are preoccupied with status.

Religion is a divisive force in society, both in civilian life and in the army. Jerry is a Catholic. Alec is a Protestant. Jerry is distrusted, often called a Fenian because he is Irish and a Catholic. Protestants are expected to honour the king while Catholics are seen as potential rebels by the state. This emphasises the divisive force of religion in society. Religious differences also explain Alicia's attitude to the war. Alec's mother is insistent that Alec join the war effort to fight for king and country. This sense of pride is emphasised through the directive that every soldier is issued: 'Do your duty bravely. Fear God. Honour the King'

(p. 73). This important belief system is constantly emphasised throughout and is linked to religious affiliation.

The violence of war is graphically portrayed in this novel. Major Glendinning represents the callous attitude of the aristocratic class. Bennett's words are chilling: 'After all there's a man killed every minute' (p. 82). This harsh line captures well the difficulties for soldiers during World War I, when their lives were valueless.

Jerry poses a threat to the established order. Influenced by Pádraig Pearse, he is a republican and uses his time in the army as training for a future rebellion in Ireland. Bennett, though English, shares his revolutionary fervour. This suggests that the powerless, working-class soldiers are becoming radicalised due to their experiences of war.

Major Glendinning may have reason to fear. His primary concern is to establish order among the rank and file. In the key moment entitled 'A Simple Lack of Choice,' Glendinning's concern is for the impending attack: 'It must succeed and for it to succeed there must be no flaw in the machinery' (p. 148). Glendinning's prejudiced view sees Jerry as a 'flaw,' as he broke military rules by going in search of his missing father: 'How you damn Irish expect to be able to run your own country when you can't control your own wasteful emotions, I can't imagine' (p. 152). In associating Irishness with emotion, he is patronising and derogatory, highlighting the ingrained prejudices of the time.

Alec is constrained by the social world in which he lives and his privileged background is the source of his isolation. On the battlefield, he is similarly isolated as an officer in the army. Neither Alec nor Jerry feels very much at home in this social world. Not surprisingly, Alec becomes a defeated figure at the end of the book. He pays the ultimate price for rebelling against military rule. He also rejects religion. He feels that he is not 'in the mood for soul wrestling, that is a pastime for those who have time to spare' (p. 2).

How Many Miles to Babylon? vividly depicts an authoritarian world where the aristocratic class make the final decisions.

CLASSROOM activities

1. What is good about Alec's life in the novel?

2. What is negative about it?

3. Alec is kept way from other children by the 'traditional barriers of

class and education' (p. 3). What do you think is meant by this line? What does it tell the reader about life then?

4. Alec is startled when his mother tells him that Frederick is not his father. Yet he is glad that he could 'escape the eyes of the ancestors on the walls' (p. 48). What do you think Alec meant by this line?

5. In what way is Alec's life both privileged and restricted?

6. What do you think of Major Glendinning's attitude towards his men?

7. Describe society at that time in your own words.

8. Could Alec have acted differently to avert tragedy for Jerry and himself? Justify your answer.

9. 'This book charts the lives of the powerful but sympathises with the powerless.' To what extent is this statement true?

CULTURAL context: The Lonesome West

This play highlights the social world of a small rural community in Ireland. This community does not reflect the wider world of the 1990s, but rather a small community's sense of isolation from the rest of the country. Modern Ireland is in a state of flux. The Catholic Church is still important in society but it no longer commands the same respect it had in the past. The old authorities of Church and State appear to be crumbling, but the country's soccer team lifts people's spirits when it reaches the quarter-final stage of the World Cup, Italia '90.

The Lonesome West portrays dark and harsh aspects of life. Most of the story is set in a scantily furnished old farmhouse in County Galway. The focal point is the fireplace and tattered armchairs. A photograph of a black dog is prized. The play is set in a small, parochial world where the rules of wider society appear not to apply.

The breakdown of the family unit is explored throughout the play through the portrayal of a negative and dysfunctional family situation. Valene and Coleman constantly come to blows, usually over the most trivial of topics. Fr Welsh pleads for tolerance and reconciliation but his plea goes unheard. The spiral of violence is rooted in a family history of dysfunctional behaviour.

Valene and Coleman's father had been arrested for screaming at nuns and now, while in a rage, Coleman has shot his father. Through Fr Welsh's intervention, Valene and Coleman are forced to re-examine their behaviour towards each other. Deep down Fr Welsh thinks 'that ye're love is still there under all of that' (Scene 5) and hopes that his letter will avert disaster. By the end of the play, the vicious family cycle is broken, highlighting the importance of individual responsibility in bringing about a better world.

In previous generations, the priest and the guard represented the respectable classes and were pillars of the community. In *The Lonesome West*, however, the priest struggles to bring a sense of cohesion to a desperate and divided community, and both he and the guard commit suicide.

Class is still determined by how much people own. Re-read the key moment entitled 'Who Owns the House?' detailed in Chapter 2. Valene gloats at his prospective economic status, achieved only after a violent death. All of the characters are poor. There is constant reference to money, which tells us it is in short supply. Both Valene and Coleman regard the stove as a luxury, which suggests that they are accustomed to poverty. Coleman is also aware of his constant state of want. This is conveyed in his use of the image of bare cupboards to represent life. The whole community appears to be starved of social opportunities.

Both Valene and Coleman are presented as lonesome and lost figures. Neither is married and Fr Welsh's description of their lives is apt: 'ye've lived in each other's pockets the entire of ye're lives.' He describes this as a 'lonesome existence' (Scene 5). Past loves are lost. The community is barren and broken. Marriage and family life, the very fabric of society itself, is in disarray in this small community. Following Fr Welsh's suicide, the fear of Girleen's possible suicide is suggested darkly.

> *'ye've lived in each other's pockets the entire of ye're lives'*

Religious values, usually among the most cohesive aspects of society, no longer inspire confidence. In this parish, the priest is a desperate figure; unsettled by the violence of some of his congregation, he fails to instil faith in the wider community. It is not a stereotypical portrayal, however. Coleman claims that unlike many priests he does not 'go abusing poor gasurs' (Scene 1). Fr Welsh's personal compassion is contrasted with the institutional view of the Church on the topic of suicide. The priest relates the Catholic Church's stance on Tom Hanlon's soul. His personal attitude is humane, but he is aware that the Catholic Church takes a dim view of suicide, linking it to eternal damnation: 'According to the Catholic Church anyways he is, the same as every suicide. No remorse. No mercy on him.' Valene's religious fervour suggests that religion has some influence in society still. In Scene 1, pride of place is given to a 'long row of dusty, plastic Catholic figurines.' Coupled with Valene's concern for Fr Welsh's soul, this suggests that certain values are cherished by each generation, despite the less cohesive sense of society. Overall, however, the power of the Catholic Church is on the wane. Fr Welsh complains to Girleen that 'nobody ever listens to me at all,' making him seem a desperate and tragic figure (Scene 4).

Violence is the most dominant aspect of the social world of this text. The play may not represent wider Irish society but rather the deprived pockets of society that have been left behind in the race for social, economic and technological advancement. Valene and Coleman's frustrations are projected onto each other. They are lonely in a world where they have never had the opportunity to marry and this frustration spills over into violence. Their emotional brokenness is mirrored by Fr Welsh's, who is violent towards himself. In the key moment entitled 'The Murder of Coleman and Valene's Father,' Valene and Coleman's overall alienation and struggle to communicate beyond insult and verbal aggression is evident (Scene 2). Fr Welsh is also aware that the community has descended into chaos and feels that God has no 'jurisdiction' in this parish (Scene 1).

In depicting life in this small rural community in this way, the play is examining life in Ireland from a particular angle. Even in the most dysfunctional of situations, hope is forever possible. Valene and Coleman's tenuous reconciliation emphasises that no one is beyond redemption.

CLASSROOM activities

1. From your study of *The Lonesome West*, what impression of society are you given?

2. What would you regard as negative in the depiction of family life?

3. Do you think Fr Welsh really has a 'terrible parish' (Scene 1)? Give reasons for your answer.

4. How important are religious values in this small community? Justify your answer.

5. How alienated is Fr Welsh from the social world of the text?

Emma CULTURAL context

Jane Austen's novel *Emma* is set in Highbury, in privileged society. The novel is dedicated to the Regent, the future George IV who took control from his father, George III, when he became ill. The Regency was a time of political uncertainty and social unrest, sparked by the Luddite riots, when workers rioted in opposition to the mechanisation of industry which was costing them their jobs. However, this novel portrays a life far removed from the political and social uncertainties of the Regency period. The life of the socially well-connected central character, Emma Woodhouse, has had 'very little to distress or vex her' (Ch. 1). The novel acts as a social commentary on the superficiality of the established classes. England is rising rapidly on the world stage and a new middle class is emerging.

Britain is depicted as a very class-conscious society. Class divisions are upheld; the rich and poor are not expected to associate. This is reflected in Mr and Mrs Elton's sneering attitude towards Harriet. Distinction is drawn between the established classes and the new bourgeoisie who have recently acquired wealth. The Coles fit into the latter category. They are described as 'friendly, liberal, and unpretending; but, on the other hand, they were of low origin, in trade, and only moderately genteel' (Ch. 25). Trade, or business, is associated with this newly wealthy class. The novel highlights their lack of acceptance by the privileged, where wealth is already established by birth and inheritance. Notice Emma's general demeanour towards the Coles: 'The Coles were very respectable in their way, but they ought to be taught that it was not for them to arrange the terms on which the superior families would visit them' (Ch. 25). Notice that despite Emma's public humiliation of her, Miss Bates is willing to accept her visit almost like a privilege. It suggests that a person's place in society is firmly established.

Emma

Jane Austen

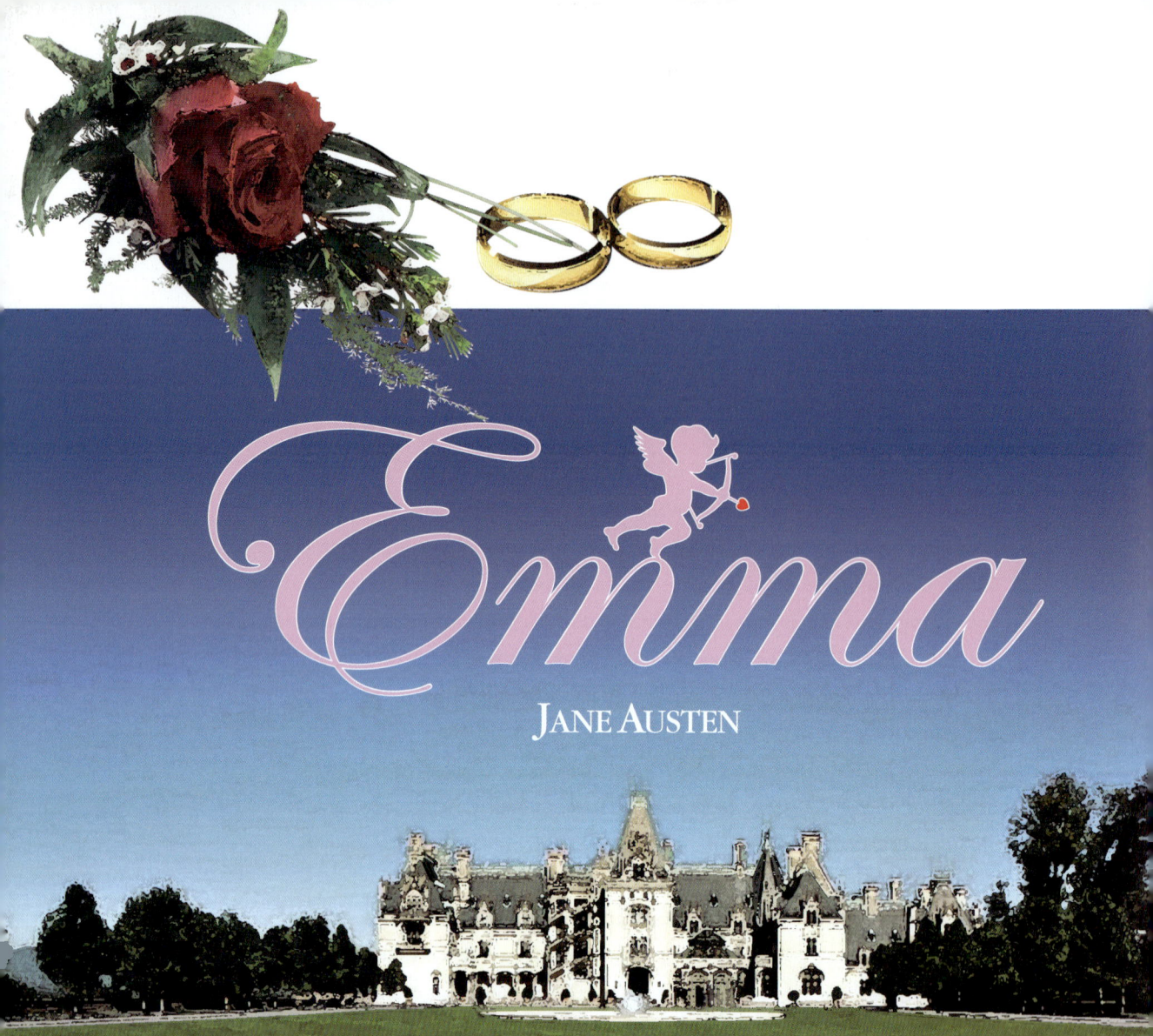

FIRST PUBLISHED:
1815, Blackwell. *Emma* was well received by the critics and public and proved to be Austen's most lucrative novel, earning her the grand sum of £40. Her books reached the peak of their popularity during World War II, as the life she depicted stood in contrast to the horrors of war.

ABOUT THE AUTHOR:
Jane Austen's (1775–1817) works of romantic fiction, set among the landed gentry, are highly prized not only for their light irony, humour, and depiction of contemporary English country life, but also for their social commentary – on the role of women, for example. She is one of the few novelists in world literature who is regarded as 'classic' and yet is widely read. None of the books published in her lifetime had her name on them – they were described as having been written 'By a Lady'.

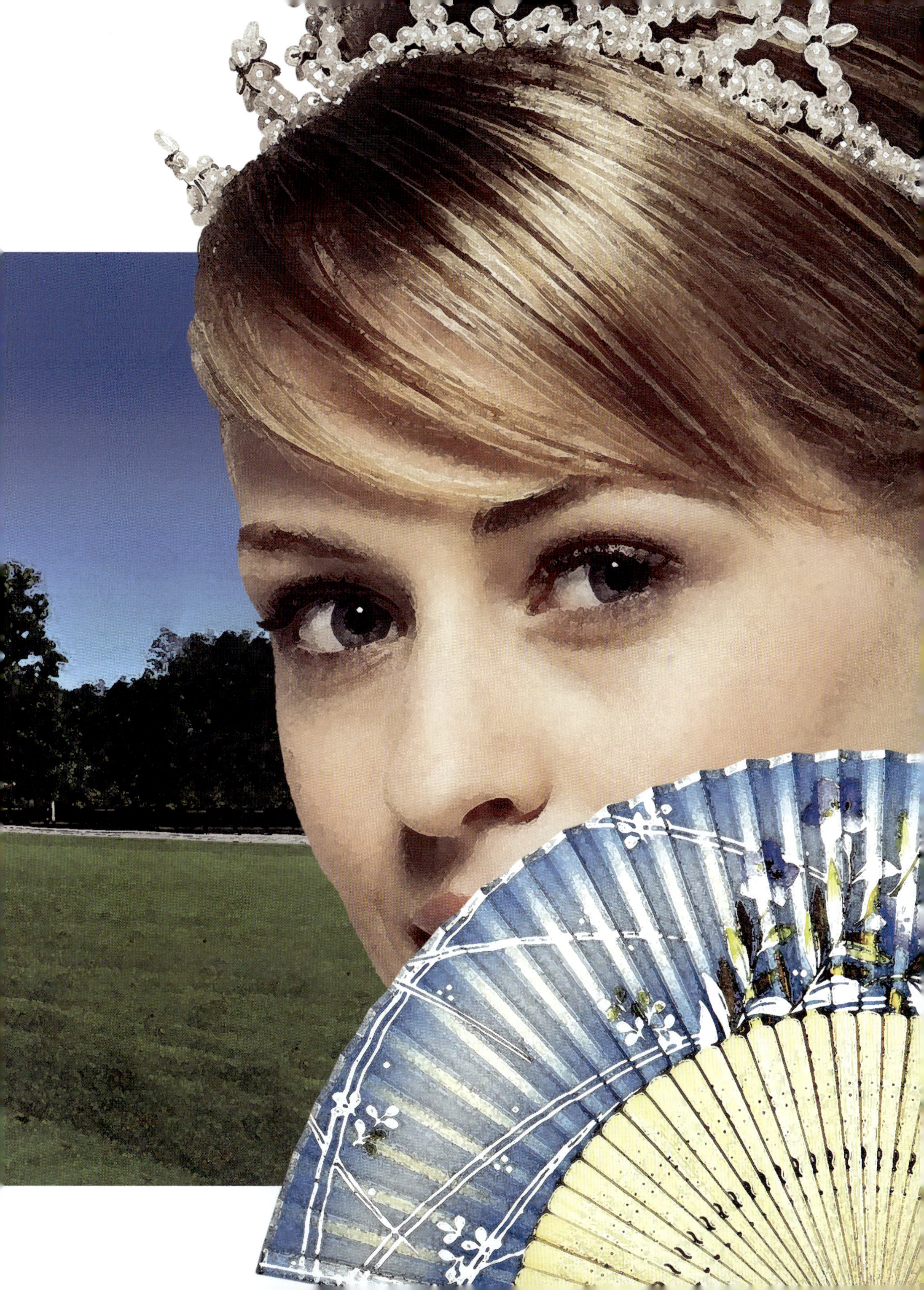

Emma Woodhouse is very society conscious. Her meddling in Harriet's romantic affairs has resulted in giving the impressionable young woman an overdeveloped sense of superiority. She tells Emma that she no longer holds a torch for Mr Martin, the local farmer: 'I hope I know better now, than to care for Mr Martin, or be suspected of it' (Ch. 47). A fearful Emma is dismayed and distraught to learn that Harriet loves Mr Knightley. Even though her general attitude is coloured by her jealousy and her feelings for Mr Knightley, there is some accuracy in her portrayal of a possible unfavourable public reaction from many in the locality: 'It was horrible to Emma to think how it must sink him in the general opinion, to foresee the smiles, the sneers, the merriment it would prompt at his expense, the mortification and disdain of his brother, the thousand inconveniences to herself' (Ch. 47). It paints a very shallow view of society, where public favour is courted and where the custom is to marry within one's social class.

> It paints a very shallow view of society, where public favour is courted and where the custom is to marry within one's social class

Religion is viewed negatively in the novel, largely due to the unfavourable characterisation of Mr Elton. Mr Elton is most conscious of society's hierarchies and responds in a largely unchristian manner towards Harriet. Re-read the key moment entitled 'Mr Elton's Rejection of Miss Smith in Favour of Miss Woodhouse' outlined in Chapter 2. Mr Elton is mortified to learn of the proposed match between himself and Harriet. He is castigating of Harriet Smith, regarding her as his social inferior and pledging his interest in Emma instead. Emma, for her part, is superior in her attitude towards Mr Elton. Anglicanism is the established religion in nineteenth-century England. Mr Elton's portrayal emphasises that many clergymen were merely given their titles. All life centres on rank and social position.

A good family name is considered essential and this is a stigma that Harriet faces on many occasions. Jane, despite the disadvantage of being an orphan, is offered greater educational advancement due to the kindness of her benefactor, Colonel Campbell. Colonel Campbell was held in high regard by her father, Lieutenant Fairfax, who was killed in action and is believed to have saved the colonel's life. Jane has 'fallen into good hands, known nothing but kindness from the Campbells and is given an excellent education' (Ch. 20).

Emma is a privileged character and is afforded many freedoms by society. The author alerts the reader to this: 'The real evils indeed of Emma's situation were the power of having rather too much her own way, and a disposition to think too well of herself' (Ch. 1). Her freedoms encourage her to impose her will too readily on an impressionable Harriet, leaving her open to Mr Elton's unwanted advances and the fear of losing Mr Knightley. However, as the story progresses, Emma realises that she has to moderate her behaviour and learn where her true heart resides.

CLASSROOM activities

1. Describe the social world of the text.

2. Which class in society is best explored? Does this restrict our understanding of the social world of the text? Justify your answer.

3. 'Through the character of Harriet, the reader becomes aware of the importance of social position and family heritage in Jane Austen's day.' Describe how this is shown throughout *Emma*.

4. 'The novel would have been very different if seen largely through the eyes of Jane Fairfax instead of Emma Woodhouse.' Do you agree with this statement? Refer to the text as a whole in your answer.

5. How negative is the portrayal of religion in this text?

6. Which key moment outlined in Chapter 2 is pivotal in describing the social world of the text for a modern readership? Justify your choice.

Tess of the d'Urbervilles

CULTURAL context

Thomas Hardy portrays Tess as a solitary figure. The social world of the text alienates the young Tess. Despite being dynamic and extrovert, life's traumas have an unsettling effect on her. The novel is set in rural Dorchester during the late Victorian era. It attacks the hypocritical morality prevalent in society. Hardy depicts the historical context in his harsh portrayal of life and alludes to the destruction of the old ways of rural life brought about by technological and industrial advances. Hardy's acute character analysis, his in-depth exploration of issues and his graphic portrayal of social alienation make his novel a precursor to modern works of literature.

The concept of the family portrayed is very limiting by modern standards. Re-read the key moment entitled 'Tess as Mother to Her Dying Infant, Sorrow' outlined in Chapter 2. Think for a moment about the horrific implications of being a nameless child. A name is intrinsic to a child's identity. There is a social stigma attached to Sorrow's identity. In this context, Sorrow is an appropriate name. Tess feels the pain of isolation as a single mother in late Victorian society. It is a touching and painful moment for Hardy's heroine. Tess fears for her child and, realising that her 'darling' is about to die, she courageously performs the baptismal ceremony herself. In reality, the text stresses the lip-service paid to family values in the harsh, moralising established Church of late Victorian society.

The novel also describes a generation gap. Both Tess and Angel have different beliefs from those of their parents. The generation gap between Tess and her mother is highlighted early on in the novel. Tess is shown to be outward looking, tolerant and progressive while her mother is depicted as closed, insular and backward looking: 'When they were together the Jacobean and the Victorian ages were juxtaposed' (The Maiden, Ch. 3). Tess is unaware of the harsh reality of life when she goes in search of her 'relatives', the d'Urbervilles. Her mother is a poor role model in this context. Tess admonishes her mother for not teaching her the ways of the world, thus leaving her vulnerable to Alec: 'Why didn't you warn me? Ladies know what to fend hands against, because they read novels that tell them of these tricks; but I never had the chance o' learning in that way, and you did not help me!' (Maiden No More, Ch. 12). This emphasises her childlike innocence and the inability of her parents to assist her. Tess is worlds apart from her mother. Equally, Angel Clare rejects the exact precepts of Christianity held by his parents. Instead of entering the Church, as is his family tradition, he wants to become a farmer.

Class is shown to have been important in late Victorian society. The key moment 'Tess's Father Meets the Parson' shows how Jack Durbeyfield is delighted to discover that he is related to the 'ancient and knightly family of the d'Urbervilles' (The Maiden, Ch. 1). His pride emphasises the importance of class and ancestral heritage. Notice Jack's fascination with the idea of his past high-ranking family status. There is a cruel twist to the tale. Tess searches out the supposed surviving members of the d'Urberville family, believing them to be her long-lost relatives of high stature, but Alec's father, Simon Stroke, made his money as a successful merchant and simply attached the name d'Urberville to his own.

There are also class tensions. Angel Clare is dismissive of the pretensions of the aristocratic classes. Alec uses his privileged social position to exploit women of a lower standing, such as Tess. There has been a history of such exploitation among the privileged classes. In this way, class is portrayed as a negative influence in society.

> Alec uses his privileged social position to exploit women of a lower standing, such as Tess

Many of the characters are in desperate situations in this text. There are no social supports available. Many of the labouring classes are destitute, the Durbeyfields being the main example. They are constantly travelling from place to place in search of work. Notice the way the Durbeyfields are mercilessly thrown out of their home after the main tenant dies.

Religion is a dominant force in society. There are tensions between the established Anglican Church and those of an evangelical persuasion. Religion is portrayed very negatively, with an overt emphasis on eternal damnation. Tess faces social exclusion from religious society when she has a baby out of wedlock. To some extent, her father's meddling in Tess's affairs is responsible for the parson not baptising Sorrow, but it leaves her in an impossible position and she performs the ceremony herself. This is not enough for the religious community. The child is buried in a 'shabby corner of God's allotment where He lets the nettles grow, and where all unbaptized infants, notorious drunkards, suicides and others of the conjecturally damned are laid' (Maiden No More, Ch. 14). The novel champions the underclass in society who are excluded socially on religious grounds.

Women's role in society is limited. They bear full responsibility for child-rearing and their vulnerability in a male-dominated society is graphically portrayed through the trials and torments of the determined and strong heroine. Tess's harsh treatment at the hands of the lustful Alec indicates the double standards of the day. As evident in the key moment 'Alec's Pursuit of Tess,' poor women have been treated in a similar way to Tess throughout history: 'Doubtless some of Tess d'Urberville's mailed ancestors rollicking home from a fray had dealt the same measure even more ruthlessly towards peasant girls of their time.' (The Maiden, Ch. 11). Alec victimises Tess here, but her determined reaction is unexpected. Angel's attitude towards Tess, while better, still does not prevent him judging her at a crucial moment in the story. In the key moment 'Tess's Revelation to Angel,' he is horrified by her deception, but, in contrast to this, his previous transgressions with an older woman are not considered shameful.

The social world of the text deeply alienates the heroine. Tess is a strong and determined character but her innocence is shattered when Alec assaults her and she has to face the shame of having a child out of wedlock. The words of the novel graphically illustrate the abrupt change in Tess's character: 'An immeasurable social chasm was to divide our heroine's personality thereafter from that previous self of hers who stepped from her mother's door to try her fortune at Trantridge poultry-farm' (The Maiden, Ch. 11). Misfortune follows her from beginning to end.

Tess is alienated from the social world of the text, but she offers a spirited response to her many trials and tribulations. She is between two worlds; she speaks two languages, her dialect at home and higher primary school English when she speaks to those in the upper classes. After Sorrow's death, Tess becomes a changed, more reflective person. This is heard in her tone of voice: 'Symbols of reflectiveness passed into her face, and a note of tragedy at times into her voice' (Maiden No More, Ch. 15). However, the phrase: 'quite failed to demoralize' is interesting, as it points to her inner resolve to cope with calamity and misfortune. To the reader, she does not simply become the 'dairymaid Tess, and nothing more' (Maiden No More, Ch. 15). Ultimately she is defeated by the negative forces at work in society, but not before she gives vent to her anger by murdering Alec. Tess is a complex character who defies simple definition. The past and her ancestors have a powerful effect on her life and tragic demise. This is emphasised in the final page: '"Justice" was done, and the President of the Immortals (in Aeschylean phrase), had ended their sport with Tess.'

> Tess is alienated from the social world of the text, but she offers a spirited response to her many trials and tribulations

However, in the wider social context, her life has little importance, as the final paragraph of the novel highlights. It is the author, Hardy, who gives her value and unparalleled significance.

CLASSROOM activities

1. Describe the social setting of the novel.

2. How important is the family in Victorian society?

3. 'Hardy demonstrates society's inadequacies in dealing with the complexity of Tess's entire situation.' To what extent is this statement true in the context of the text as a whole?

4. How important is class in Tess and Angel's relationship?

5. What is the most negative aspect of the late Victorian era?

6. 'Tess's social situation is restricted and desperate, but she is a determined heroine whose natural inclination is to behave unconventionally.' To what extent is this statement true? Refer to the text in your answer.

7. Which key moment outlined in Chapter 2 can be described as pivotal in exploring cultural context?

8. Describe how Hardy's novel offers a fitting critique of rural life in Dorchester in the late Victorian era.

Oedipus the King
CULTURAL context

Oedipus the King is a tragedy. Oedipus is on a journey of self-discovery, but it results in his own destruction. The play describes mythical Greek society and highlights the importance of allegiance to the gods and the struggles of human experience. Piety and patriotism are seen as parts of the essential fabric of society.

Theban society is hierarchical, but not despotic. Oedipus's power and authority result from his success in defeating the Sphinx. The priests are conscious of his authority when they plead with him to help them confront the plague that is now destroying Thebes: 'You cannot equal the gods, your children know that, bending at your altar. But we do rate you first among men,

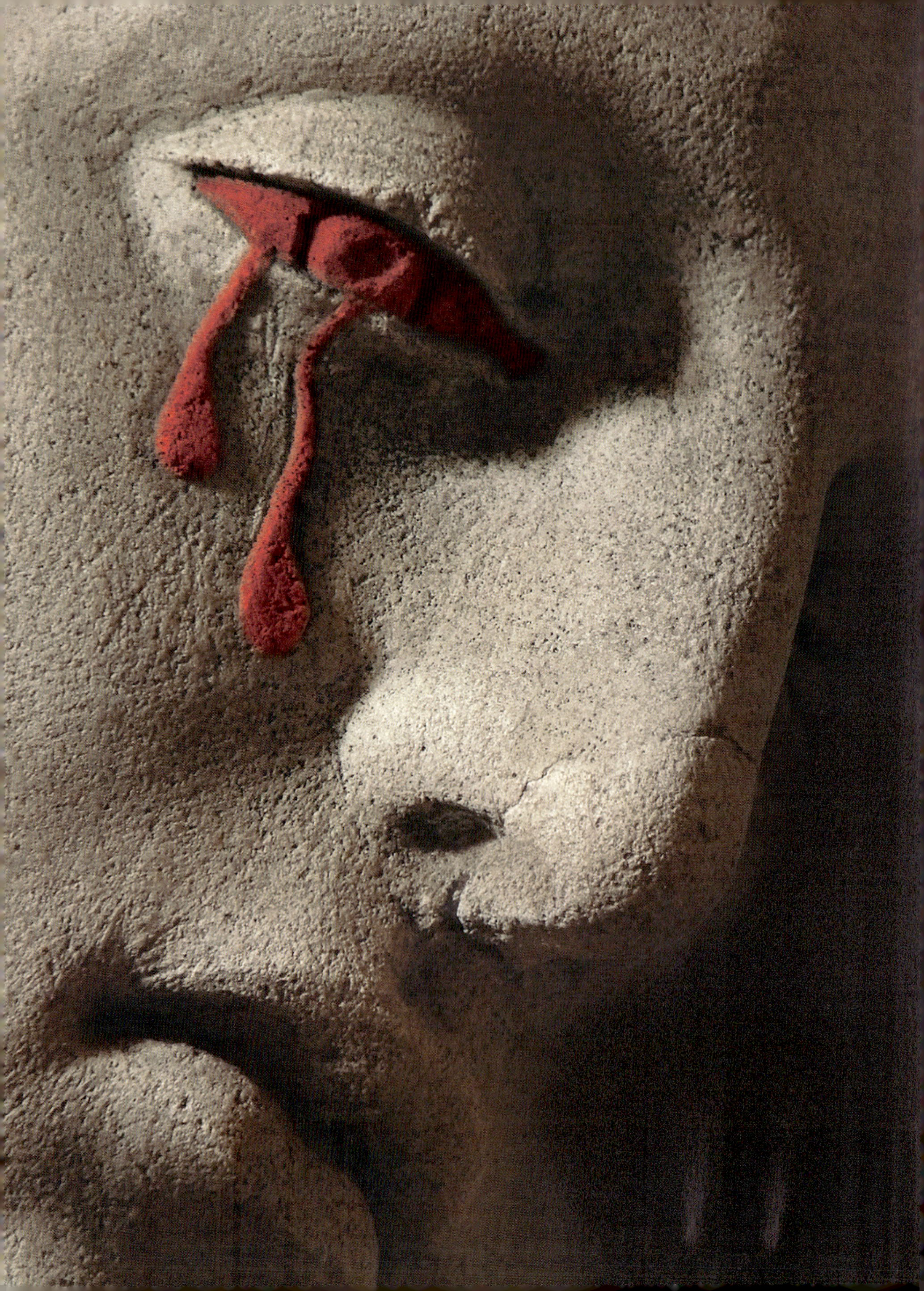

OEDIPUS THE KING

SOPHOCLES

FIRST PERFORMED:
Around 430 BC in an open-air theatre, Athens. The play was written for one of the many drama competitions that took place during religious festivals.

ABOUT THE AUTHOR:
Sophocles (496 BC–406 BC) was born into a wealthy family near Athens. He received a good education, according to the old Greek system, in which music, dancing and gymnastics training played an important part. As a young man he became the most fêted playwright of the age. He wrote 123 plays during the course of his life, but only seven have survived in a complete form. His dramas are full of the spirit of Athens in the classical period. He sees men (and to some extent women) as powerful, rational, creative beings, the masters of the world around them, and the proud creations of the gods. Sophocles also recognises the terrors of war and barbarism, which can sometimes overcome men and women. In his plays, he pleads for the triumph of reason over wild emotion and anger.

both in the common crisis of our lives and face-to-face encounters with the gods' (39–45). However, there are limits to Oedipus's power. Creon tells the angry king that he does not control all of Thebes: 'My city too, not yours alone!' (705). Oedipus rules with Creon and Jocasta. Any move towards dictatorship would have been sternly rejected. Yet the lower class in society is quite vulnerable. When the fearful shepherd is unwilling to disclose the truth, he is threatened with torture by the king.

The importance of kingship in society is emphasised in Oedipus's reaction to Laius's ghastly murder. Oedipus is horrified at the thought of the former king's murder not being investigated properly. He believes that a lowly thief would never attempt to kill a king without some encouragement from those from higher strata in society: 'A thief, so daring, so wild, he'd kill a king? Impossible, unless the conspirators paid him off in Thebes' (140). This emphasises the importance of the right to rule.

Jocasta, however, operates in a male-dominated society. She has a moderating influence in the play, acting as peacemaker between Creon and Oedipus. The family is important in the context of wider political and social power, but Jocasta has to grapple with the horror of the play's revelation. She acts to protect Oedipus: 'You're doomed – may you never fathom who you are' (1170–75).

In order to prevent the prophecy that he would murder his father and marry his mother coming true, Oedipus left Corinth and arrived in Thebes. He acts in ignorance of his own identity. While this has ramifications for the family, it has political consequences as well. As the king, Oedipus is seen as a proud man. Re-read the key moment entitled 'Seeing the Truth' outlined in Chapter 2. The difference in worldly authority is emphasised. Notice the contrast between Oedipus's pride and the prophet's humility. Tiresias is important as a seer and his prophecies come true, much to Oedipus's dismay. Oedipus's offence is seen to be an affront to the gods, who are uninterested in motives. Oedipus is full of self-loathing. His personal piety comes to the fore: 'O god – all come true, all burst to light!' (1305). All human efforts have been in vain.

> 'You're doomed – may you never fathom who you are'

Institutional violence stems from kingly authority. In Oedipus's interrogation of the shepherd he threatens torture for what he sees as an attempt to hide the truth. The murder of King Laius is seen as an affront to society and must be punished. In this context, the gods send a plague to Thebes because this crime has to be punished. Another form of violence is violence against the self. Oedipus is so horrified at the revelation that he blinds himself; he is unable to look upon the truth. His self-loathing is evident. He speaks of being imprisoned in a 'loathsome body' (1520) and highlights the corruption of the self: 'O Polybus, Corinth, the old house of my fathers, so I believed – what a handsome prince you raised – under the skin, what sickness to the core' (1527–30). Jocasta commits suicide. This stresses the violent nature of society.

> His self-loathing is evident. He speaks of being imprisoned in a 'loathsome body'

Oedipus is deeply alienated from society. In his effort to uncover the truth about his family, he sows the seeds of impending doom. At the beginning of the play, Oedipus is a powerful figure, certain of his identity, a father and proud of his achievements. In effect, he becomes the character he feared: 'I am a man, an alien, no citizen welcomes me into their house, law forbids it' (900–905). The text emphasises the importance of the gods in the very fabric of society itself and from whom there is no escape. This is the lesson that Oedipus learns, to his own personal cost.

CLASSROOM activities

1. Describe the essential aspects of Theban society.

2. In what way is Oedipus's power constrained?

3. Compare and contrast the attitudes of Tiresias and the shepherd towards Oedipus.

4. Comment on the importance of religion in Theban society.

5. Comment on Jocasta's role in the tragedy and what it shows about women's role in general.

6. Explain the different forms of violence in this text.

7. How strongly is Oedipus alienated from the social world of the text? To what extent do you consider this his own fault?

CULTURAL context 32A

***32A* is set** in Raheny, an urban community in Dublin, in 1979. The play presents the thinking of the time, when family values and marriage were embedded in Irish culture.

Family is given central importance in this film, suggesting its wider significance as part of the social fabric of society. Not all families correspond to the traditional model, however, which shows a degree of tolerance and social change. Single-parent families are depicted; Ruth's parents have split up due to domestic violence, leaving bitterness in its wake. However, family tensions surface in Maeve's traditional family over Dessie's drug taking, which suggests wider social tensions.

The traditional model of marriage is still very much valued in Irish society at this time. However, Ruth's mother was unhappily married and shuns any future contact with her estranged husband. Ruth finds herself caught between her warring parents, though there is no example of direct confrontation. Re-read the key moment entitled 'Ruth's Mother Uncovers Ruth's Deception,' outlined in Chapter 2. Old wounds re-surface as Ruth struggles to come to terms with her mother's reaction. In contrast, Maeve's parents are happily married. If anything, Maeve's father is overly protective of his wife and very concerned for her health and well-being. Both parents struggle to respond to their wayward son and are deeply frustrated by his ongoing rebellious behaviour.

This text defines the youth culture of the 1970s and the emerging generation gap, when young people's attitudes and values were sometimes in marked contrast to those of their parents. This is most obvious when Maeve finds herself emotionally and socially out of her depth on her date with Brian Power. She is seen to respond like a child. The conversation between two older girls about another's pregnancy highlights tensions and a straying from traditional values. In this case, the young mother is told to give up her child, suggesting that in this era older attitudes still persist and are accepted by the younger generation.

Viewers are encouraged to follow Maeve's path to greater emotional maturity. When she enters an older boy's world, Maeve is emotionally and socially out of her depth. Brian's world is centred on the local park and the Grove, a nightclub. In the park, Brian's friends smoke cannabis and are free from parental control, depicting a picture of rebellious youth culture. Maeve, however, is isolated in the Grove. When Brian dances with Jackie she is portrayed as Brian's social equal, in contrast to the immature Maeve.

As always, youth culture is best explored through the music of the time. Blondie's version of 'I'm a Woman' forms an appropriate introductory soundtrack, as both it and the film's title highlight sexual awareness among the young. Another song, 'Shout It Out,' stresses Maeve and Ruth's coming of age. Many more pop and rock songs are used throughout the film, underlining the preoccupations of the younger generation in the film and offering an attractive way of adding to our understanding of the issues raised.

> When she enters an older boy's world, Maeve is emotionally and socially out of her depth

In contrast to youth culture, class is ill-defined. The film is set in a largely middle-class suburban neighbourhood, characterised by small shops and local economic development. However, it is a time of economic uncertainty and increasing emigration. Ruth's father is forced to emigrate, which tells us that he struggles to survive financially.

Religious values are given priority. Maeve, Orla, Claire and Ruth all attend a Catholic convent school; free secondary education is offered to all in the 1970s. Discipline is maintained by the strict Sister Una, but Maeve breaks the rules when she secretly meets Brian Power. Religion is still part of the fabric of society, exemplified by Pope John Paul II's visit to Ireland in 1979.

In *32A*, gender roles are clearly delineated. Maeve's housekeeping duties are firmly established even before her father punishes her with even more chores. It is Maeve who irons her older brother's shirt and is responsible for looking after her younger siblings when her mother is in hospital. Her father's confrontational approach reflects the traditional parental role within the household. It is a male-dominated society.

However, the female point of view is central to the film. Maeve and Ruth are on a journey to maturity and both characters reflect the social world of the text. Trouble begins when Maeve moves away from the old familiar world and enters the alterative permissive lifestyle represented by Brian Power.

32A depicts the culture of 1970s Ireland. Its characters echo the traditional attitudes to marriage and the family which were common at the time. However, the film is given a decidedly modern twist by having the story viewed from a female perspective.

CLASSROOM activities

1. From your study of *32A*, what impression are you given of society?

2. What are the deep-seated tensions associated with family life in the 1970s?

3. Describe the youth culture of *32A*. To what extent are its attitudes similar to those of people today?

4. How male-dominated was society in the 1970s?

5. Describe the social tensions depicted in *32A*.

CULTURAL context: The Constant Gardener

The Constant Gardener is largely set in Africa. It is portrayed as a violent and despotic society where the impoverished multitudes struggle for survival. It is a sharply divided world on almost every level: social, economic and political. The film's hero, Justin Quayle, realises this as he travels in search of the truth.

Re-read the key moment entitled 'The Treatment of Wanza,' outlined in Chapter 2. A girl named Wanza lies dying in a busy and underfunded hospital in Africa. Tessa alerts Sandy Woodrow to the ongoing scandal: Wanza has been given a drug which is being tested on human beings. An atmosphere of secrecy persists. Wanza's life is easily disregarded as she is powerless in society. Though it is a matter of life and death, the starving millions are afforded no voice.

There is a wide disparity between rich and poor. Notice the difference between the busy, bustling hotel frequented by the elite in Africa and the poverty-stricken conditions of the masses.

The elite have very little concern for the impoverished millions. In the key moment entitled 'Sandy's Revelation to Justin,' Sandy's attitude demonstrates indifference to the high number of deaths in Africa: 'Look at the death rate. Not that anybody's counting.' He justifies the medical project in Africa on the grounds that it serves British commercial interests well. The poor in Africa are the weakest in global society. Life itself is a constant struggle. Even the socially depressed regions in the UK are given priority over the medical needs of the struggling poor in Africa. Racism colours the thinking of Sandy Woodrow and Sir Bernard Pellegrin, who are in positions of power, while the humane Justin Quayle is merely a low-level diplomat in the high commission.

> The poor in Africa are the weakest in global society

Most of the Africans depicted live in perpetual squalor. Their small huts are very cramped and barely adequate to support a starving and growing population. The poor are given scant access to resources. The key moment 'The Lack of Choice for the Sick' details how the poor woman at the front of the queue is denied treatment because she will not consent to take the drug Dypraxa. The denial of proper treatment means a denial of the right to life. The doctor refers to the 'rules.' Justin is aware that the rules militate against the sick and poor in Africa.

The role of women in wider society is acknowledged in the film. Tessa operates, however, in a predominantly male culture. Her determination to fight for the rights of the poor in Africa sets her against the personal interests of the powerful. Sandy is attracted to Tessa and sees her as a potential mistress. Sir Bernard's comments in his letter to Sandy highlight his chauvinistic attitude. Marriage is still part of the fabric of society both in Africa and in the wider world. Political and social opportunities for women have increased in the modern era.

Violence is a constant reality in Africa. The key moment 'One Little Girl and the Dangers of Africa' depicts how the marginalised are exposed to the greatest dangers, while the aid agencies are given priority. Raiders ransack a village in southern Sudan, where the rule of law has broken down. Children are stolen and a dazed man looks at his burning village. Whole communities are torn apart. This key moment captures the life of one little girl. Justin tries to bring her with them on the plane, even attempting bribery, but to no avail. Her future is bleak. If she is lucky, she will make it to a refugee camp. As in the medical centre, the rules disregard the rights of the dispossessed.

The powerful in society are represented by Sir Bernard Pellegrin. Sir Bernard is Foreign Secretary with special responsibility for Africa. He is a powerful figure in the British establishment. The implication is that he colluded in the brutal murder of two aid workers, Dr Arnold Bluhm and Tessa Quayle. Sir Bernard is publicly humiliated at the end of the film, but this is only a partial victory. In one way, it serves to highlight the importance of democracy in holding people to account for their actions. The general public, however, is kept in the dark. It is implied that the financially ruined businessman, Curtiss, whose company is culpable in the deaths of many of Africa's poor, is made a lord. Most successful of all is Sandy Woodrow, who escapes public scrutiny.

The powerless in society are the struggling millions, most especially the sick who depend on medication for survival. African children are denied the rights afforded to their counterparts in the first world. Children like Wanza and Kioko are reduced to living life on the very margins of society. Kioko is very scared when confronted by the police at the medical centre. He is questioned by the officers as if he were a criminal, but he is powerless to prevent such questioning and his protests go ignored. The police can operate in a despotic manner without the normal restraints in operation in the first world. Tessa's cousin makes fitting observations: 'No murders in Africa, only regrettable deaths.' He argues that the lives of the African poor are 'bought so cheaply.' This clearly conveys the glaring inequalities in society. The poorest are denied even the dignity of a proper burial. Wanza and sixty-two others are buried in unmarked graves, their deaths concealed as if they never existed.

> *'No murders in Africa, only regrettable deaths'*

Justin is deeply alienated by the social world of the text, both socially and politically, where betrayal is rife. He is a widower who searches for the truth in the context of his wife Tessa's and Dr Arnold's brutal murder. Justin is in conflict with powerful institutional forces, represented by Sir Bernard Pellegrin and Sandy Woodrow. Sir Bernard has undue influence on the situation, while Sandy is content to work within the parameters of diplomacy. Justin finds himself isolated with only the support of Tessa's friend, Ghita, in his search to uncover the truth. He operates in the context of a lawless, violent society where human life is cheap and the suffering of the African poor is continuous. Justin finds himself on the run and is afforded no protection. He becomes a heroic figure who meets a tragic end. However, he uncovers corruption in powerful circles and so brings about some change, but this is only a partial victory.

CLASSROOM activities

1. Explain the importance of the contrast between the first and third worlds in the wider context of the text as a whole.

2. How restrictive, in your view, is African society? Explain your answer.

3. Which key moment highlights the glaring inequalities in African society? Justify your choice.

4. Compare the advantages of the powerful with the disadvantages of the powerless, as conveyed in *The Constant Gardener*.

5. Assess the importance of the minor characters in examining the social world of the text.

6. How alienated is Justin from the social world in which he lives? Explain your answer.

Casablanca
CULTURAL context

***Casablanca* is set** in the real Moroccan city on the north African coast. Europe is under the despotic control of the Nazis but Casablanca is nominally under French Vichy rule. The Vichy régime is a puppet administration for the Germans. Casablanca is the waiting port for many refugees fleeing Nazi-occupied Europe and hoping to settle in freer democratic societies. It is described as a 'tortuous refugee trail' to reach Casablanca, where they 'wait' for passport visas to escape. Their waiting appears an eternity. The fascism of the Nazis requires strong military authority to uphold its dictatorship.

Class still provides important distinctions in totalitarian society. Money is an advantage. It offers a chance for the refugees to buy a passage to a new life. Many refugees struggle to buy the right transits on the black market, where corruption is rife. A rival club owner informs Rick that people are the most lucrative commodity. Major Strasser is a powerful figure, who tries to impose Nazi authority. Another powerful figure is Captain Renault, who is supposed to work in the interests of the German Reich in Casablanca. Even Captain Renault is prepared to become corrupt for personal favours, financial or otherwise. He describes himself as a 'poor corrupt official.' Corruption is endemic in societies where life revolves around money.

> Corruption is endemic in societies where life revolves around money

Despite the importance of class, other divisions emerge. Major Strasser of the Third Reich arrives in Casablanca in search of Victor Laszlo, a Czech resistance leader. National identity and patriotism are important in this context. The French in Morocco sing the French national anthem in the midst of German soldiers. It is a dangerous moment as it explores an undercurrent of tension between different national communities. The Germans invaded Czechoslovakia and Victor Laszlo fights for the right of his country to be free. Unlike the major, he does not wear a military uniform. Resistance movements operate in a secretive fashion, hoping to play their part by working with the Allies to subvert German authority. This tension is also expressed at the beginning of the film where there is violence between the Free French Movement and the Vichy authorities.

Ilsa operates in a male world. Re-read the key moment entitled 'Rick and Ilsa's Love.' Notice Rick's response to the woman he once loved. Ilsa is desperate to plead Victor's case in this scene, but her options are limited. She refers to her clandestine marriage to Victor, how it could not be made public for fear of the reaction of the authorities. Notice how her marriage to Victor could have made her a target.

The external world of the text is portrayed as a very negative force. Military rule is despotic. The atmosphere is tense with danger. Human life is cheap; resistance fighters are gunned down in the streets by French police. Violence is accepted under totalitarian rule. In the key moment 'Rick's Precious Moments with Ilsa,' a sense of the cultural context of the time is evoked with the song 'As Time Goes By.' Ilsa is distressed at the thought of the approaching

German army and a flavour of the moment is captured by anxious people listening to the loudspeaker and the frantic action at the train station as they flee Paris. It signals an end to French democratic rule and the beginning of German military occupation. Civilians are easily caught in the crossfire in wartime and military authority is emphasised throughout.

Casablanca is a divided world. It is a corrupt, conflict-ridden society where tensions emerge over race and political affiliation. Essentially, German authority is resented in Casablanca, a former French colony where French national identity is strong. In this context, the major tries to impose authority through Captain Renault. Rick's neutral stance dominates his thinking for most of the film until Ilsa's declaration of love reminds him of his former allegiance to the Allied cause.

Rick puts himself outside the social world of the text. In 1935, he ran guns to Ethiopia and in 1936 he fought in the Spanish Civil War against Franco, the Spanish dictator. Re-read the key moment entitled 'A Surprise Ending?', where Rick acts aggressively towards Captain Renault in order to save Ilsa's life. He shoots Major Strasser. Rick is effectively isolated here as he is surrounded by the Vichy police. His anti-fascist political allegiances come to the fore. He acts out of love for Ilsa and in commitment to the Allied cause. However, danger is averted when Captain Renault offers him the hand of friendship in his darkest hour. It highlights Captain Renault's dissatisfaction with the Vichy régime, which is captured well when he throws the water into the bin. It demonstrates how the tides are turning against Hitler and Nazi authority in Casablanca.

CLASSROOM activities

1. Describe the social setting of the film *Casablanca*.

2. What is the biggest distinction in society, as depicted in this text? Is it racial, social or economic?

3. To what extent is society in *Casablanca* male-dominated?

4. Describe the effects of institutional violence on the social world of the text.

5. What do you learn about the Vichy régime?

6. How alienated is Rick from the social world of the text? Refer to three key moments in the text in formulating your answer.

14

Answering the
cultural context
question

Answering the cultural context question

Your task is not simply to tell the story or highlight the cultural context of any text. You need to compare the texts clearly under certain headings. The trick is to provide the examiner with as many comparative points as possible.

All characters exist in a social world. This social world has a positive or negative impact on the lives of the central characters in each text. Most societies form social hierarchies. Stories create characters that the reader or the audience come to like or dislike. Cultural context shapes the plot. The social world of the text explores the level of class consciousness, the power of marriage, religion or the family within society, together with the powerful groups that hold the strongest influences over the lives of the characters in the text.

This chapter will:

- Outline ten steps to help you tackle the cultural context question
- Examine the 2009 Leaving Certificate question in relation to *Tess of the d'Urbervilles*, *Sive* and *Casablanca*.

CULTURAL CONTEXT question — 2009 Leaving Certificate

'The main characters in texts are often in conflict with the world or culture they inhabit.'

In the light of the above statement, compare how the main characters interact with the cultural context of *at least two texts* you have studied for your comparative course. *(30 marks)*

Understand the question
STEP 1

You need to be sure what the question demands of you:
- What are the key words in the question?
- What is the question asking you to do?
- How can you connect the question with your knowledge of the subject?

The key phrases in this question are 'main characters' and 'in conflict with the world or culture.' The question is asking you to compare the texts and evaluate how the characters respond to or drift from the social world of the text. The world or culture of a text can be defined as the social environment. The social environment is what is external to each character.

Planning your answer
STEP 2

You should first plan the main points that you intend to highlight in your essay and then link your plan to the question, as outlined below. It is important to

Tess of the d'Urbervilles	*Sive*	*Casablanca*
Tess is against the social world of the text. Tess is isolated from society.	Sive is the most supported, but suffers the social shame of being a 'bye-child.' Sive is isolated from society.	Rick's past political involvement makes him questionable to Major Strasser. He isolates himself from society.
Tess exists outside of society.	Sive exists outside of society.	Rick exists outside of society.
Tess has the disadvantage of class.	Sive has the disadvantage of class.	Rick does not have the disadvantage of class. He is an outsider, an American.
Tess has a precarious social position as a woman.	Sive has a precarious social position as a woman.	Rick has a precarious social position as a club owner in the political turmoil of WWII Morocco.
Tess has to deal with negative belief systems: as a single mother to Sorrow.	Sive has to deal with negative belief systems: as a bye-child forced to marry Seán Dóta.	Rick has to deal with the negative belief system of the Third Reich.
Tess in conflict with the social world of the text.	Sive in conflict with the social world of the text.	Rick in conflict with the social world of the text.

plan for the following reasons:
- Planning helps you trace the constituent elements of cultural context in the texts
- A plan will help guide your essay
- A plan helps reveal possible comparisons between the texts
- It enables you to keep your answer relevant to the question asked.

STEP 3 First impressions: writing the essential opening paragraph

The first paragraph is very important in an essay. It should assist in introducing the remaining paragraphs. You need to show the examiner that you have understood the question and what it is you are required to answer.

Points for reflection include:
- Are the characters in conflict with the social world of the texts?
- How unhappy are they in these social worlds?
- Which text shows the central character to be most in conflict with the social world of the text?

STEP 4 Writing the middle section of your answer

Refer to the question at all times. Refer to your plan as often as is required. Use this book to help plan answers to past exam questions, specifically Chapter 13. It is also essential to refer to a series of key moments to highlight the manner in which the cultural context is treated in your texts. Use Chapter 2 to refresh your memory of the key moments in each text. You should also:
- Expand upon one point per paragraph
- Make clear comparative points in each of your paragraphs.

Points for reflection include:
- The degree to which each of the central characters is in conflict with the social world of the text
- The descriptions in the texts of each cultural world depicted.

STEP 5 Lasting impression: writing the conclusion

The conclusion is essential as it brings all the main points in your essay

together. It is important to write a conclusion as it:
- Helps draw the points in your essay together
- Reconstructs the points in your answer in a different way.

Re-read the question
STEP 6

Make sure you re-examine the question.
- Have you answered all aspects of the question?
- Is there any aspect that has not been examined?

Look at the plan
STEP 7

Ask yourself whether there is any aspect of the plan that you have not included in your answer. Make sure all aspects of the plan relate to the question.

Re-read the middle section of your essay
STEP 8

This is the section in your answer that should provide the most detail.
- Make sure you have made as many comparative points as you can in each of the paragraphs.
- Did you refer to the question statement in each of your paragraphs?

Re-read the opening and concluding paragraphs
STEP 9

The opening and concluding paragraphs are important in your essay. They are essential for making a general and lasting impression.

Is there anything else?
STEP 10

Check if there is anything that has not been included in your essay which could be important. If you are happy with your answer, move on to the next question.

CULTURAL CONTEXT question

2009 Leaving Certificate

'The main characters in texts are often in conflict with the world or culture they inhabit.'

In the light of the above statement, compare how the main characters interact with the cultural context of *at least two texts* you have studied for your comparative course. *(30 marks)*

SAMPLE answer

Comparing the Social Worlds in *Tess of the d'Urbervilles*, *Sive* and *Casablanca*

The texts I have chosen are Thomas Hardy's *Tess of the d'Urbervilles*, John B. Keane's *Sive* and Michael Curtiz's *Casablanca*. The social worlds of the texts are shown to be dark and depressing. Essentially, Tess is a strong, tragic heroine who battles with the ingrained prejudices of rural late-Victorian society. Similarly, Sive has to face the reality of the social stigma of illegitimacy and Mena's menacing influence in her life. Both Tess and Sive are powerless figures who are alienated by the social world of the texts in different ways. In contrast, Rick's position in society affords him greater power and influence in *Casablanca*, but it is an alienating world where suspicion and betrayal are rife in a totalitarian society. For different reasons, the main characters in *Tess of the d'Urbervilles*, *Sive* and *Casablanca* find themselves in conflict with their social worlds.

All characters exist on the outside of society. Tess and Rick are distrusted on account of their actions, while Sive is prejudged on account of her birth. Family name is viewed negatively in *Tess of the d'Urbervilles* and *Sive*. For Rick, it is his political record which makes him an outsider. Angel castigates Tess for her 'effete aristocracy' while Sive is forced into a marriage with Seán Dóta on the grounds that it will provide her with a name. Both societies represent a harsh view of illegitimate children and their mothers. Tess is conscious of the humiliation of being a 'spouseless mother' to a 'nameless child' while Sive is made conscious of society's prejudices by a spiteful Mena: 'I'm telling you your father was nothing. He was no father. He had no name. You have no name. You will have no name till you take a husband.' Rick suffers in a different sense; he has fought against anti-fascist forces in the past, making him a target for the Germans. In all texts, the central characters are separated from their social world, setting up a conflict between them and social demands and pressures.

All characters have to face the challenges that emerge in their social worlds and to a large extent, though in different ways, they are shown to be in conflict with them. All suffer as a result of the clear distinctions within the social fabric. Tess and Sive's world is class-conscious. Money is the most valued commodity in all societies. People are defined according to their social class in *Tess of the d'Urbervilles* and *Sive*, while in *Casablanca* this is complicated by nationality and political allegiance. Mena's emphasis on those of a richer class is contrasted with Angel's abiding hatred of the class system. She castigates those of a lower social class. However, both Mena's and Angel's comments have a negative effect on the main characters, Tess and Sive, and serve to isolate them more from the social community. Rick does not have the disadvantages of class but he is still an outsider, as an American, in Casablanca. In *Casablanca*, the distinctions revolve less around class and social position – as is evident in *Tess of the d'Urbervilles* and *Sive* – but rather in relation to nationality. Here a clash emerges between the German Reich and subject national groups, such as the French and the Czechs. Rather than being central to the action, as is the case with Sive and Tess, Rick tries to adopt a neutral position. This is commented upon by a rival businessman: 'In this world today, isolation is no longer a practical policy.' However, Rick's political allegiance to the Allied cause becomes obvious in the final stages of the film. His decisions affect the lives of others such as Victor and Ilsa. These decisions have a positive outcome, whereas Alec, Mena and Thomasheen's decisions have a negative effect on Tess and Sive.

All these characters are in conflict with their social worlds. Life is very challenging in all texts. Both Sive and Tess have to grapple with poverty, while Rick's position as a club owner is rather precarious in Vichy Morocco. In different ways, this puts all the characters in direct conflict with the social worlds of the texts. In *Tess of the d'Urbervilles*, Tess and her family face eviction, which serves to highlight the precarious and desperate lives of English labourers. Likewise, Mena speaks about the poverty-stricken masses: 'Will you thank God that you won't be for the rest of your days working for the bare bite and sup like the poor women of these parts?' In effect, a harrowing and harsh working life is what characterises Tess's life in Hardy's novel. Rick has none of these disadvantages, but even as a club owner his livelihood is under constant threat. He is indiscriminately closed down by the Vichy régime. Military occupation erodes the freedom of the individual in *Casablanca*, including Rick's, while the lives of Tess and Sive are miserable even without military occupation. Sive tries to resist the suggestion that she should marry Seán Dóta, but Mena's and eventually Mike's insistence makes life impossible for her. Tess's resistance to her social world is more overt than Sive's. She writes letters to Angel, refuses Alec's advances on occasions, but like Sive, she has to succumb to powerful forces. Alec, Mena, Thomasheen and Major Strasser are all instrumental in creating havoc for the central characters.

Sive and Tess suffer due to the limited roles offered to women in society, while Rick risks his position by providing support to a desperate refugee and her husband when she asks for help. Her husband is trying to win money in Rick's casino. Rick fiddles the numbers so that this young man wins the money, enabling him and his young bride to travel to freedom. Rick acts against the social order here by helping the dispossessed, while Sive and Tess are already excluded due to their poverty. This sets them in conflict with the social world of the text. Sive and Tess are denied their childhoods. Mena tells Sive: 'What would a grown up woman like you want with spending your days in the middle of children.' She is denied the chance to finish her education. Tess changes into a different person after Alec's unwanted advances. There is an 'immeasurable social chasm' between Tess the maiden and Tess the adult. As women, both Tess and Sive are in conflict with their social worlds. Both have to come to terms with harsh treatment and unwanted advances. Sive has to deal with Seán Dóta while Tess has to come to terms with Alec's scandalous treatment of her. Sive speaks of her torment to Nanna: 'When we passed by the cumar near Donal's he made a drive at me! He nearly tore the coat off me.' She describes Seán as an 'ould sick thing,' while Tess dismisses Alec as her 'four months' cousin.'

While Tess and Sive have to come to terms with bad treatment, Rick risks his position to provide a lifeline to a young woman and her husband, providing them with much-needed cash to buy their transit out of Casablanca and on to the free world. Like Tess and Sive, he rejects the harshness of his society's norms. He says he will refuse to partake in the black market – 'I don't buy or sell human beings' – despite this being lucrative; human beings are 'Casablanca's leading commodity.' In different ways, Tess, Sive and Rick are in conflict with the social worlds of the texts.

All characters have to deal with negative belief systems within their prevailing cultures, though this is particularly true of all the family in *Sive*. Mena and Mike's overtly mercenary approach compounds Sive's difficulties. Marriage is viewed in terms of social position. Here the immediate family context, rather than wider society, is unduly negative. Tess's situation is different. Both families link marriage to social position. Jack is proud of the d'Urberville family ancestry while Mena is insistent on the social advantages of Sive marrying Seán Dóta. Sive is in a similar position to Tess's child, Sorrow, though she grows up to feel this humiliation while Sorrow dies. Through Mena, Sive feels her rejection while Tess is conscious of the fear of hell and damnation propounded by the religious. Tess outwardly rejects this negative view, calling it: 'Crushing! Killing!' The painter who writes down these religious inscriptions tells Tess that no allowances are made: 'I cannot split hairs on the burning query.'

In a different vein, Rick has to come to terms with the negative belief system of the Third Reich. This is the most negative of all texts, with its emphasis on militarism, extreme German nationalism and totalitarian government. Finally, Rick actively resists the occupation by offering Victor the letters of transit, enabling him to continue his fight as a resistance leader. Rick pledges himself to the Allied cause. Equally, Tess responds actively by refusing Alec's advances and refusing to be his 'creature:' 'I have said I will not take anything more from you, and I will not – I cannot. I should be your creature to go on doing that, and I won't.' Sive is more passive than Rick or Tess. She is despondent and lifeless in her last scene in the play. Unlike Rick and Tess, she is not openly resistant to the negative social forces at work in her life. Liam describes her last hour as traumatic. He relates that he saw her 'running across the bog with only the little frock against the cold of the night.' Unlike Sive, both Rick and Tess react aggressively. Rick kills Major Strasser; Tess murders Alec. Sive, by contrast, inflicts violence against herself as a means of protest. Tess is resigned to her fate at the end of the novel, realising that she will be executed. In this sense, Rick is the most successful in his resistance against the prevailing forces in society.

To conclude, Tess, Rick and Sive are all in conflict with the social world of the text in different ways. All are outsider figures for different reasons. The conflict with the social world becomes a gripping story in itself in all three texts.